THE ANCESTORS OF NANCY ABDILL

Abdill Family History, Volume III

The Ancestors of Nancy Abdill

a family's tale of

TRANSATLANTIC ADVENTURE

and the lives they built *on the other side*

Featuring two centuries of stories

FROM THE

DNIEPER

TO THE

HUDSON

in lands known then and now as

Russia, Poland, England
Ukraine and Prussia

By Richard J. Abdill III

with added first-hand accounts of

THE OLD COUNTRY

First edition

2017

Minneapolis, Minnesota

Cover design by Anna Gindes.

Cover image, portrait: Nancy Abdill, circa 1963. From the collection of Ann Dondero.

Cover image, background: Ellis Island circa 1920, via the Library of Congress, National Photo Company collection, reproduction number LC-DIG-npcc-00224.

First edition, 2017

ISBN: 978-0999129500

Library of Congress Control Number: 2017912550

For Nana.

*"Don't ever tell anybody anything.
   If you do, you start missing everybody."*

—J.D. Salinger,
   The Catcher in the Rye

Contents

Abdill Family History

This is the second volume in a series of books detailing the ancestry of the author and his siblings, though they have not been published in order. The planned series:

- I: **The Ancestors of Henry Stone**: Published April 2017. A study of all the known ancestors of Henry Stone (1866–1940), a great-great grandfather of the author.
- II: **The Ancestors of Richard Abdill**: Projected 2019. Completes the study of the family of the author's father: The remaining ancestry of Sally Abdill (b. 1929), plus the lineage of Richard Abdill Sr. (1928–2014).
- III: **The Ancestors of Nancy Abdill**: Published November 2017. The known ancestry of Nancy (Siegel) Abdill (b. 1959), mother of the author.
- **Abdill Family History**: A casebound, archival-quality compilation that will combine and update the information of all previous volumes.

Introduction

Hello! My name is Rich. If you're reading this, we are probably family, and I probably have some interesting information for you.

If you're a Siegel, the information here links us back to immigrant relatives that have been unknown to our family for decades. If you're an Arbeiter, our newly found relations go back even farther, to somewhere around the 1750s. Given that many *Ashkenazim*[i] in Poland didn't formally adopt surnames until the 1820s, we've likely found the first direct ancestor to use the last name "Arbeiter."

I started looking into my family's history in June 2016. The first volume was completed in early 2017 and covered a portion of my father's relatives—more than 2,200 names, with another full volume to go before his tree is complete. By contrast, all of my mother's known ancestors are included in these pages. I traced my father's family back to the year 600; I can confidently say the four dozen ancestors in this book were more difficult to find.

The people from the first volume were easier to track down because, in short, they didn't require all that much tracking. The Abdills have been living in New Jersey for more than 160 years; ancestors of the Stone family first

---

[i]In broad terms, *Ashkenazi* Jews are generally within the ethnic subdivision that includes the Jews of eastern and central Europe, as contrasted by the *Sephardi* Jews of areas like Spain.

arrived in Virginia in 1607 and lived there until[ii] 1955. My mother, on the other hand, had only one grandparent born in this hemisphere.

Before we get any farther in the history, however, there are some notes about the organization of the book that should be covered.

The numbering system

You'll see what appears to be a pretty complex numbering scheme used for identifying people. Once you get the hang of it, it's a powerful framework that should be helpful in understanding who's related to whom.

Since this is predominantly a collection of my direct ancestors, it uses *Ahnentafel* numbering,[iii] a system designed to trace ancestry backwards from someone ("all the ancestors of baby Jimmy"), rather than other, more popular systems for tracing ancestry forward ("all the descendants of Olde James").

Everyone is assigned a number, starting with me (1) and moving backward, to my father (2), mother (3), and so on—because everyone in the family tree has only two biological parents,[iv] the number *2* is an important one: To find the number of a person's father, simply **double that person's number**; to find their mother, **double the person's number and add one**. (This also means spouses are one number apart.)

A simple example: Ann Arbeiter is number *7*. Her father, Solomon, is $7 \times 2 = 14$. Solomon's father is $14 \times 2 = 28$. To find someone's mother, the process is similar: Each woman in the tree has a number one greater than her husband's. For example, Solomon's number is *14*, which means his wife, Claire Reinstein, is number *15*. So, if you

---

[ii]Technically, there was likely a gap between 1612 and 1630.
[iii]Also sometimes referred to as the Sosa-Stradonitz Method.
[iv]So far.

wanted to find Ann Arbeiter's mother, you would take her number, *7*, and double it (to *14*, Solomon's number), then add 1, to get Claire's number, *15*. Siblings do not get a number, nor do spouses who are not a direct ancestor. It's nothing personal.

You'll notice that some entries in the book are not consecutive: To maintain the numbering system, people who are missing from the tree still have their place "reserved." Schleme Sigalow, for example, is number *48*, but we don't know who his biological parents were—so, numbers *96* and *97* remain blank, because those numbers are where his parents would be located. By extension, the parents of numbers *96* and *97* are also unknown, and their parents, and so on, so all the numbers of Schleme's ancestors (96/97, 192/193, etc.) are missing.

Generations

The Ahnentafel numbers in the book also have "generational indicators"—those are just to add a little clarity to a number like "58," which at a glance isn't much help. Leib Jacobowitz's actual reference number going forward is *6-58*, which simply means he is number *58* in the tree and is in the sixth generation. His parents would be in generation 7, his grandparents in generation 8, and so on. I am the only person in generation 1, so my number is *1-1*; my father, because his number is *2* and he is one generation removed from me, is *2-2*. To continue the example from above, Ann Arbeiter is *3-7*. Solomon Arbeiter is *4-14*, because he is one generation older than his daughter. Claire Reinstein, Solomon's wife, is number *4-15*; she is in the same generation (4) as her husband, but her Ahnentafel number (15) is one greater than his (14).

Format and Organization

All direct ancestors have a small biography and appear side-by-side with their spouse and a list of any known children. The child in the direct line of descent is indicated in capital letters. So, for example, the children of Abraham and Sarah Arbeiter are listed like this: "Rebecca, SOLOMON, Benjamin," because Solomon Arbeiter is the child of theirs that is a direct ancestor of mine. Most times a person is referenced, their Ahnentafel number directly follows their name, in italics, like this: "Sarah Jacobs *5-29.*"

Most "Ahnentafel charts" using this system just start with number 1 and go backwards in order. This approach is the easiest to navigate if you're using the book as a reference and are looking up individual people, but reading it from front to back doesn't make as much sense: As the tree grows "out" and the number of people in each generation grows, people get farther and farther away from their parents in the text. In the 10th generation of such a list, for example, there could be as many as 512 biographies before the next generation even starts; this number grows exponentially with each successive generation.

To avoid this, the chapters are instead organized by surname, starting with the youngest person we know by that name. In the "Arbeiter" chapter, for example, we start with the most recent (male) Arbeiter in the tree, Solomon *4-14.* We then move on to his parents, Abraham *5-28* and Sarah *5-29*, then Abraham's parents, and so on. The families of the wives in each chapter are broken out into their own chapters, according to their last names as well. So, while Claire Reinstein *4-15* married Solomon *4-14* and is included in the "Arbeiter" chapter, her ancestors are in the next chapter, for the "Reinstein" family. The overlapping person (Claire, in this case) is included in her husband's chapter.

I admit this is approach probably puts an unfair focus on the male ancestors, a pattern that you'll likely see repeated throughout the book. My only excuse is that this annoyingly patriarchal approach mirrors the societies of the time: In addition to the husband's name dictating the family's, many of the women here were homemakers without any documentation except for (if we're lucky) birth, death, and census records. Until about 1940, the citizenship of many women wasn't even decided individually: If she married an American citizen, she became an American citizen. But if a woman—even one born in America— married an immigrant alien, her citizenship was revoked.

In any case, it is clearly an uphill battle to obtain details about the lives of the women in this book. When there was enough information to make informed inferences about what their existence was like, I did my best to include it; most of the time, however, we will have no idea.

"They were strangers"

Still, our forebears on this side of the tree have remarkably similar stories: Eastern European Jews feel the ground burning under foot. Pushed by weakening economic opportunities and a rising tide of religious violence, they escape via the English Channel, stowed in sardine-tin steerage decks alongside all their belongings; without exception, they brought young children with them. They arrive a week or two later, their crowded steamships sloshing through the sea-washed, sunset gates of New York Harbor, past the famed mother of exiles on Bedloe's Island. They're transferred from there onto barges that take them to the winding queues of the Ellis Island immigration facility. Their first views of New York are the southern shores of Brooklyn, where many of them later rent apartments and raise their children, where their grandchildren and great-grandchildren would be born.

They took whatever jobs could be found: Sol Arbeiter was a newsboy, hocking papers on the street corners of Harlem. Helen Steinman got a job as a department store clerk; her sisters worked in the city's tumultuous garment industry, as did Harry Reinstein and his children David and Anna. The New York they arrived in had no Empire State Building, no Chrysler Building, no subway—the streets were full of carriage horses, and Queens was still a wilderness. When Henry Steinman arrived in 1892, the Statue of Liberty had not yet turned green.[v]

The rhetoric used to malign them was not new then and is still readily recognizable today. Writer Irving Howe, himself the son of Russian immigrants, examined the objections in *World of Our Fathers*, his sprawling examination of Jewish immigration to America: "The 'new' immigrants, helpless in urban slums, seemed to many native Americans both symptom and cause of a spreading social malaise. Could they be expected to honor the democratic outlook of the Founding Fathers? Would they not disdain the traditions of individualism on which the nation had thrived? Were they not hopelessly marred by ignorance, dependence, superstition?" Even progressive reformer Henry George was driven to complain about countries "shipping off its people, to be dumped upon another continent, as garbage is shipped off from New York to be dumped into the Atlantic Ocean."

Though he had complaints about the systems of economic injustice that oppressed the poor, George's point was simple—America already had enough beggars. "Wherever you go throughout the country the 'tramp' is known; and in this metropolitan city there are already, it is stated by the Charity Organization Society, a quarter of a million people who live on alms," he wrote. "What, in a few years more, are we to do for a dumping-ground? Will it make our difficulty the less that our human garbage can vote?"

But the poorest and most beleaguered of Eastern Europe continued to arrive, most of our relatives among them.

---

[v] Made of copper, the statue was the color of a penny for its first two decades.

They brought a strange language, stranger customs, and a brand of Judaism that was discomfiting even to other Jews. Still, the "American" way of life was not destroyed—like it had so many other times before, it simply evolved to accommodate the newest Americans. The country's colonial roots have left it with a unique population, one in which a wide majority are here because their ancestors either traveled to America or were transported here against their will. Each generation has had its maligned batch of foreign misfits, and each has formed another stratum in the story of a country uniquely situated to absorb them. It would serve us well to remember that our family exists as we know it because, when their home refused to keep them and their neighbors couldn't help, the Reinsteins and Newmans and Arbeiters and Siegels and Steinmans looked to the United States, and found an outstretched hand.

Starting with this generation, we have a good picture of most family members who came to America. But the generation before is a relative mystery, obscured by limited foreign records and a lack of oral history. Most never came to America, so in most cases we have to rely on the data of their children to offer hints about their lives.

Fittingly, our uncertainty of the past likely mirrors their uncertainty of the future: As we are finding now in the attempt to document the foreign lives of our relatives, departing Europe was a hard break with a lengthy past—impoverished families sold all they owned in exchange for their tickets to America. There were no jobs waiting for them,[vi] no apartments lined up at the other end. Harry Reinstein *5-30* arrived in 1904 and told inspectors he had $5 to his name—when they checked, they found it was actually $2.

Jay Arbeiter, Harry's grandson, still has vivid memories of Harry's children getting together in big parties: "Hy and

---

[vi]Curiously, regulations changed in 1885 made it almost impossible for immigrants to arrive with guaranteed employment.

Anna and Pearl, my mother,[vii] Ruth, and Hy Dreizen and Sam Reinstein, and people by the name of Task... Joe and Goldie Task... They had what they called a 'cousins club,' and they would meet once a month," he said. "You'd go there, and there'd be 30 people in the room, and the men would be playing pinochle and the women would be in the kitchen... They didn't know people, they didn't speak the language. They were strangers. They relied on one another, both financially and socially... They did this because they had this bond, they came over from the old country—they had nothing, they had nobody. They had each other."

Almost everyone in the generation of the "cousins club" were immigrants, and those that weren't had parents who had grown up and married on the other side of the ocean. They missed the births of their nieces and nephews back home, the funerals of their parents and siblings. Eventually, they watched from the Empire State as German tanks rolled through their hometowns, as their cousins slowly disappeared, as the symbols of their life and culture were torn down. By 1943, the graves of all four of Abraham Arbeiter's grandparents were destroyed by the Nazis, plus those of all eight great-grandparents, spread out miles apart in the Polish countryside. The erasure of Jewish cultural landmarks wasn't a coincidence: If you stand in the former Jewish graveyard of the Arbeiters' hometown—now just a field—looking across the street to the untouched Christian burial ground provides a heavy-handed illustration of how intentional the move was.

For reasons I don't quite have a handle on, this discovery laid a particularly heavy weight on my mind. It's not only the distant Americans in the family who don't know where our relatives are buried—*no one* does. A gravestone does more than mark the location of a box in the ground: It's the only tangible evidence most of us will leave behind that we existed at all. A marker in the ground that says "Zelman

---

[vii]Claire (Reinstein) Arbeiter *4-15*.

died" carries a far more meaningful message: "Zelman lived." If we think of it in that context—which the Nazis certainly did, as they flattened cemeteries and gave away the rubble—then the only gravestone those ancestors have left is the stack of paper you hold in your hands.

And so, slowly, what started as a hobby project began to take on more meaning. I make no claim that this is a *good* family history book—just that it is the first, an attempt to understand a little bit more about where we came from and what it took to get here. All the known immigrant ancestors in the family—at least 11 in our direct line— arrived between 1900 and 1912, with other relatives arriving over the previous decade. They went years without seeing each other, as siblings and parents came over ahead of the rest, bringing everyone else later with the money they were able to scrape together by living in one-bedroom squats in some of New York's most notoriously fetid housing.

Henry Steinman came to the U.S. as a 15-year-old and didn't see his parents again until he was 23; his father Markus didn't meet his first grandchild until she was 12. Abraham *5-28* and Sarah Arbeiter *5-29* left both of their families behind in London and Poland when they came to Brooklyn; when Abe departed in early 1907, he never saw his mother or older brother again.

They were here, alone, looking for a future. And now, 110 years later, all we can do is offer our thanks.

—**Rich Abdill**
June 2017
Minneapolis, Minnesota

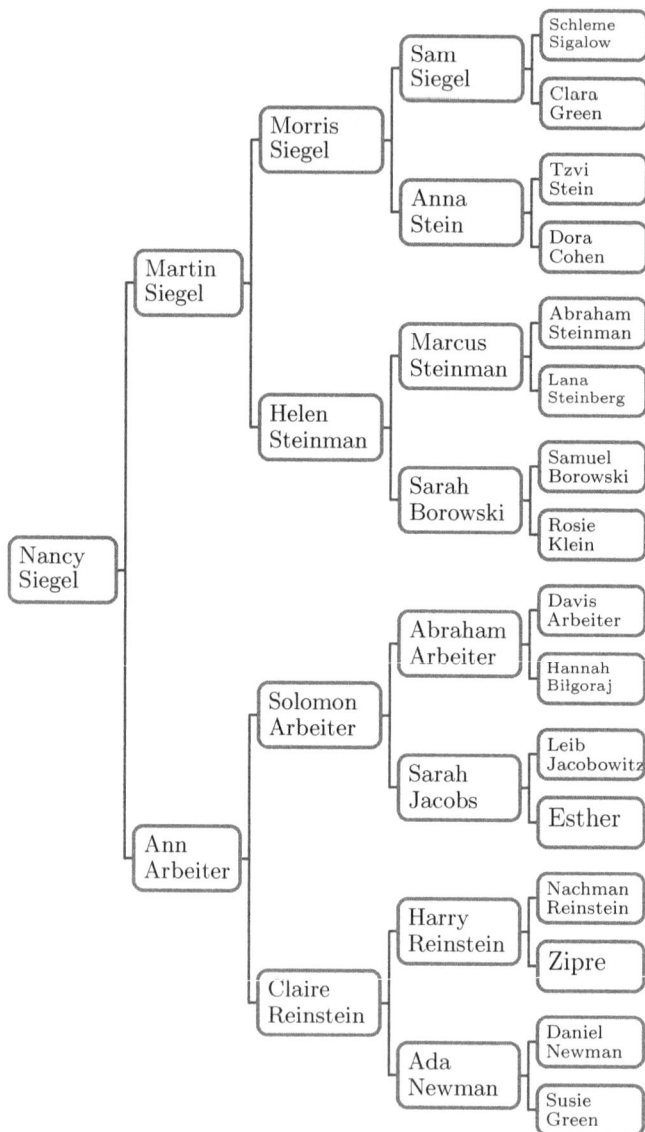

Figure 1: Most of the direct ancestors of Nancy Abdill.

Chapter 1

Arbeiter

The story of our Arbeiter ancestors starts with a ledger. The family's origins had been obscured for decades—Abraham Arbeiter immigrated here from London, that we knew, and "arbeiter" is a germanic word for "worker," so somewhere in Europe seemed likely, maybe Prussia or Poland. There were no clues, and Abe had been dead for 70 years.

So, this ledger. It looks interesting, but not particularly helpful: Printed in large letters at the top, it says, LIST OR MANIFEST OF ALIEN PASSENGERS FOR THE U.S. IMMIGRATION OFFICER AT PORT OF ARRIVAL. Under that, someone has filled out, for what might have been the 30th time that day, the information for the ship: The S.S. *Celtic*, arriving at port of New York, 27 May 1907, after departing from Southampton, England. Each line has a passenger, and each passenger has a number. Down on line 17, we see the entry we're looking for: Abraham Arbeiter, age 28, a hairdresser bound for New York. In the "Race or People" column, someone from the shipping company has written "Hebrew."

A fun artifact to have, but nothing revelatory—nothing, were it not for a thin slip of paper glued, slightly crooked, onto the page's right margin, a slip overlooked a dozen

times before it was read. At first, Abe's entry here looks
equally mundane—brown hair, fair complexion, et cetera—
except for a small, cursive entry on the far edge, under
"Place of Birth": "Plotzk, Russia." The clue we needed.
The clue that opened up ancestry going back to the 18th
century, for a family that had before struggled to crack the
20th.

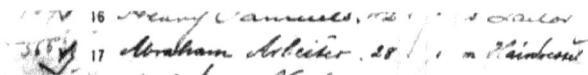

Figure 1.1: Part of Abraham Arbeiter's entry in the 1907 ship
manifest documenting his trip to the United States.[1]

We pick up the story in the Pale of Settlement, the
region of the Russian empire designated in 1791 as the only
allowable location for the residency of Jews. The area included the modern countries of Ukraine, Moldova, Poland,
Lithuania and Belarus, and was abolished around the time
of World War I and the fall of the czarist regime. Particularly, we are in Bieżuń,[i] a small town on the Wkra River
in central Poland, about 80 miles northwest of Warsaw in
the Polish governorate of Płock.[ii] 20-year-old Ryfka Chrzanowska is living there with her middle-aged parents. She
is engaged to a 23-year-old from the town of Wyszogród.
It's not known how they met, but, while the fabled Jewish
matchmakers were still in use across Eastern Europe, hints
of more modern courtship rituals were starting to take
hold—parents were beginning to give up some of their control over the alliances forged by marrying off their children,
and the children were slowly gaining more discretion over
their choice of mate, possibly via letter-writing or short,

---

[i]The "ż" in "Bieżuń" is pronounced like the "s" in "usual," and
the "u" is pronounced as if it were "oo." The emphasis is on the
second syllable.

[ii]Płock, the city and governorate, is pronounced in Polish with
an "sk" sound at the end, like "Plotsk," or potentially "Pwotsk."

supervised "dates."[2] (The introduction of "romantic love" as a factor in marriage arrangements was seen by many as a signal of the failure of traditional values.)[3]

On February 15, 1843, Ryfka's fiancé, Zelman Arbajter, traveled with his family along the looping 60-mile road between his town and hers, and the couple was married. The record of the union provides small hints about those attending: For example, Ryfka's father, Szoel, was the only relative able to sign his name in Polish, suggesting he may have had a comparatively advanced education. Under his signature, his wife Ruchla signed her name in compact, tidy Yiddish characters. Under that, the Yiddish signatures of Zelman's parents, Berek and Ruchla Arbayter.[iii] Beneath the family's signatures are the two witnesses: Lachman Gertman, the elderly caretaker of the Bieżuń synagogue, signed his name in jagged, jumpy letters; beneath him, an 83-year-old hatmaker named Zyskinder Krywiec signed using what can only be described as large, Yiddish smudges.

After the wedding, it appears Zelman and Ryfka stayed in Bieżuń, at least for a time. This may have been part of a tradition known as *kest*, in which either the groom's or bride's parents gave the newlyweds free room and board, usually for between two and five years.[4] Zelman's parents were living in Wyszogród at the time, so the couple probably stayed with Ryfka's family. The following year, 1845, Zelman and Ryfka's first child, Dawid, was born in Bieżuń.

Two decades later, Dawid returned to Wyszogród, the town of his father's family, and married Hana Itta Biłgoraj on August 24, 1864. It's not clear when Dawid moved back to Wyszogród, but if it was not specifically because of his marriage, the most likely time would have been in the wake of the January Uprising of 1863, which triggered a crackdown across the region and inspired a small exodus from Bieżuń in particular.[5]

[iii]The spelling of everyone's surnames in these records varies widely; consistent spelling of last names is a more modern invention.

Figure 1.2: An 1820 Russian map depicting the heart of the Płock governorate. Warsaw is in the bottom-right corner; Wyszogród is just west of it, and Bieżuń is in the top-left corner.[6]

Hana's family had been in Wyszogród for generations: Dawid and Hana both had grandfathers who worked as butchers in the town, and Hana's father, Szulim Haim, joined the family business and did the same. She had been born in the town in 1846, and she and her new husband may have stayed with her parents as Dawid set himself up as a *handlarz*, or peddler.[iv] On market days (probably Tuesday and Friday),[7] Dawid likely traded with the rural

---

[iv]In Polish, the "rz" digraph is pronounced more like "zh," like the way the "s" is pronounced in the English word "usual." Using English spelling conventions, *handlarz* is probably more recognizable as "handlaj."

Poles who came to town with fresh produce.[8]

Dawid and Hana's first child, Isak, was born in 1871. At some point, the family may have traveled extensively, though the circumstances are unknown—their second child, Łaja, was born in 1873, and her town of birth is recorded as "Jarosław." In addition to the city of Jarosław located 250 miles south of Wyszogród, there are multiple villages known as Jarosław or Jarosławiec. It's unclear which of these, if any, was Łaja's birth place, but none are particularly close to Wyszogród.

At some point during this time, Dawid became a tavernkeeper in the Wyszogród area, though its location is unknown.[v] Rural taverns were common in the Pale, and alcohol was one of the few industries in which Jews were allowed to operate unencumbered by special restrictions.[9] Frequently, these taverns were more than simple bars, and operated as inns and kosher food establishments, a valuable resource for the throngs of traveling Jewish merchants forced to hit the road during the week.[10]

Dawid and Hana had a total of nine children. As far as we know, all but Łaja was born in Wyszogród. The town itself was home to about 4,000 people, of whom 3,000 were Jews.[11]

That's where Dawid and Hana's fourth child, Abram, was born, in the winter of 1878. It's not known what their house looked like, but the majority of buildings in town were wooden huts;[12] a wooden floor, rather than packed dirt, would have been a sign of status.[13] A brick house would likely have been out of reach—they were for the relatively wealthy,[14] but living in Dawid's inn may have afforded the Arbajters a less conventional housing arrangement. A simple guess at what their supper table may have looked like would include borscht (a beet soup, served cold), probably with a side of bread or boiled eggs,

---

[v] As the family's remaining children were all born in the town, we can assume Dawid's business was not too far removed from there.

or maybe *kreplach*, an Ashkenazi dumpling that Wyszogród residents filled with mushrooms.[15] Cucumber salad might have made an appearance as well, with a heavy cream dressing.

There was a single synagogue in town, built in the 1700s, so it is easy to imagine what the family would have seen: A tall brick building, topped by a wide, domed roof. Resident Bella Zawierucha-Gutman recalled fondly, "The stout thick walls, the large green double door and tall windows, looked all week long like an enchanted castle, fast asleep. On Shabbat and holiday the synagogue came alive."[16]

Attending a *shabbat* service, they walk through those doors, the Friday sunset at their backs. To the sides, wooden steps led to a loft where a children's choir (or cantor's helpers) would sit, a relative novelty in Poland.[17]

Walking forward, they would have to travel down a set of stairs,[18] part of an elaborate dance played with the local Poles: In countries where Jewish settlement was stable enough to allow for the construction of houses of prayer, there were frequently policies forbidding a synagogue from being built taller than any local churches. To get around this, more daring congregations would construct squat-looking buildings that extended far below ground.[19] Zawierucha-Gutman described the effect in Wyszogród: "From outside the synagogue did not look very tall, because it was square, big, with a roof with cupolas; but whoever entered it was wonderstruck with its height."[20]

From the stairs, the Arbajters walk forward, into a large sanctuary, about 60 feet square. The women climb one of the sets of spiral stairs, into their segregated section of the sanctuary above.[vi] The walls are ornately decorated—built after the depiction of human figures fell out of favor as a violation of the commandment against "graven images,"[21]

[vi]Even today, men and women in Orthodox synagogues are frequently required to sit in separate sections.

the synagogue's interior is instead adorned with sprawling blocks of Hebrew text.

Large stone columns evenly spaced around the perimeter hold up the vaulted ceiling,[22] which also features painted Bible verses. On the opposite wall, the "ark" used to store the Torah scrolls extends across almost the entire room. It's one of the most ornate structures of its kind in Poland, doubtless a point of pride in the community since its creation, intricately painted and carved by famed[23] artist David Friedlander.[24] The rococo work is huge and complex—the tree of knowledge in one spot, beasts entering Noah's ark in another, the musical instruments mentioned in the Book of Psalms. In the middle is a sculpture of two giant lions facing each other, standing on their hind legs.

In the middle of the cavernous room is a raised *bimah*, from which the *Torah*[vii] would be read at various points. This is where Abram would have climbed during his *bar mitzvah* ceremony, where he would at least have offered blessings over the Torah, and probably chanted a portion of that week's reading. It must have been a proud day; the family would have donated a pound of wax to help light the room and commemorate the occasion.[25] It's the same bimah—and maybe the same Torah scroll—where his grandfather would have gone through the same ordeal.

[vii]The Torah is the first five books of the Hebrew Bible. A segment is read every week at *shabbat* services.

Figure 1.3: A photo of Wyszogród taken at some point before 1918, when it appeared on a postcard. The building at the top of the hill on the far left is the synagogue.[26]

The education of Abram and his brothers would have closely resembled that of his father and grandfathers as well: Though the availability (and nationalist tendencies) of public schools vacillated over time, most boys received formal education only from a *melamed*, or religious teacher, who may have taught dozens of students at a time over lengthy days in the classroom, possibly from 8 a.m. until 9 p.m.[27] Except in the most well-to-do families, girls did not attend school.[28]

At least one of Abram's grandparents—his mother's mother, Sura Ester, was alive into Abram's teen years. His mother's father, Szulim Haim, died when Abram was about 9. Eventually, Abram encountered at least one uncle, his father's brother Mendel, who also left Bieżuń and ended up working as a laborer in Wyszogród some time before Abram was 10. They were likely well acquainted, and the birth of his cousins when Abram was a young teen was probably a big family event.

Abram was born during the reign of Tsar Alexander II, a liberal reformer whose assassination when Abram was a toddler may have sealed the fate of the Arbajters' eventual departure from Eastern Europe forever. The backlash from the tsar's murder in 1881 reignited anti-Semitic public policy and sentiment that had mellowed over the decades since he was crowned—one scholar said the assassination "fell upon the Jews as a national calamity... Separated from the great masses of the Russian people by race, nationality, religion, occupations and other social and psychological characteristics, they offered an unusually favorable object of attack."[29]

Innkeepers in particular were a target of scorn: Anti-Semitic riots, or *pogroms*, broke out across the countryside and almost invariably[30] included a visit to local Jewish taverns, where vodka was stolen and buildings were vandalized. In at least one village, the mob destroyed the Jewish tavern-keeper's license, then held an impromptu auction for the contents of his building.[31]

The Russian government investigated the violence that took place in the aftermath of the assassination and found that attacks on the Jews were their own fault, for having exploited the "native inhabitants," corrupting them with liquor and contributing to general delinquency that kept them from agricultural success. In short order, a committee recommended Jews be almost entirely barred from the liquor trade.[32]

Figure 1.4: An undated photo of the market square of Wyszogród, where the Arbeiters lived before moving to London. Photo credit Yad Vashem.[33]

The oppressive "May Laws" enacted in 1882 did not deal specifically with liquor, but affected the Jews of the Pale in many other ways: Jews were banned from owning or renting land outside of towns, which drove many rural entrepreneurs out of business and left countless others homeless. While the Arbajters were, for the time being, safely residing in the town of Wyszogród, Jews living in villages were forcibly expelled—and if a town was tired of its Jewish residents, Poles simply recast the "town" as a "village" and labeled Jews illegal settlers.[34]

There were also stringent caps placed on Jewish education: While the administration of the late Alexander II had aimed to promote assimilation by encouraging Jewish participation in secondary schools and universities, that policy was swiftly reversed during the reign of Alexander III.[viii][35] The "percentage rule" of the late 1880s capped the Jewish admission ratio for most schools at 10 percent,

---

[viii] Alexander III's son became Tsar Nicholas II, the "last tsar." News of his abdication during the February Revolution in 1917 was met with "great jubilation" in the Jewish immigrant community.

even in the Pale, where Jews constituted a large proportion of the population. In majority-Jewish towns such as Wyszogród, the effects were obvious and immediate. Historian Samuel Joseph explained in 1914 that the rule, "was almost as great a blow as the May Laws. It threatened the cultural ruin of Russian Jewry. Bound up as the admission to these schools was with the liberal professions and with the opportunity of escaping from the limits of the Pale, it meant that one of the main highways to freedom in Russia had been closed to the Jews."[36]

It was also probably around this time that the family began talk of relocating: Though there were few legal routes of escape, more than 200,000 Eastern European Jews arrived in America in the 1880s,[37] a number that would grow for decades. The Arbajters had few signs of hope for an improvement of conditions in their homeland. In 1891, Russia attracted rebukes from around the world for expelling the entire Jewish population of Moscow, and pogroms broke out routinely, with the tacit endorsement of the government.

In 1892, however, something peculiar happened: Going against essentially all previous precedent,[38] the Russian government afforded Jews a special privilege—the right to leave. The historically strict Russian borders had been officially opened to the Jews—they were free to go, so long as they promised never to return.[39] The first Arbajter left Poland the following year.

In 1893, Abram's older brother Isak left for London, when Isak was about 22 and Abram 15. Even with the eldest gone, the family was still huge, at least by modern standards: Abram had two older sisters, three younger sisters and a little brother. The youngest, Mariem, was 3. (When Abram was 8, another sister, Ryfka, had died as an infant.)

Even with Isak gone, however, we know very little for sure about the family's plans for the future at this point. Despite legal and logistical difficulties, it was not

uncommon for family members to leave Poland to earn
money and later return—during this period, 30 percent
of Polish immigrants to America actually went back.[40] It
was also possible that Isak had planned to stop in England
until he could afford passage to America, a common plan
that sometimes resulted in the immigrant simply staying
put in London instead. Even if Isak had been able to pull
together enough money in London to purchase passage
to New York, his departure from Poland lined up exactly
with the Panic of 1893,[41] an economic depression in the
United States that left millions out of work and brought
the "first wave" of eastern European immigration to a close
for almost a decade.[42] If the U.S. had been Isak's intended
destination, this may have inspired a change of course.

Either way, around this time the already overcast fortunes of the Arbajters began to darken further, along with
the hopes of many in the Pale: Just between 1894 and
1898, the number of Jewish paupers in Russia increased
by 30 percent.[43] This was also the time when the Russian
government finally started to crack down on the Jewish alcohol industry. In the 1880s, Jews owned or ran 60 percent
of the (legal) taverns in the Pale of Settlement; by the end
of the 1890s, that rate was down to 37 percent. In addition
to the prohibition against Jews owning or leasing land in
rural areas, where many taverns thrived, the government
also granted itself a monopoly on alcohol sales,[44] further
endangering the distilling industry and the taverns of the
Pale. All of this added up to a historically Jewish industry
being effectively boarded up. While it was common for
innkeeps to have side businesses[45] (Dawid likely moon-
lighted as a tailor),[46] by 1898 it appears the family had
definitely resolved to leave—in that year, Dawid followed
Isak to Great Britain, leaving Abram behind for the time
being, with Hana and his siblings.

Jewish writer Irving Howe considered the unique factors
that facilitated this "new exodus": It was not unique
for Jews in Eastern Europe to find themselves mired in

"persecution and poverty," so why was this time different? Given the region's history, one might expect instead to find "perhaps a new version of the orgiastic false messianism of the seventeenth and eighteenth centuries, perhaps a new phase in the ecstatic pietism of Hasidism, perhaps some unforeseeable religious outburst." Instead, millions simply packed up and left. Howe posits that the reaction was different in the late 1800s because it happened to line up with a period of "cultural renewal" in the Jewish community, creating an "explosive mixture of mounting wretchedness and increasing hope, physical suffering and spiritual exaltation. And what was new in their experience was that for the first time they could suppose there was someplace else to go."[47]

It's not known how the family was supported financially during the time Dawid and Isak were abroad, but it likely involved the two Londoners sending money home from England. Abram, still in Wyszogród, was also of working age, and had probably been working as a tailor like his father. After he too left for England in 1899, Abram did tailoring work for a short time there as well.[48]

Traveling up the Thames, 22-year-old Abram Arbajter likely disembarked in the shadow of Tower Bridge,[49] at the Port of London, then the largest dock complex in the world.[50] Here, he became "Abraham Arbeiter"[51] and dove into the soot-covered urban jungle of Whitechapel, in London's East End. The area had long been an impoverished part of the city but had gained particular notoriety over the previous decade, when all of London was fascinated and horrified by the "Whitechapel murders," a string of 11 brutal killings that drew attention to the abhorrent conditions near the docks. Many of the victims lived or were found within blocks of Abraham's future flat on Old Montague Street. At least five of them are believed to have been murdered by the unidentified killer known as Jack the Ripper.

Even with the Whitechapel killer in hibernation, Abra-

ham would have needed to be vigilant from the start—
"crimps" still prowled the London waterfront,[52] ready to
trick (or force) the drunk or the naive disembarking there
into service on a merchant vessel, raising the prospect of
an immigrant being "shanghaied"[53] before he'd even been
able to establish a place to live in the city from which he
was being kidnapped.

The immigrant exam-
inations at the London
docks, when there were any,
were nothing compared to
the rigors of Ellis Island.[55]
Even then, one British customs official said incoming
Polish immigrants didn't
have anything to examine
in the first place, saying
"the majority had only a little canvas bag tied with a
piece of string."[56]

Later in 1899, Abra-
ham married Sarah Ja-
cobowitz, a fellow Pol-
ish Jew. Their wedding
was 18 Oct 1899 in the
East London Synagogue,[57]
an Orthodox congregation
founded in 1877.[58] Though
plans called for the im-
poverished neighborhood's
synagogue to be built as

Figure 1.5: An undated photo of
the ark of the East London Synagogue. The rectangular canopy
on the left is the chuppah, a
small ceremonial tent put in
place for weddings.[54]

plainly as possible,[59] when finished it had seats for more
than 600 and featured refined Victorian architecture that
included floor mosaics, intricately carved wood features,
and Gothic embellishments[60] reminiscent of the synagogue
in Wyszogród. (The building still stands at 52 Rectory
Square in the East End,[61] though it has been converted

into an apartment building—albeit one with the Ten Commandments hung high on one of the walls.)[62]

The only documentation we have of Abraham's arrival in London puts the date at some point in 1899,[63] the same year he got married. This would have left almost no time for a recognizable courtship, much less for a courtship plus the planning of an entire wedding. A plausible explanation for this is that Abraham and Sarah met through the workings of a *shadchan*, or matchmaker—Louise Jordan Miln wrote a 1900 book examining worldwide marriage traditions and reported, of the Jews of the East End, "no man in Whitechapel drives a busier or a more paying trade than does the *shadchan*."[64]

The matchmaking trade is even more transactional than it seems at first glance; Miln explains the process that starts once a matchmaker is retained by a potential groom: "He goes to the shadchan and states who he is and what he has, and what he requires. The shadchan states his terms, and probably demands a retaining fee. He then produces a list of likely maidens on his books. This list includes names, appearance, dowries, families, and addresses... in the course of a few nights the marrying man goes to view the marriagable women. It is called 'going on view.' A Jewess of that class will say frankly, 'I am to be on view to-night'... When the bridegroom has made his choice he informs the shadchan, who opens negotiations with the bride's father."

However it came to be, Abe and Sarah ended up together. At 5-foot-3,[65] he was short, but she was shorter;[66] one can't help but wonder if the shadchan had anything to do with that. They moved to a recently built[67] flat at 80 Old Montague Street, where Abe soon got into the hair-cutting business: The 1901 census lists Abraham as a hairdresser and says he works "at home"; it's not clear if this literally meant out of the family's flat, or in the shop that was built on the ground floor of the building. He almost definitely worked with his younger brother Jacob, who was only 14 but is listed in the census as a hairdresser rather than a student.[68]

Jacob was living in a flat on Stepney Green, less than a mile to the east, with their parents. By this time, Dawid and Hana Itta were known as "Davis" and "Annie."[69] Abe's three other younger siblings were with them too: Nelly, age 19, a tailoress. Rasza (now "Rosie"), age 15, worked in cigarette manufacturing. Miriam, the youngest at 12 years old, appears to be going to school.[70] Isaac, the oldest, was living a few blocks south with his wife Betsy and the couple's four-year-old daughter, Evelyn. He'd found work as a bookkeeper.[71]

Abe and Sarah had two children by 1903, Rebecca and Solomon. Their names are the English versions of Abraham's grandparents, Zelman and Ryfka Arbajter. At this point, they were living at 17 Casson Street, a tenement two blocks west of their first flat. Evidence suggests this may not have been a positive move: A fish curing facility was across the street,[72] for starters, which would have contributed colorful scents to the neighborhood. Heading south from their house, you quickly hit the corner of the short block; turning right puts you on Finch Street, a mostly residential through-way only two blocks long. Walking down Finch, you'd see (and smell) an open-air fish market to the left, on Hope Street,[73] plus dense, tall brick tenements on either side of the road.

Charles Booth had done an astoundingly broad economic survey of London a few years earlier, and found the houses of Finch Street to be a notably poor section of the neighborhood.[74] At the end of Finch, crossing Osborn Street would put you on Thrawl Street, about three blocks away from the family's flat. In Booth's economic study, streets are color-coded in various shades of orange, red and blue to indicate the relative affluence of the neighborhood— the block around Thrawl Street is marked in thick, black ink, used sparingly throughout the map to indicate only the city's worst conditions. The map legend states the coloring used for Thrawl Street indicates the "lowest class" neighborhood, "vicious, semi-criminal."[75] This is also where Emma Smith was found, the first victim of the Whitechapel murders.

The Arbeiters did not last long on Casson Street. By the time their third child, Benjamin, was born in 1905, they had moved farther east, closer to Davis and Annie, in a tenement block along Stepney Green.

It's around this time that we start to see hints of a long-discussed family mystery—when the Arbajter family came to England (and later the U.S.), some branches spelled their surname "Arbeiter," while others used the more stately "Arbiter." (While it's not known definitively why one was chosen over the other, "arbeiter" is a German word for a laborer, while "arbiter" is an old English word for judge or adjudicator.)

There is confusing documentation every step of the way, even just looking at Abraham and Sarah's family—while they exclusively used the name "Arbeiter" in the U.S., the birth records of their three children offer three different spellings: Rebecca Arbiter in 1900,[76] Solomon Arbeiter in 1903[77] and, somehow, Benjamin *Arbeter* in 1905.[78]

In fairness, Benjamin's record can likely be attributed to a clerical error—while Betty and Sol's records were reported by Abraham, Benjamin's birth was reported to the registrar by Sarah, who signed with a symbol instead of her name. If she was unable to sign her name, it's probable she was also not yet able to read English. Illiteracy was an unsurprising condition at that time, even for a woman in her late 20s: Most women and girls in the Pale received no formal education at all,[79] and adult education classes in the English-speaking world cost time that was likely in short supply, especially in a poor household with three children younger than four years old. In addition, in such an overwhelmingly Jewish neighborhood, Sarah likely could have gotten by without knowing even how to speak English, much less read it.

There are other inconsistencies, however: There are still Rebecca and Solomon's differing records, plus the curious death records of Abraham's parents, Davis and Annie. Annie's death certificate gives the last name "Arbeiter,"[80] but her gravestone uses the "Arbiter" spelling.[81] Davis's death certificate also lists him as an "Arbeiter,"[82] but United Synagogue cemetery records list his name there as "Davis Arbiter." Records from the probate of Davis's estate also give an alternate surname of "Albeiter."[83]

Abraham's oldest brother, Isaac, has the opposite pattern: He and his family are recorded with the surname "Arbiter" as early as 1901,[84] and used that spelling consistently from then on. Even so, in the same cemetery that his parents are buried under the name "Arbiter," Isaac, for unknown reasons, appears in cemetery records as "Arbeiter."[85]

Isaac and Betsy's son Joseph used the last name "Arbiter,"[86] as did Joseph's son, Ivor.[87] Ivor traveled to the United States during World War II[88] and stayed with Solomon's family, starting the entire Arbeiter/Arbiter discussion with the U.S. branch of the family.

One-time inconsistencies aside, the short version of the explanation is simply that three brothers immigrated from Poland and wanted (or needed) to anglicize their last name, "Arbajter." Two of them, Abraham and Jacob,[89] chose "Arbeiter," and one, Isaac, chose "Arbiter." Their descendants followed suit.

It's not clear what pushed Abraham to make another trip, this time alone, but in May 1907 he left, aboard the S.S. *Celtic*, for America. It would be the last time he saw his mother Annie, who died in 1919,[90] and Isaac, who died in 1923.[91] He was hardly alone in his quest: Between 1904 and 1908, almost 24,000 Jews—maybe a tenth of Britain's entire population—left Great Britain for America, most leaving London in favor of New York City.[92]

Abraham arrived on May 27, with Sarah and the children arriving on the S.S. *St. Paul* six months later. The four of them were briefly detained at Ellis Island,[93] a fate common for women traveling with children but not a husband;[94] they were allowed to enter once Abraham could pick them up.

Visiting the family's old haunts in Europe is a tempting notion, but one that will likely fall short of expectations. The apartment building where Abraham and Sarah first lived is gone now—in addition to absorbing about a dozen bombs during the London Blitz (plus two giant naval mines attached to parachutes),[95] the area around Old Montague Street was almost entirely demolished in the decades after World War II.[96] The area around Stepney Green is part of a London "conservation area,"[97] but the buildings in the area of the old tenements appear to be far newer than 1901.

Of the Arbajters in Poland, the simplest explanation may be an old musical adage, usually cited in reference to jazz: "Music is the space between the notes." The same could be said of post-war Poland—in a country of more than 35 million, there is plenty of music being played, but the silences are where we find the Jews.

Rabbi Byron Sherwin wrote about several trips he took to Poland in the 1980s and 1990s, to search for evidence—if not physical, then at least spiritual—of his Jewish ancestors, in a land devoid of Jews. Sherwin makes multiple references to "split vision," imagining the world of the past beside the realities before him. This appears multiple times as a more literal dichotomy, such as when he was traveling with two professional acquaintances, a priest and a rabbi, down a street in Warsaw: "[The rabbi and I] speak in Hebrew. He and the priest converse in Polish. Young Poles cast curious gazes at us as we walk to the rabbi's house for lunch. The rabbi wears traditional Hasidic garb. The priest says to me in English, 'You see, there is no anti-Semitism in Poland.' The rabbi says to me in Hebrew, 'After everything that has happened to us here, you see how they still hate us. They are afraid that we might return.'

Polish anti-Semitism, Jewish anti-Polonism—these topics accompany me wherever I go."[98]

Later, reaching the former location of the Warsaw ghetto, Sherwin sees the "split vision" again: "Warsaw before the war—the most Jewish city in the world. Warsaw now—a *Judenrein*[ix] city awakening from communism... I think of what one of the survivors of the Warsaw Ghetto uprising once said, 'If you could lick my heart, the poison would kill you.' "[99]

Decades after Sherwin's trips, these dynamics still simmer below the surface. In 2014, Warsaw allocated more than $120,000 for a project to replace structures in the city that had been built out of Jewish tombstones—even then, some residents were skeptical; one told a reporter simply, "What's the good of destroying everything? The Hebrew is only on one of the arbour posts."[100]

In 2017, emboldened by the success of far-right politicians agitating against Islam and immigration, resurgent Polish white nationalist organizations held their largest rally ever—police estimated 60,000 demonstrators marched through the capital, some holding banners with slogans such as "Europe will be white or uninhabited" and "Clean blood."[101] A reporter asked one of the demonstrators why he had come; he responded, "To get the Jews out of power."[102] 72 years after the Red Army liberated the city from Nazi control, chants of "Sieg heil" again echo through the streets of Warsaw.[103]

In particular, our family's story in Wyszogród is one of absences: There were almost 3,000 Jews in the town before the Nazis arrived; today, some estimates say there may be as few as 5,000 in the entire country,[104] down from a pre-war population of more than 3 million.[105] The synagogue on the hill is gone, destroyed at the command

---

[ix] *Judenrein*, meaning "clean of Jews," was a term used by Nazi Germany to indicate the "impurity" of Jewishness had been removed from a region.

of German invaders in 1939.[106] The site where it stood remains undeveloped, a politely maintained lot near the river[107] that tells a more captivating story than a temple ever could.

The Jewish cemetery in town is equally deserted, though to call it "vacant" would be something resembling an error: More than a century of Jews are buried there,[108] including Ryfka Arbajter, the younger sister of Abraham Arbeiter *5-28*. However, we will never know where—today, there is only a field. The Nazis destroyed most of the stones (or *matzevot*) during the war, and there are stories across Eastern Europe of Jewish cemeteries being "quarried" for building materials even years later. Entire matzevot have been found, Hebrew writing still visible, in the masonry walls of stables, the floors of homes,[109] and, sometimes, in other cemeteries, having been flipped around and re-engraved after the war for Christian burials.[110] In Wyszogród, sections of sidewalk were made with markers torn from the graves of the town's Jews.[111] There was an older Jewish cemetery nearby, in use by the town until it filled up in 1830. When the Nazis arrived, they dug up the graves and tossed the bones into the river. Officials were reportedly bribed to allow the townspeople to retrieve the remains and re-inter them in the "new" cemetery, though the stones are lost and part of the original cemetery is now used to store garbage.[112]

It's easy to find the new cemetery. Abraham's grand-parents[x] are buried there, and at least two[xi] of his great-grandparents. Abe's cousin, Haim Aron Biłgoraj, was buried here in 1914.[113] Haim Aron's wife, Brucha, and three of their children[xii] were killed in the Holocaust and buried elsewhere—the most likely location is with the rest of Wyszogród's Jewish residents, in the burn-pits of the

---

[x]Szulim Haim *7-114* and Sura Ester Biłgoraj *7-115*.
[xi]Szulim Haim's parents, Szymon *8-228* and Rasza Biłgoraj *8-229*.
[xii]See the *HaShoah* appendix for more information about them.

Treblinka extermination camp,[114] raising the grim notion
that those laid to rest in a defiled cemetery may have been
the fortunate ones.

An obelisk was erected in the center of the site in 1989,
dedicated to the town's Holocaust victims. Nearby, a small,
unassuming monument from 1947 sits among the shrubs,
designed to look like a gravesite.[115] On a long, flat slab, an
engraving reads, *Ten cmentarz został zbezczeszczony przez
hitlerowskich barbarzyńców w latach 1939-1945*, which trans-
lates to, "This cemetery was desecrated by Nazi barbarians
in 1939–1945." Above that, a simple, rounded gravestone
stands, perpendicular to the slab. In unadorned capital letters, it says only, *Nawet umarłym nie dali spokoju*: "Even
the dead were not left in peace."

*Figure 1.6: A photo likely depicting the interior of the Wyszogród
synagogue. Along the back wall is the aron ha-kodesh, the elaborate structure used for holding the Torah scrolls.*[116] *According to
testimony from former residents, the Nazis forced Wyszogród's
Jews to personally dismantle the ark around Hanukkah 1939;
its destruction provided firewood for the town.*

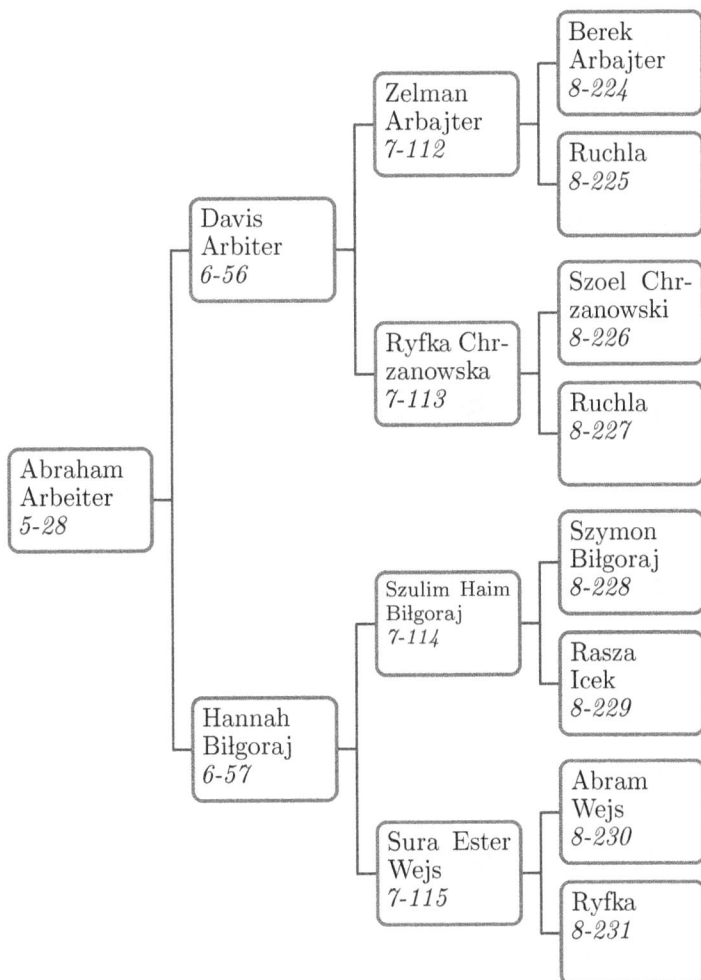

Figure 1.7: The known ancestors of Abraham Arbeiter (5-28), the great-grandfather of Nancy Abdill (2-2).

Solomon Arbeiter (4-14), Claire Reinstein (4-15)

Solomon Arbeiter was the middle child of Abraham and Sarah Arbeiter, born 10 Oct 1903 in the Whitechapel district of London, England.[117] He left England for America with his mother and siblings 9 Nov 1907. In the 1910s, Sol got work selling newspapers in Harlem,[118] near where the family was living at 1293 Amsterdam Ave.[119]

Clara Reinstein was born 30 Mar 1908 in the family's home at 99 Gerry St.,[121] in Brooklyn. She married Solomon on 6 Feb 1927[122] and gave birth to their first child, Sylvia, 19 Jan 1929.[123]

Sylvia's death later the same year was the topic of quiet family stories for decades: There had been a vaguely explained accident in which her carriage was knocked over; Sylvia hit her head,[124] the story went, and she died, simple as that. However, her death certificate, obtained in 2017, yielded additional information that no one in the family had known: Sylvia's primary cause of death is listed as "acute meningitis, probably T.B. in organs," with the secondary cause "acidosis due to acute intestinal intoxication." There is a form of non-contagious meningitis that can be caused by a traumatic brain injury, so it is possible the fabled accident was still the primary cause.

Figure 1.8: Claire and Solomon Arbeiter, possibly at their wedding in 1927.[120]

However, it appears Sylvia was also gravely ill independently of her injury—tuberculosis ("T.B.") was still not widely vaccinated against, and it would be decades before the necessary antibiotics were invented to fight the disease.

Sylvia's tuberculosis may be why there is no further elaboration on her meningitis: In the early 20th century, the New York City Department of Health maintained a list of diseases requiring more details if they were the "sole cause of death," because "any one of these may be the result of an injury, and thus be a subject for investigation by a Medical Examiner. If it is not, the certificate should make that plain." Meningitis was on the list, but tuberculosis was not; there is no evidence that there was an investigation.

Figure 1.9: Ann 3-7, Sol 4-14 and Jay Arbeiter in about 1936.[125]

In any case, it is striking to consider that Claire had given birth to, and then buried, her first child before she was 22, and Solomon had just turned 26. The couple had a total of three children:

- **Sylvia**, b. 19 Jan 1929, d. 1 Nov 1929 in the Bronx.[126]
- **ANN ETTA** *3-7*, b. 8 Nov 1930 in Queens, d. 21 Apr 2017 in St. Petersburg, Florida. Probably named after Solomon's paternal grandmother, Hana Itta Arbeiter *5-29*, who in England went by the name "Annie." See the "Siegel" chapter for more.

- **Jay David**, b. 28 May 1935. Possibly named after Solomon's paternal grandfather, Dawid Arbajter *5-28*, the husband of Hana Itta. Married Joan Berman (b. 8 May 1937),[127] with whom he had two daughters: Lisa (b. 8 Dec 1963) and Gail (b. 4 Sep 1965; married Jamie Goldstein, three sons: Daniel, Benjamin and Adam). Divorced; married Suzanne Schleiff in 1992.

Though the family was under the impression Solomon worked for the *New York Daily News* for most of his career, Sol is listed in the 1920 census as an office clerk,[128] and in 1930 as a "junk dealer";[129] his son Jay has no recollection of these jobs being discussed. He does remember, however, hearing that Sol had at one point gone into business with David Reinstein, Solomon's brother-in-law, in a candy store venture[130] in the 1920s—David is listed as the "storekeeper" of a candy store in the 1930 census,[131] when Sol was already in the "junk" business. Goldie (Newman) Task, who was Claire and David's aunt, was running a candy store with her husband in 1940;[132] it's possible they were also somehow involved.

Solomon and Claire separated in about 1947,[133] and were officially divorced in 1955.[134] Solomon got remarried, to Aina Kristina (Eriksson) Myhrman, probably at some point between 1955 and 1968.[135] Aina was born 10 Oct 1909 in Stockholm, Sweden,[136] to Helmer and Anna (Larsson)[137] Eriksson.[138] They immigrated to the U.S. in 1925 and lived in Brooklyn.[139] It appears she eventually started spelling her name "Ina,"[140] probably in the 1930s.[141]

Ina married Rolf Engelbrekt Myhrman 27 Apr 1929 in New York[142] and had two daughters: Barbara (b. abt 1930) and Ingegerd (b. abt 1932).[143] Ina and Rolf divorced in 1938, when they appear to have been living in Dade County, Florida,[144] though Ina and their children were living in New York again in 1940, with the Erikssons.[145] Sol moved to Florida at some point after his separation from Claire *4-15*; it's not known whether he and Ina met in New York, or if she had returned to Florida first.

Claire moved to Metuchen, New Jersey in the 1970s.[146] Richard Abdill *2-2* remembers Claire speaking in Yiddish to a family friend, joyful to be able to have a conversation in what was likely her first language.[147] Yiddish is a relatively unique construction, associated with the culture of the Ashkenazi Jews rather than a particular geographic region. "Old Yiddish" likely became the colloquial language of Eastern European Jews some time around the 13th century, born of elements pulled from German, Aramaic, and several regional dialects, before modern Yiddish coalesced some time around 1700.[148] It seems worth noting that, after family members spoke the language for what could have been 900 years, Claire was the last one.

Solomon died 26 Jan 1973 in South Florida;[149] Ina lived until 8 Dec 2002.[150]

Claire lived in Metuchen, New Jersey and died 5 Oct 1992.[151]

Figure 1.10: Ann Dondero 3-7, Nancy Siegel 2-3 and Claire Arbeiter 4-15 in about 1986.[152]

Figure 1.11: The signatures of Solomon 4-14 and Claire (here, Clara) Arbeiter 4-15 from their 1927 marriage certificate.

(a) From May 1937. Front row: Claire 4-15, Ann 3-7 and Jay Arbeiter. Back: Arthur Gladstone, Claire's brother-in-law, and Sol Arbeiter 4-14.[153]

(b) Ann Dondero 3-7 with her brother Jay Arbeiter, at the bar mitzvah celebration of her son Mark.[154]

Figure 1.13: Ann 3-7, Jay and Claire Arbeiter 4-15.[155]

Abraham Arbeiter (5-28), Sarah Jacobowitz (5-29)

Abraham Arbeiter was born "Abram Arbajter" in the Polish town of Wyszogród on 22 Jan 1878.[157] He was probably named after Abram Wejs *8-230*, his mother's grandfather.

He and his family moved to London, England in the late 1890s, and he married Sarah Jacobowitz there in 1899.[158] (At some point, she and her children began offering her maiden name as "Jacobs," not "Jacobowitz.")

Sarah was born 12 May 1880[159] maybe in a small village called Kizminsk.[xiii]

Abraham and several relatives were working as hairdressers when he left for America[160] 18 May 1907, aboard the ship *Celtic* out of the large port in Southampton, England.[161] He was followed several months later by Sarah and the couple's three children:[162]

Figure 1.14: Sarah Jacobs, in a photo she gave to her son Sol 4-14 in 1932.[156]

- **Rebecca**, "Betty,"[163] born in London 2 Nov 1900,[164] died 6 Mar[165] 1983.[166] Probably named after Ryfka Arbajter *7-113*, Abraham's grandmother. Married first Jacob Wasserman on 20 Jun 1920;[167] he died in 1928 of complications from appendix surgery,[168] possibly in Oklahoma.[169] The couple had one son, Harold (5 Sep 1921–19 Jun 2002).[170] Married next

---

[xiii]See the "Jacobs" chapter for more about this potential location.

Louis Buchalter 20 Aug 1931,[171] then Arthur Jarwood (11 Nov 1907–27 Jun 1998).[172]

- **SOLOMON** *4-14*, b. 10 Oct 1903, London, England;[173] d. 26 Jan 1973, Dade County, Florida.[174]
  Probably named after Zelman Arbajter *7-112*, Abraham's grandfather. Married Claire Reinstein *4-15*,
  then Ina Myhrman; see previous section for more
  details.

- **Benjamin**, b. 24 Mar 1905 in London,[175] d. 20 Dec 1987
  in New Port Richey, Pasco County, Florida.[176] Married Sylvia Greenberg (22 Feb 1911–31 Jan 2001)[177]
  in abt 1927;[178] had one daughter, Elaine, b. abt
  1928.[179] Ben and Sylvia appear to have split up at
  some point in the 1930s, and living family members
  do not remember having heard of her. May have had
  a son[180] and at some point remarried, to someone
  named "Mary."[181]

*Figure 1.15: The Arbeiter siblings and their spouses, in 1968.
L–R: Marty Siegel 3-6, Ben and Mary[182] Arbeiter, Ann Siegel
3-7, Sol 4-14 and Ina Arbeiter, Arthur and Betty Jarwood.[183]*

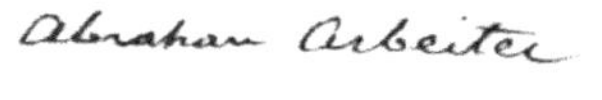

Figure 1.16: The signature of Abraham Arbeiter 5-28 from his World War II draft registration in 1942.[184]

Once they arrived in America, the children found a home waiting for them at 375 W. 126th Street, in Harlem. They were part of a major relocation happening in conjunction with a construction boom in the area: In 1900, about 17,000 Jews lived in Harlem.[185] By 1910, there were more than 100,000, broken up into multiple distinct neighborhoods.[186] Until the Great Migration kicked in after World War I and brought hundreds of thousands of African Americans to the northeast, Jewish immigrants were the largest ethnic group in Harlem, which at the time was the second-largest community of new Jewish immigrants in the country (second only to the Lower East Side).[187]

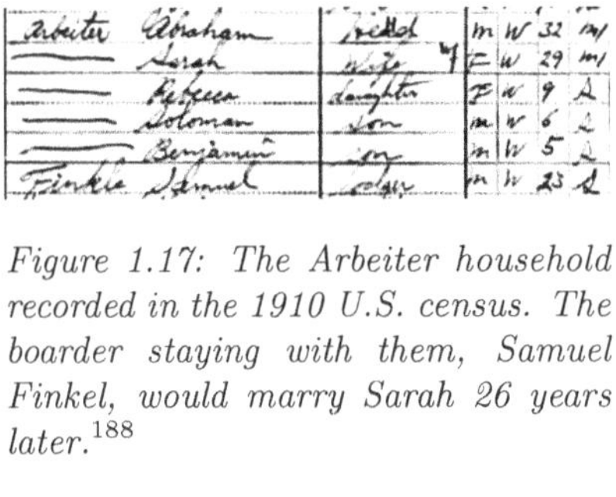

Arbeiter	Abraham	head	m	W	32	m1
—	Sarah	wife	F	W	29	m1
—	Rebecca	daughter	F	W	9	S
—	Solomon	son	m	W	6	S
—	Benjamin	son	m	W	5	S
Finkle	Samuel	boarder	m	W	23	S

Figure 1.17: The Arbeiter household recorded in the 1910 U.S. census. The boarder staying with them, Samuel Finkel, would marry Sarah 26 years later.[188]

Abe and Sarah's grandson Jay Arbeiter said the family was, at least for a time, deeply religious: "My grandfather, when he came over, was very religious. He was Orthodox. My mother told a very funny story that when my parents were first married, my father's parents [Abe and Sarah] came over for dinner—and she was just a new bride at the time—but they came over and they were eating, and my grandfather said, 'This is the most delicious veal I've ever had.' And she, my mother, said, 'Oh, that's not veal,' you know, 'That's pork.' And he turned white and tried to go into the bathroom to throw up." He added, "In later years, by the way, he was totally areligious, if not sacrilegious."[189]

Abraham and Sarah appear to have separated around

1925: Sarah and their children are recorded twice in the 1925 New York state census—once with Abraham in Mamakating, an upstate resort town,[190] and once in East Harlem with Sam Finkel, Sarah's future husband.[191]

Sam Finkel was born 15 Sep 1886 in Russia[192] and came to the U.S. in 1908.[193] Interestingly, he was listed in the 1910 census as a boarder living with Sarah and Abraham,[194] so it appears he knew the family for decades before he and Sarah were married. At the time, taking in boarders was common enough to not even warrant a second glance—in 1910, 32 percent of Jewish homes in the city had at least one.[195] While there aren't any statistics about women marrying men who had rented a room in their home, there are numerous accounts of "nervously jocular references" in popular Yiddish fiction and theater of the moral risks of the male boarder.[196]

Sam and Sarah were officially married in spring 1936,[198] though Sarah in 1929 opened a bank account and gave her husband's name as "Sam."[199]

They were living in upstate New York by 1939,[200] where they ran a junkyard. Jay Arbeiter remembers visiting occasionally: "She had a hard life," he said. "When we would visit her, she had a junkyard in Newburgh, and in the winter, she'd be sitting with a kerosene stove in a little shed, with gloves with no fingers, her fingers coming out of the palms of these gloves, buying and selling junk to people."[201]

Figure 1.18: Abraham 5-28 and Blanche Arbeiter.[197]

They both died in Newburgh, Sam on 11 Feb 1949,[202] and Sarah 14 Jan 1963. They're buried nearby at Congregation Agudas Israel Cemetery in New Windsor.[203]

Abraham also remarried after the divorce, to Blanche Salter, a widow about 14 years his junior. She was born Blanche Friedman[204] abt 1892 in New York;[205] she married Bernard "Barney" Salter probably 4 Jan 1913.[206]

Barney died 14 Dec 1918,[207] after the couple had two children: Henry, born abt 1914,[208] and Joseph, born 13 May 1915.[209] There is no further documentation of Henry, who may have died as a child, but Joseph was living with Abe and Blanche in 1940.[210] He died 23 Aug 1983.[211]

The years between 1925 and 1940 are something of a mystery: Documentation of the marriage between Abraham and Blanche has not been found, and none of the members of the family are accounted for in the 1930 census. They were likely married at some point before November 1937,[212] but other than that we do not catch up to them until 3 years later.

Blanche died 26 Oct 1959,[213] and Abraham on 8 Sep 1966.[214]

"Aunt Betty & Uncle Lou"

An accounting of the Arbeiters in New York would be incomplete without including the presence and influence of Louis "Lepke" Buchalter (b. 6 Feb 1897,[215] d. 4 Mar 1944). The short version is simple: Betty Arbeiter married a gangster—a good one, at that—and lived well for decades by the proceeds of murder and extortion. The longer version isn't actually much more complicated.

Louis was born to a poor Jewish family on the Lower East Side; his penchant for petty crime as a teenager got him acquainted with the lower levels of the New York underworld, and he slowly gained more and more power as he helped the fledgling mafia ecosystem gradually evolve past lead-pipe strong-arm services and into the more sophisticated racketeering we are familiar with today.[216]

Lepke encountered Betty somewhere in the smoky jazz clubs of New York, where Betty worked and Lepke met with his underworld associates. Betty was a hostess at Club Kentucky,[218] the popular West 49th Street jazz joint[219] most well known for the young leader of its house band, Duke Ellington.[220] She also worked for nightclub entrepreneur Ben Marden,[221] whose businesses included the Silver Slipper,[222] known as a glamorous[223] midtown club where one could find easy liquor through the era of Prohibition,[224] and the Cotton

Figure 1.19: Jay, Betty and Ann Arbeiter 3-7 at Camp Allegro.[217]

Club,[225] the famous Harlem venue that hosted musical greats such as Ellington, Cab Calloway, Fats Waller and Count Basie. While the details of their meeting are unknown, chroniclers of Lepke's life believe these clubs were involved.

When they were married in 1931, Louis was already on his way to the top of what would become known as "Murder Inc.," the most prolific squad of goons and assassins in the history of the American mob. It's estimated that the Syndicate, as it was more commonly known at the time, was responsible for upwards of 1,000 murders nationwide,[226] to say nothing of the intricate web of extortionary rackets in place all over New York under Lepke's personal direction.

At the same time, "Uncle Lou"—five-foot six, soft-spoken[227] and sentimental—was a friendly and benevolent presence in the lives of his in-laws: He legally adopted his step-son, Betty's son Harold Wasserman,[228] and carried a picture of him inside his platinum, diamond-studded

35

pocket watch.[229] He made sure his niece Ann *3-7* could go to Camp Allegro,[230] the expensive summer camp run by his sister;[231] Ann fondly recalled her summers there even decades later.[232] He and Betty lived well: The FBI found on one trip to a Southern resort they spent upwards of $1,000 per week,[233] for example, and Betty later testified about conversations she had at the heavyweight boxing match between Max Baer and Jim "Cinderella Man" Braddock. (She claimed to have won $50 betting on Braddock, a 10-to-1 underdog.)[234]

There is evidence of less altruistic connections to the Arbeiters as well: FBI files suggest Betty's brother Ben was a "bodyguard and driver"[236] for Lepke, and their mother Sarah *5-29* reportedly helped set up bank accounts with her husband Sam Finkel that may have been used to funnel money between parties.[237] (It's important to note that there is no documentation of these assertions ever being brought up in court, and the accused are no longer around to defend themselves. The accusations should be taken with a grain of salt.)

Figure 1.20: Louis Buchalter (right) in 1940. According to the Library of Congress, he is handcuffed to FBI Director J. Edgar Hoover.[235]

While the family narrative 80 years later would lead one to believe the Arbeiters were naively unaware of the dealings of "Uncle Lou," it would have been hard to miss the clues: He was a millionaire, for starters, without any particular business—some estimates guess that the annual proceeds from his labor rackets, split with partner Jacob "Gurrah" Shapiro, may have totalled as much as $50 million.[238]

In addition, the bar mitzvah for Betty's son Harold was attended by many of the contemporary mafia's biggest names: Bugsy Siegel was there, as was Meyer Lansky and Abner "Longie" Zwillman. Also in attendance was Lucky Luciano,[239] the first boss of the Genovese crime family, then at the height of his power.[xiv,240] In *Lepke*, a 1975 movie about Buchalter's life, Abe Arbeiter *5-28* was played by Milton Berle.

Eventually, Louis stopped coming around: He ended up on the run in late 1936, triggering an international manhunt after multiple convictions for violating antitrust laws with his rackets and, later, for conspiring to smuggle heroin into New York. By summer 1939, Lepke's killing spree of potential witnesses had inspired FBI Director J. Edgar Hoover to name him "national Public Enemy No. 1."[241] Eventually, Lepke's surrender was negotiated by famed New York columnist Walter Winchell, and he turned himself in directly to Hoover in front of a hotel. One of the first things he reportedly said to Hoover was, "I would like to see my wife and kids, please."[xv,242]

The surrender happened 24 Aug 1939—it was the last day of freedom he would ever have. He was convicted 30 Nov 1941 of the murder of candy store owner Joseph Rosen, and, on March 4, 1944, he was strapped to the electric chair at Sing Sing Correctional Facility[243] and executed. Prosecutor Burton Turkus noted, in his 1951 memoir: "Before then, no executive of organized crime

---

[xiv]Allegedly, it was Luciano who four years later concocted the scheme that tricked Lepke into surrendering by convincing him, with the help of Lansky and Zwillman, that he would not have to face the murder charges being prepared by the state.

[xv]This is probably an error on Winchell's part—it seems unlikely that Lepke would have asked to see his "kids" when he had only one.

ever sat in the chair. Since Lepke, there has been no other."[xvi,244]

There are people who would prefer the Buchalters not be mentioned in this book; by all accounts, the occupation and fate of Lepke was never talked about, even decades after his death—it wasn't until Ann's daughter Nancy *2-3* was an adult that she even knew of him.[245] It's understandable to want to avoid the topic, and the aim of this work is not to air anyone's dirty laundry in the name of historical gossip. It makes sense that Louis and his bloody legacy are left out of polite family conversation—however, this book is not polite family conversation. This isn't *supposed* to be happy—it's just supposed to be true, and we would do a disservice to our descendants to lie to them by omission. Even if it's embarrassing to be connected to him, to scrub him from history is a far graver sentence than to avoid bringing him up at the dinner table, and it is a fate none of us have the right to impose.

So, Lepke and Betty are in the book. Not because it's salacious, but because they're family.

[xvi] Before his murder conviction, Louis had been convicted on drug charges and sentenced to more than a decade in federal prison. Because of a complicated series of *habeas corpus* technicalities regarding federal authorities turning him over to New York for execution, Louis had to receive a pardon from President Franklin Roosevelt before he could be sent to the chair. Turkus called it "probably the longest and certainly the most bizarre and needless controversy ever waged between national and state authorities over one man."

Figure 1.21: The Reinstein family at the Riobamba Club in the early 1940s. Lepke (the brother-in-law of Claire Reinstein 4-15) owned the club, which in 1943 hosted the debut of young singer Frank Sinatra. Clockwise from bottom-left: An unidentified woman, Anna and Arthur Gladstone, Milton and Ruth Kaufman, an unidentified woman, Pearl and Harry Gitlin, Claire Arbeiter 4-15, an unidentified man.[246]

Visit Lepke In Death House

Mrs. Betty Buchalter and her son, Harold, reach the gate of Sing Sing prison, N. Y., for a death house call on her husband, Louis Lepke) Buchalter, leader of the notorious "Murder, Inc." Lepke was given at least two more days of life by a last-minute gubernatorial stay, pending an appeal to the U. S. Supreme Court.

Figure 1.22: A newspaper photo of Betty and Harold leaving Sing Sing Correctional Facility a few days before Louis Buchalter's execution.[247]

Davis Arbeiter (6-56),
Hannah Biłgoraj (6-57)

Davis and Hannah are the Arbeiters who took the family out of Eastern Europe—though Polish documentation suggests most of the family immigrated in 1904, they had actually arrived in time for the 1901 British census.[248] They certainly moved to England at some point after 1889, when their youngest child was born, and probably after 1891, when they do not seem to have been accounted for in that year's census in England.

Davis Arbiter was born "Dawid Arbajter" in 1845, in the small Polish village of Bieżuń,[249] in the Płock Governorate. Hannah was born 15 Jul 1846 with the name "Hana Itta Biłgoraj" in Wyszogród.[250] Though they told census-takers in England they had eight children,[251] it appears there was a ninth, who died as a child. The other eight, as far as we know, immigrated to London with their parents:

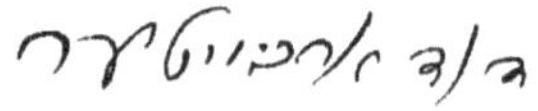

Figure 1.23: The signature of Dawid Arbajter 6-56 from the 1878 birth record of his son Abram 5-28.

- **Isak**,[252] "Isaac,"[253] b. 1871 in Poland,[254] died 17 Nov 1923 in London after being hit by a motorcycle.[255] Worked in Wyszogród as a *krawiec*,[256] or tailor. In London, he spent at least several years working as a jewelry dealer. Married Betsy abt 1896 and had three children: Eveline, Esther,[257] and Joseph.[258] Joseph's young son Ivor[259] left London 18 July 1940[260] to stay with Solomon *4-14* and Claire Arbeiter *4-15*; Joseph and Solomon were first cousins. (The family story has always been that Ivor came to escape "the Blitz," the prolonged German bombing of London in World War II, but Ivor left weeks before the Battle of Britain began, and almost two months before the "Blitzkrieg" campaign launched. Ivor's journey was likely more connected to the general evacuation efforts that started the previous year.)

- **Łaja**, b. 1873, potentially in Jarosław,[261] Poland. She is listed in Poland as having gone to London with the rest of the family, though no records of her presence there have been found. She may have been the 36-year-old "Leah Arbiter" who died in Whitechapel in summer 1906.[262]
- **Ruchla**, b. 22 Nov 1875 in Poland.[263] Like Łaja, she was recorded as having emigrated to England, but no documents have been found indicating her presence there.
- **ABRAM** *5-28*,[264] "Abraham," b. 22 Jan 1878[265] in Poland, d. 8 Sep 1866 in New York. Worked as a barber. The only known Arbeiter sibling to travel to America. Married Sarah Jacobs; see profile in previous section.
- **Nauma**, "Nelly," b. 11 Jan 1881 in Poland.[266] Worked as a "tailoress" in London for a time.[267] May have been the "Nancy Arbiter" who died in Whitechapel in summer 1918.[268]
- **Jakow**, "Jacob," b. 11 Jan 1881 in Poland,[269] d. 21 May 1946 in London.[270] Worked as a barber;[271] married Sarah abt 1908,[272] had three[273] children.
- **Rasza**, "Rosie," b. 3 May 1886 in Poland.[274] Was working as a "cigarette cutter" in London in 1901.[275] Likely married Hyman Applebaum summer 1906;[276] one son, Davie.[277] They lived near Rosie's brother Isaac, who may have been in business with Hyman.
- **Ryfka**, Rasza's twin sister,[278] b. 3 May 1886 in Wyszogród.[279] Probably the same "Ryfka Arbajter" who died there later in 1886.[280]
- **Miriam**,[xvii] b. 15 Jan 1890 in Poland.[281] Married Morris Peters 1910;[282] one son, Hyman.[283]

[xvii]Her given name was recorded in Poland as "Mariem."

If we take Wyszogród's residential records from the
1890s at face value, then we have a pretty clear timeline of
the family's emigration: Isak left first, in 1893, followed by
his father Dawid *6-56* in 1898, Abram *5-28* in 1899, and
the rest of the family together in 1904. However, almost
the entire family is enumerated in the 1901 English census—
whether the other dates can be trusted is an open question,
but we know Isak, at least, was in London before abt 1896,
when he got married.[284]

It's interesting that Abram is recorded as leaving in
1899—it's unclear where officials obtained that information,
but it would seem that if he was specifically recorded as
leaving that year, that everyone else actually had remained.
This would mean his siblings and mother would have arrived
in London just in time to appear in the 1901 census.

Hannah (or "Annie") died 30 Mar 1919.[285] Dawid (who
went by "David" when he first arrived in London[286] and
then adopted the name "Davis") died 27 Dec 1929;[287] his
£125 estate passed to his son Jacob.[288]

They are buried beside each other in East Ham Cemetery in London. Both have large gravestones with lengthy
epitaphs, but for some reason Davis's, despite being 10
years younger than Hannah's, is almost entirely unreadable.
His name and the Hebrew inscription is gone except for a
few scattered characters, but the bottom half of the stone
is still partially readable and includes a short poem:[289]

> His hand was open as the day
> A generous heart, a nature brave
> And when from earth he passed away
> Our hearts went with him to the grave

The lines are a selection from "In Memory of Charles
H. Sandford," a poem by American writer George Pope
Morris.[290] If Hannah's intact gravestone is any indication,
there must be a lot missing from Davis's—hers includes a
lengthy Hebrew inscription reading, in part, "The worthy

woman who fears God should be praised, wholesome and pure were her deeds, she extended her hand to the poor, and lent a hand to the afflicted, the Torah of God was precious to her..."[291]

In English, it says below her name that she is "deeply mourned by her sorrowing husband, children, grand-children, relatives & friends," and also includes a poem:[292]

> A light is from the household gone
> A voice we loved is stilled
> A place is vacant in our home
> Which never can be filled

The source of this verse is unclear, but it appears in American epitaphs and obituaries as early as 1857,[293] and in the United Kingdom at some point after that.[294]

Zelman Arbajter (7-112), Ryfka Chrzanowska (7-113)

Zelman Arbajter was born abt 1820. Ryfka was born abt 1823, to Szoel *7-114* and Ruchla Chrzanowski *7-115*.[295] We don't know for sure where either was born, but they were married in Bieżuń 15 Feb 1843.[296] The couple had at least two children:

- **DAWID** *6-56*, b. 1845 in Bieżuń; assumed the name "Davis Arbeiter" in England. See profile above for more.
- **Mendel**, b. 25 Mar 1866 in Bieżuń, d. 18 Feb 1909. Moved to nearby Sochaczew at some point, and ended up in Wyszogród,[297] where Dawid was raising his family. Worked as a *robotnik*, or laborer.[298] Married Estera Sura Grinbaum in 1888,[299] had four children: Moszek Aron (b. 20 Dec 1888),[300] Lipa (b. 8 Nov 1890,[301] d. probably 16 Aug 1914, see below), Hena Ryfka (b. 1895)[302] and Bela (b. 15 Jul 1903).[303]

Lipa Arbajter

It appears at least one son of Mendel Arbajter fought in World War I: Lipa, a first cousin of Abraham Arbeiter *5-28*, is probably the "Licpo Arbajter," killed 16 Aug 1914,[304] who was recorded in documents currently held by the Russian State Library:[305] Though the name is slightly different, the soldier's father is listed as "Mendel," he is from Wyszogród, and our Lipa would have been 23 at the time, a standard age for military service.

When war broke out late in the summer of 1914, Poland itself was not a country: Its lands had been split over the previous 150 years between multiple powers,[xviii] some of which were on opposing sides in the war. The war's first[306] Polish military unit, the First Cadre Company, was founded 3 Aug 1914 by famed leader Józef Piłsudski, who formulated an (ultimately successful) plan to join forces with the Central Powers—Germany and its allies— in an effort to free Poland from Russian rule: Piłsudski's "Polish Legions" fought with the Austrian military against Russia, and when the war ended in 1918, Poland became an independent country for the first time since the 1700s.

Lipa Arbajter appears to have been among the first soldiers to join these forces—his death on August 16 is timed less than two weeks after the unsanctioned formation of the First Cadre Company, and 11 days before the Polish Legions were even officially started. While we don't have any information about where he was killed, if he was fighting with the First Cadre Company his death was likely about 125 miles south of Wyszogród, somewhere near Kielce, the first city liberated from Russian rule. The unit helped capture the city on August 12, but the next day was forced to retreat by Russian forces. Three days after that, "Licpo" died.

[xviii]See the "Shifting borders" chapter for details.

Berek Arbajter (8-224), Ruchla (8-225)

Berek Arbajter was born abt 1804 and worked in Wyszogród as a butcher. He died 28 Apr 1855, also in Wyszogród. Ruchla was born at about the same time as Berek, and died sometime after he did.[307] They had four known children:

- **ZELMAN** *7-112*, b. abt 1820.[308] See profile directly above.
- **Mosek**, b. 1825 in Bieżuń, d. 11 Feb 1890.[309] At some point Mosek moved to Wyszogród, where Zelman's children were living in the late 1800s.
- **Myndla**, b. abt 1835.[310]
- **Mordka**, b. abt 1842.[311]

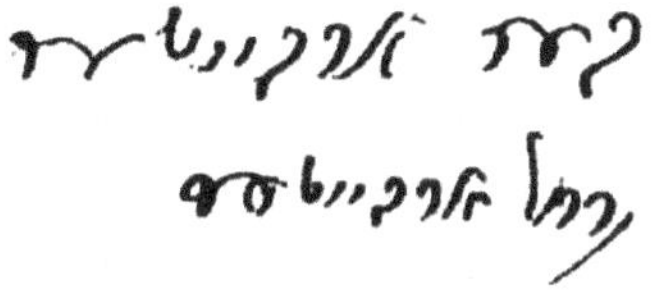

Figure 1.24: The signatures of Berek 8-224 (top) and Ruchla Arbajter 8-225, from the 1843 marriage record of their son Zelman 7-112.

Family of Mosek Arbajter

Zelman's brother Mosek married Łaja Ficman[312] and had
six children:

- **Josek**, b. 1 Oct 1863.[313] Probably known formally
  as "Josef"; "Josek" is the Polish diminutive form, or
  nickname.[314]
- **Tauba**, b. 2 May 1871.[315]
- **Raca**, b. 8 Feb 1874.[316]
- **Fajga**, b. 20 Mar 1877.[317]
- **Sura Mindla**, b. 15 Sep 1861.[318] Married Szlama
  Zauraj.[319]
- **Ruchla**, b. 14 Oct 1859. Married Abram Icek Akaw-
  iec,[320] had six children:
  - Alta Haja, b. 9 Mar 1882, d. 3 Jan 1892.[321]
  - Hena Malka, b. 15 Feb 1886, d. 16 Dec 1918;[322]
    married J.D. Baum).[323]
  - Moszek, b. 4 Dec 1890; moved to Gostynin.[324]
  - Ruda, b. 15 May 1894.[325]
  - Hana Maria, b. 18 Jan 1897.[326]
  - Golda, b. 1899.[327]

Chapter 2

Biłgoraj

"Biłgoraj" is a name that has been unknown to our branch of the tree for generations—for context, the mother of Abraham Arbeiter *5-28* was Hana Itta (Biłgoraj) Arbeiter *6-57*; this is her family. Though the "Ł" character in the name closely resembles an English "L," common pronunciation is actually the equivalent of "w." In addition, the trailing "aj" in the name is pronounced as "ai." If we were to spell "Biłgoraj" the way it sounds to Americans, it would probably be "Biwgorai," with the emphasis, as is the case in many Polish words, on the second-to-last syllable.[1]

It's notable, though not particularly revealing, that the family's name is shared by a town in southeastern Poland, near the current border with Ukraine. While "toponyms" like this can reflect a family's geographical origins, we have no confirmation this is the case with the Biłgoraj branch of our tree, nor any indication of how far removed the family in Wyszogród was from actually living there.

Szulim Haim Biłgoraj (7-114), Sura Ester Wejs (7-115)

Szulim Haim Biłgoraj was born 18 Dec 1821, probably in Wyszogród. He worked as a *rzeźnik*, or butcher, and died 9 Jun 1887.[2]

Sura was born in 1825 to Abram *8-230* and Ryfka Wejs *8-231*.[3] Szulim likely died in 1887 in Wyszogród,[4] and Sura on 20 Sep 1895.[5]

Records suggest they had four children:

- **Zelmen Ber**, b. 10 Jun 1844. Worked as a wagon driver.[6] Married Dwojra Lichtman, had four children: Laja Rasza (b. 4 Feb 1865),[7] Ryfka (b. May 1867),[8] Hawa (b. 16 May 1878)[9] and Hana (b. 5 Mar 1882; moved to Rembowo).[10]

- **HANA ITTA** *6-57*, b. 15 Jul 1846, d. 30 Mar 1919 in London.[11] Married Dawid Arbajter; see profile in "Arbeiter" chapter for more.

- **Szymon Boruch**, b. 5 Nov 1848, d. 25 Feb 1908. Worked as a butcher.[12] Married Masza Winter, had four children: Lewek Icek (b. 4 Sep 1876),[13] Abram Haskel (b. 1 Jun 1878),[14] Haja Gitel (b. 20 Dec 1880, d. 19 Aug 1886)[15] and Szulim Haim (b. 1 Feb 1889).[16]

- **Icek**, b. 22 Jul 1853. Worked as a butcher like his brother and father.[17] Married Ruchla Laja Brikman, had seven children: Haim Aron (b. 20 Jun 1878, d. 29 May 1914),[18] Ryfka Maria (b. 17 Sep 1880, married Mortka Golberg; moved to Żyrardów),[19] Hana (b. 19 Aug 1882; moved to Warsaw),[20] Noech (b. 20 Oct 1883,[21] married Mindla Lisser),[22] Matys (b. 17 Jun 1885, d. 15 May 1886),[23] Szmul (b. 15 Jun 1889, d. 20 Jun 1890)[24] and Rasza (b. 15 May 1887; moved to Warsaw).[25]

Szymon Biłgoraj (8-228), Rasza (8-229)

Szymon Biłgoraj was born abt 1770,[26] probably in Wyszogród. While we don't know the parents of Szymon *8-228*, it's possible he had a brother, **Lewek Zachariasz**, who married a woman named Hanna and had at least one son, Icek Szulem (b. 16 Oct 1814, d. 21 Jan 1896).[27] There's no documented connection between Lewek and Szymon, but they are the only two Biłgoraj men in Wyszogród at the turn of the 19th century.

We don't know anything of Rasza's origins, though it's likely she was younger than Szymon: While we only have birth information for two of the couple's four known children, Szymon was 53 when their son Lajzer was born, according to the age given on his death certificate 20 years after that.

Szymon and Rasza had four known children:[i]

- **Dwoyra Fayga**[28]
- **Sura**[29]
- **SZULIM HAIM** *7-114*,[30] b. 18 Dec 1821.
- **Lajzer**,[31] b. 1825, d. 9 Jun 1893. Worked as a *furman*, or driver.[32] Married Maria Moszkow (b. 1826, d. 28 Mar 1886),[33] two known children: Lewek Zachariasz (b. 9 Nov 1852) and Ester Itta (b. 1858,[34] d. January 1889).[35]

Szymon worked as a butcher, and died 13 Dec 1846 in Wyszogród.[36] A "Rasza Bilgoraj" died later, in 1864,[37] though it has not yet been confirmed that she is the one in question.

---

[i]It's possible there were more children; these are the ones listed on Szymon's 1846 death certificate.

Icek (9-458)

The father of Rasza *8-229* is among the most distantly related ancestors we know of for Nancy Abdill *2-3*; whoever he was, he would be Nancy's fifth-great grandfather, though his identity right now is only speculation. Rasza's surname is recorded in only one known location, the entry for her son, Szulim Haim Biłgoraj *7-114*, in the Wyszogród books of residence. There, Szulim's parents are listed as Szymon Biłgoraj and "Rasza Icek"; in the entry for their other son, Lajzer, she is listed only as "Rasza." There is reason to believe this is not a "surname" as we understand it now, but rather the name of Rasza's father. See the appendix "Rasza's father" for an evaluation of the evidence.

Chapter 3

Chrzanowski

You may have noticed the varied spelling of this surname throughout the book. The main reason for this is simple—in Polish, surnames are considered adjectives, and adjective ending in vowels in that language are gendered. So surnames ending in "–ski" (and its variants, such as "–cki" and "–zki"), when appended to a female, would end instead with "–ska," "–cka" or "–zka."[1]

Jakob Szoel Chrzanowski (8-226), Ruchla Szmuelowiczow (8-227)

Szoel Chrzanowski was born abt 1787,[2] though we are not sure where. The suffix of his surname ("–ski") suggests it could be a *toponym*, or a surname based on a place, usually a familial hometown.[3] Chrzanów, Poland is the most likely candidate, though it's unclear when (or even if) the family lived there—it's almost 250 miles south of Bieżuń, where Szoel and Ruchla were present for their daughter's wedding in 1843, so it may have been several generations earlier, if at all.

Ruchla was born probably about 10 years later than Szoel.[4] The surnames recorded for her in the birth records

of her children hint at the name of her father, the mostly
likely identity being that of **Szmul** *9-454*: There are three
surnames attributed to Ruchla at different times: "Szmu-
low,"[5] "Szmuelowiczow"[6] and "Berkow."[7] The "—ow" and
"—owiczow" suffixes indicate that the name is a *patronymic*,
or name based on the person's father.[8] While it's possible
her father's name was something like "Szmul Berek," it was
also not unheard of for a woman to use the patronymic of
her *father* on occasion, instead of her own, so it's possible
"Szmul" was her father, and "Berek" was her father's father.
It's also possible one or both of these was simply a regular
surname, but the variance in the references to Szmul may
indicate it was a true patronymic. We don't know for sure,
and neither of those names appear in other records of the
town.

Szoel and Ruchla were married some time before 1823,
when their first known child was born. They had at least
six children, all born in Bieżuń:

- **RYFKA** *7-113*, b. abt 1823. Married Zelman Arbaj-
ter 15 Feb 1843; see "Arbeiter" chapter for details.
- **Ruchla**, b. abt 1830. Married Jcick Bekier 1849 in
Bieżuń;[9] at least one child, Abram (b. 1857).[10]
- **Lewin**, b. 1833.
- **Chaim**, b. 1836, d. 1837.[11]
- **Hana Laja**, b. 1839.[12]
- **Ester**, b. 1841, d. 1843.[13]

Szoel died in 1857, in Bieżuń;[14] Ruchla's fate is unknown, though she was alive in 1843 to sign the marriage
certificate of their daughter Ryfka.

The younger children

We know the names of the parents of Ryfka *7-113* are
Szoel and Ruchla Chrzanowski, based on her marriage

(a) Szol Chrzanowski 8-226   (b) Ruchla (Szmuelowiczow)
Chrzanowska 8-227.

Figure 3.1: The signatures of the Chrzanowskis from the 1843 marriage record of their daughter Ryfka 7-113.

certificate. The only "Szoel Chrzanowski" in the records of Bieżuń is a "Jakob Szoel Chrzanowski," married to a Ruchla: The most obvious connection is that it is the same couple, though we can't be sure given the information available. The most incongruous fact is that the couple also appears as the parents of a child born in 1841, almost two decades after Ryfka's birth, raising the possibility that these Chrzanowskis would be too young to have been Ryfka's parents as well.

This concern is mostly mitigated by the ages attached to those birth records: Though inconsistent, there are four separate instances where the couple's approximate birth years are given, once for each of Ryfka's younger siblings. In the 1841 record for the youngest (known) child, Ester Chrzanowski, Szoel and Ruchla's ages are given as 54 and 44, respectively. That would place their birth years at about 1787 and 1797, which presents no conflicts with Ryfka's birth year and makes it clear both parents were relatively old when their youngest child was born.

There is one other notable age disagreement regarding Szoel: In 1857, a "Jakob Szoel Chrzanoski" died in Bieżuń, age 76. Assuming this is the same person, it would put his year of birth around 1781, which is pushing the bounds of plausibility regarding his parentage of the younger children in the list. However, the deceased Szoel is listed has having been married to a "Ruchla," so it appears to be the same person with many different years of birth.

Jakob (9-452),
Bajla (9-453)

We only know of the parents of Szoel Chrzanowski *8-226* because of their mention in the index of a set of documents that includes Szoel's death record. It's likely they were born somewhere around 1750, though we have no evidence. They are listed here without surnames because most Polish Jews did not formally adopt last names until about 1821, when Jakob and Bajla were likely already deceased.

As fifth-great grandparents, Jakob and Bajla are in the most remotely related generation of Nancy Abdill's direct ancestors.

Chapter 4

Jacobowitz

Leib Jacobowitz (6-58), Esther (6-59)

Curiously, what we know of the parents of Sarah (Jacobs) Arbeiter *5-29* comes almost exclusively from the FBI: Records from an investigation into Sarah's son-in-law, Louis Buchalter, show that the Bureau looked into a bank account Sarah opened in 1929; according to the Harlem Savings Bank at 125ᵗʰ Street and Lexington Avenue, Sarah said her parents were named Leib and Esther.[1] It's worth noting, however, that Sarah also reportedly told the bank her year of birth was 1888, when it was much more probable to have been eight years earlier than that. She also said her husband's name was "Sam," though she wouldn't legally marry Sam Finkel until 1936. At the least, Sarah's gravestone says she is the daughter of "Leib,"[2] so we can likely believe at least that part.

Sarah[i] told U.S. census-takers in 1910 that Leib and Esther were born in Germany, though in the 1920 census, this answer changed to "Russia." Given Sarah's other statements about being born in Russia, it seems safer to

---

[i] Or someone in Sarah's household, at least.

go with the latter, though the change may have been due to anti-German sentiment in the U.S. following the first world war.

When Sarah arrived in the U.S., she reported being born in a place that may have been called Kizminsk,[ii] in the Sverdlovsky District, Oryol Oblast, Russia. There is no remaining evidence of the town, but, if the name of the *shtetl*[iii] was accurately recorded, this is our only guess.

There are references to Kizminsk on the collaborative family history website MyHeritage.com (which uses its Russian name, Кизминск); these are the only references we can find, but they point specifically to this "oblast," or region.

Latvian genealogy researcher Patrick Munits explains: "...given that such a precise geographical location was specified it is likely that the village indeed existed there at one time. Keep in mind that it [is] also a region of Russia that has seen steady population decrease for decades. It is also in the general area of some of the most intense battles of WWII, so many villages have simply been erased from the face of the planet."[3]

It appears the couple had at least two children:

- **SARAH** *5-29*, b. 12 May 1880, d. 14 Jan 1963 in Newburgh, New York.[4] See profile in the "Arbeiter" chapter for more.
- **Dinah**, date of birth unknown, but was still living in 1907, when Sarah gave the name of her sister, "Dinah Birron," as a personal contact in England upon arriving in the United States.[5]

[ii]It is listed as "Kisminsk" in a ship manifest entry for Sarah's arrival in New York.

[iii]"Shtetl" is a Yiddish word for a small, majority-Jewish town in eastern Europe, not as small as a village (or *dorf*). *Shtetlekh* were diminished by industrialization and loss of population to growing cities; they were destroyed by the Holocaust.

Sarah's gravestone describes her as the daughter of Leib,[6] but no additional records have been found for Leib, Esther or Dinah Jacobs, nor for the Birron or Birren family that Dinah appears to have married into. Given that both sisters appear to have spent time living in London, England, it seems probable that their parents would also have moved there, but we have no indication that they did.

"Jacobs" is also an anglicized version of her last name, which she adopted later in life: In records from England, in the years just after she'd married Abraham Arbeiter *5-28*, her surname is recorded as "Jacobowitz,"[7] "Jacobovitch,"[8] and, once, as "Yacobovitz."[9] In America, her maiden name was always listed as "Jacobs," with the exception of the license for Sarah's 1936 marriage to Samuel Finkel, in which she gave her maiden name as "Jakus."[10]

Chapter 5

Reinstein

It is a mercifully cool summer day. Breezy, not even 75 degrees,[1] and it's already after noon. It is July 5, 1905—a Wednesday during the garment industry's busy season,[2] when 30-year-old tailor Harry Reinstein would normally be dragging himself toward the halfway point of a 12- or 14-hour shift. But today is not an ordinary day—today, he is at New York's Ellis Island Immigration Station, waiting to pick up his mother, wife and three children, more than a year after they'd been separated so Harry could prepare the family's way in the *Goldene Medine*—the land of gold.

The waiting room is at the bottom of the "Stairs of Separation,"[3] a well-known fixture of the processing center that, despite its ominous name, looks entirely mundane—an unadorned set of steps, divided by railings into three sections. When Harry had passed inspection the previous year, he walked down the steps on the far left, to a barge that shuttled him back to the Battery and into his new life in New York. Those bound for the railroad[4] or New Jersey were separated (hence the name) and sent down the far-right steps. The remaining Reinsteins, when they arrived July 3, had taken neither—they were sent down the middle stairs, reserved for detainees,[5] which is what brought Harry to the island today.

Harry arrived in New York on March 11, 1904. 77,544 Russian Jews arrived that year, the highest annual total yet seen.[6] His exact motivations are unclear, but many at that time cited fears sparked by the Kishinev pogrom,[7] an anti-Jewish riot the previous year in which Russians, believing local Jews had killed two local children to use their blood in baking Passover matzo, emerged from Easter church services and began to assault the entire Jewish population of the town. Dozens were killed, and well over 1,000 homes and stores were looted and destroyed. It was part of a decades-long rejection of the Jewish minority in the Russian empire, who had lived there for hundreds of years but were still seen as outsiders to be regarded with suspicion, if not outright contempt. Government policies began to restrict Jewish economic opportunities even farther than they already had, anti-Semitic newspapers rang alarms about the Jewish menace, and communities throughout the Pale of Settlement were the subject of routinely unpunished violence and discrimination. Millions fled, most of them to the United States.

Mary Antin, an immigrant who had come to America in 1891, described the pervasive discussions popping up about the mythical land of freedom across the ocean: "America was in everybody's mouth. Businessmen talked of it over their accounts; the market women made up their quarrels that they might discuss it from stall to stall; people who had relatives in the famous land went around reading their letters for the enlightenment of less fortunate folk... children played at emigrating; old folks shook their sage heads over the evening fire, and prophesied no good for those who braved the terrors of the sea and the foreign goal beyond it; all talked of it, but scarcely anyone knew one true fact about this magic land."[8]

When Harry found a home on Hester Street,[9] in a tenement on the Lower East Side, the area had already been completely transformed as the "Jewish Quarter"—

in particular, Jews from Eastern Europe, with defined blocks even for specific regions of specific countries. Historian Selma Berrol explained that the Tenth Ward, unlike the more established Jewish community in London's East End, "was divided into Hungarian, Galician, Rumanian, Levantine, and Russian sub-ethnic districts 'in a pattern suggesting the cultural, if not the physical geography of the Old World.'"[10] Another chronicler observed, later on: "The Russians disliked the Poles, the Poles disliked the Russians, the Russians and Poles collectively disliked the Lithuanians, and everybody who was not Hungarian found the Hungarians toplofty and condescending."[11]

The city's unprecedented demographic shift happened slowly, then all at once: In 1870, researchers estimated there were about 60,000 Jewish people living in the city. In 1880, the tally had risen to 80,000 Jews—by 1910, there were 1.1 million.[12] The Reinsteins' arrival fits a broader pattern almost exactly: Researchers found that 1904 and 1905 in particular contained an uncharacteristically high ratio of Jewish men compared to women and children, which at least one study attributed to the plan of "sending over the men as an *avantgarde* to prepare the way for their families... In 1906, however, the number of males decreased by 2,000, but that of females increased by more than 25,000. In this tremendous increase of females is registered the effect of the *pogroms* of 1905–6, in which years the movement became a veritable flight."[13] When the remaining Reinsteins fled in June 1905, the Russian Revolution was in full swing, workers' strikes had broken out across the empire, and the series of peasant uprisings had started that would eventually destroy thousands of agricultural "manors" across the country. Several months after their arrival, more than 600 pogroms broke out, mostly in Ukraine, and mostly against the Jews. It was conditions like these that inspired an immigrant to write in his diary, upon reaching the U.S., "Sympathy for Russia? How ironical it sounds! Am I not despised? Am I not urged to leave? Do I

not hear the word *zhid*[i] constantly? Can I even think that
someone considers me a human being capable of thinking
and feeling like others? Do I not rise daily with the fear
lest the hungry mob attack me?...It is impossible...that
a Jew should regret leaving Russia."[14]

The Reinsteins' current problem, however, was much
simpler: They just wanted to get out of the building. Ada
and the children had arrived at Ellis Island on July 3. They
all passed inspection but, like many other "unescorted
women and children," they were detained until a relative
could vouch for their safety (and financial support).[15] The
S.S. *Astoria* must have arrived too late for Harry to receive
word and make it to the island that day—despite the thousands of lost, shuffling bodies in every hallway of the facility,
Ellis Island closed at 5.[16] Normally, this would not have
been an issue—the family would have been assigned cots,
fed several meals, and left without incident the following
day. However, the next day, the Reinsteins were still there:
The facility was closed—it was Independence Day.[17]

This meant the family would have to spend another
day locked on the third floor of the main building, in the
dormitory above the Great Hall's famous vaulted ceilings.[18]
The dorms, one for men, another for women and children,[19]
were cacophonous with anxiety. One account explained,
with possible hyperbole, the collision of cultures to be
witnessed: "An Italian child who had never seen running
water was suddenly made to take a shower. Two men
were impressed by bed springs—they had never seen them
before. All night long they bounced up and down on it for
fun. The mixture of ethnic groups angered some people. At
dawn a Turk wakened people with his Muslim prayers. And
Englishmen complained of being in a room with Italians
who were eating garlic. In the mess hall it was impossible
to suit the palates of 60 different national tastes. They

---

[i]Though its context and adoption varied, *zhid* was commonly
recognized in the Russian language as an anti-Semitic slur.

would all eat kosher meat and Italian bread. But Italians wouldn't eat oatmeal, Scandinavians disliked spaghetti, and 30 Muslims ate nothing but boiled eggs."[20]

Still, while the inspection process could be terrifying (one reporter described it as "the nearest earthly likeness to the final Day of Judgment, when we have to prove our fitness to enter Heaven"),[21] the experience wasn't necessarily a hostile one: One in three inspectors were immigrants themselves, and all inspectors spoke an average of three languages.[22] If an inspector encountered a traveler he couldn't communicate with, someone from the facility's "full-time army of interpreters" would intercede.[23] There was also oversight and assistance from groups such as HIAS, the Hebrew Immigrant Aid society, which would likely have been of enormous help to Harry in particular, when he arrived in America without any verified family to support him.[ii] HIAS established a bureau on Ellis Island in 1904, where agents were stationed to assist immigrants through the inspection process and to find their way in the city. They ran a soup kitchen in Manhattan, and provided clothes to anyone in need.[24] Their shelter was open around the clock and was available for anyone who needed a bath or a place to receive mail. They supplied free newspapers, plus stationery for writing home. If New York was not the immigrant's final destination, they would make sure an uncertain traveler had someone to accompany them to the train station.[25] It's also possible that when Ada and the children were detained, an aid society agent was the one to find and notify Harry of their arrival.[26] One author summed up their universally praised services, offered to a grateful community: "Thousands of sons and daughters, as also their sons and daughters, would find life a little easier, a little more comfortable because of the men who waited

---

[ii]Harry told officials from the steamship company that he was meeting a cousin in the city; the person's identity is unknown, and it would not have been unusual for him to not actually exist.

at Ellis Island with those blue caps on which the Yiddish letters for HIAS had been embroidered."[27]

The Reinsteins were likely helped by another aid society as well, on the other side of the Atlantic—German Jews watching the mad rush of eastern refugees fleeing through their ports set up numerous agencies to assist them and reduce the frequency with which they were fleeced by scammers. The largest of these by far was the *Hilfsverein der Deutschen Juden*, established in 1901.[28] The group helped coordinate trustworthy services for the immigrants in ports such as Bremen and Hamburg,[iii] where thousands of people without anywhere to stay could instead be found sleeping in rail stations, doorways and public parks.[29] From 1905 to 1914, an estimated 700,000 Eastern European Jews traveled through Germany; of those, 210,000 received aid directly from the *Hilfsverein.*[30]

It is 1:05 p.m. Finally, the Reinsteins are freed: An "Inspector Coe" is satisfied that they have somewhere legitimate to go. After at least a year and a half apart, Harry watches his family emerge from the innards of the facility: Pearl, age 5. David, age 4. Ada, 28 years old,[31] probably carrying Anna, age 2. She had just spent two weeks traveling 4,500 miles, across an entire continent and another entire ocean, with three pre-schoolers.

However, there was an absence: Zipre Reinstein, Harry's mother. They had purchased a ticket for her, but she never made it aboard the *Astoria.* It's not clear why she was not able to make the journey, nor if she traveled to port with the family but was turned away before departure. She is even listed on the *Astoria* manifest, though is crossed off— generally, an indication that the decision not to board was made too late to amend the passenger list.[32] Ann Dondero *3-7*, Harry's granddaughter, said she remembered hearing

---

[iii]While all the Reinsteins left for America from Glasgow, German and Dutch ports were popular points of departure to get to the United Kingdom.

something of an ancestor being blocked from emigrating because of an eye condition—interestingly, further research suggests that to be the most likely explanation for Zipre: Trachoma, a highly contagious bacterial eye infection, was rampant among immigrants and was the cause of thousands of rejected passengers. It would also make sense that Zipre was struck off before being allowed to board—when the U.S. began forcing steamship companies to pay for the return trips of immigrants rejected at Ellis Island, the companies began performing more stringent inspections at European ports prior to departure.[33] (Of those who made it to Ellis Island, trachoma caused another 20,000 rejections in 1904 alone.)[34]

In any case, it appears the Reinstein family's Ellis Island reunion, likely one of the most joyous occasions of their lives, was also when Harry found out he would never see his mother again.

The family probably went from there to an apartment at 39 Essex Street,[35] around the corner from Harry's former lodgings. The six-story building is still there,[36] though it is in significantly better shape than it was then, when it was in a section of town so run-down that it's now a five-minute walk from the city's Tenement Museum.

The housing in which they landed was particularly dangerous to children, who were more vulnerable to the frequent outbreaks of diseases such as diphtheria, tuberculosis (the "Jewish disease"),[37] and, most frequently, measles.[38] Skin diseases were also common, such as impetigo, scabies and ringworm.[39]

New York's Tenth Ward housed well over 700 people per acre,[40] considered at the time to be the most densely populated location on the planet.[41] A survey of families in the area found that 50 percent of them slept three or four to a room; another 25 percent said five or more people slept in each room.[42] One reporter described the experience of merely visiting the neighborhood: "The supreme sensation of the East Side is the sensation of its astounding populousness... The architecture seemed to sweat humanity at every window and door. The roadways were often impassable. The thought of the hidden interiors was terrifying."[43]

Much of the blame for the impassible roadways were the pushcarts: They were positively everywhere, full of food, clothes, and anything else a poor vendor could buy for cheaper than they could sell it—goods of every kind were for sale at the *chazer* (pig) market, where "everything but pig could be bought off pushcarts,"[44] pushed by peddlers shouting, *Kafe, weiber, kafe*—"Buy, ladies, buy." If a resident was forced to work long hours and couldn't get to Hester Street until after dark, they would find the vendors still there, their wares spread out under naphtha lamps.[iv,45]

In addition to the terrifying novelty of Manhattan in particular, America in general was a source of daily wonder to many immigrants: rocking chairs are cited in multiple accounts as being particularly mysterious to recent arrivals,[46] including one that explained, "There were five of us newcomers in the room, and we found five different ways of getting into this American machine of perpetual motion." That same immigrant was likewise mystified by a friend's gift, "a queer, slippery kind of fruit which he called *panana*."[47] (One account from Ellis Island claims that when bananas were distributed in the dining hall, the immigrants ate them with the skins on.)[48] Still, American fruits were popular among the immigrants, especially compared to vegetables—except for carrots, beets and cabbage, most veggies were roundly rejected by the Jewish community of the time. (Eventually, lettuce and tomatoes were accepted as being "good for the children.")[49] When another immigrant first saw a woman chewing gum, his first thought was to wonder "what kind of mouth disease she possesses,"[50] and there was confusion about the status of corn on the cob, which back home was barnyard fodder.[51]

[iv]Naphtha is a kerosene-like fuel used in "flare lamps" until the early 20th century.

In addition, the idea of going to a restaurant was so foreign to immigrants that they didn't have a word for it until New Yorkers introduced *oysesn*—literally "out eating"—into the Yiddish lexicon.[52] For most Russian immigrants, New York would also have been where they had their first-ever encounter with a black person.[53]

Alarm clocks were also a new concept to many Jewish immigrants—if not mechanically, then certainly culturally. The "intensity and hurry" of America was seen by many as "an entirely new world outlook,"[54] particularly for those from small towns. One writer explained: "The *shtetl* had been wretched enough, and every impulse to romanticize it must be resisted. But at least it was a thoroughly known place where one's ancestors lay buried, it did not loom up to terrifying heights before one's eyes, it required no special knowledge of machines in shops or on trolleys, and it seldom had much to do with the rigors of the clock. The *shtetl* encouraged that indifference to time which a true religious existence demands and a life of pauperdom enables. To many of the immigrants, when they first arrived in the United States, the sheer noise of the streets, the bulk of the buildings, the constant pushing and elbowing and rushing of daily existence, were terrifying."[55]

The immigrants who came to the Lower East Side from Russia were practically universal in their faith in Orthodox Judaism and observance of kosher dietary laws,[56] or *kashrut*. There was a stark divide between these "downtown" immigrants and the "uptown" Jews, who had immigrated earlier in the 1800s from Germany. The Germans, as a group, were more economically stable and far more enthusiastic about assimilation—to the deep confusion of their Orthodox "downtown" counterparts, the December living rooms of many German Jews were decorated with Christmas trees.[57] They had worked hard to "fit in," and saw the rush of Russian Jews, who spoke loudly in Yiddish and "arrived looking like bindle stiffs—hobos with their worldly possessions, slung over their shoulders in gunnysacks,"[58] as something of a liability. Even Julia Richman, the uptown Jewish educational reformer who had requested specifically to be assigned to the Lower East Side, said these "newcomers" were "full of menace to the entire Jewish community of New York."[59] The editorial board of *New York Times*, then owned by German Jews, shouted their disapproval even louder, calling the new arrivals "hatchet faced, pimply, sallow cheeked, rat eyed young men of the Russian Jewish colony who, weaned on nihilism and dynamite throwing, long...to demolish law and order," and warning that "such individuals damage the image of Jews as a group."[60]

It appears the Reinsteins, at least, managed to keep their heads above water with Harry's income as a tailor, probably in small shops sometimes housed in tenement apartments. Despite the prolific output of the city's garment industry, individual businesses remained tiny for decades: When Harry arrived, a typical sweatshop had only a dozen or so workers.[61]

Still, the garment industry employed 53 percent of Russian Jewish men, plus 77 percent of their female counterparts who were employed outside the home.[62] While many "Columbus tailors"[63] took up the trade after arriving in America, Harry was by 1910 working as a cutter, one of the most skilled positions in the industry. This, combined with his claim on arrival to be a tailor by trade, strongly suggests he was among the "tailors" coming in who was actually telling the truth.[64] Tailoring was, after all, a common Jewish trade even for those just arriving— a common Yiddish saying was allegedly, "*Ver geyt keyn Amerika?*"—who goes to America?—"*Die shnayders, shusters, un ferdganovim*"—the tailors, shoemakers and horse thieves.[65]

Interestingly, the term "sweatshop" is actually a more specific situation than it sounds, and has nothing to do with the temperature—contractors (or "sweaters") would take jobs for piecework from manufacturers, then pass on the assignments to the workers, making garments in tenements or small shops. Manufacturers would "sweat" as much profit as they could from the contractors, who then "sweated" as much labor as possible from the workers in order to maintain the shop's razor-thin profit margins.[66]

The family moved to Brooklyn probably May 1, 1907—Harry's address in March 1906 is still listed in Manhattan,[67] and in June 1907 as Brooklyn.[68] At the time, "Moving Day" was still a solid New York institution: Almost all private leases in the city expired on the exact same day, May 1, leaving the entire city to scramble out of their old apartments and into the new ones at the same time, jockeying for room on horse-drawn moving carts and dodging the tumbling furniture of every other household in the middle of its transition. Lawyer and diarist George Templeton Strong wrote, "Every other house seems to be disgorging itself into the street; all the sidewalks are lumbered with bureaus and bedsteads."[69] Frontiersman Davy Crockett, then a U.S. congressman from Tennessee, accidentally found himself in town on Moving Day 1834 and was completely baffled, saying, "it seemed to me that the city was flying before some awful calamity. 'Why,' said I, 'colonel, what under heaven is the matter? Everybody appears to be pitching out their furniture, and packing it off.' He laughed, and said this was the general 'mooving day.' Such a sight nobody ever saw, unless it was in this same city. It seemed a kind of frolic, as if they were changing houses just for fun. Every street was crowded with carts, drays, and people. So the world goes. It would take a good deal to get me out of my log house; but here, I understand, many persons 'moove' every year."[70]

The Reinsteins' departure to the east was part of a much broader push out of the Lower East Side that received another boost in 1908, when the city's first subway line connected Manhattan to Brooklyn Borough Hall.[71] Between 1900 and 1920, the Jewish population of Brooklyn grew by 22 percent.[72] It appears Harry had learned English by 1910,[73] and Ada at some point attended night classes to learn it as well, according to stories remembered by her granddaughter Ann *3-7*. In addition to the challenges of learning a new language, the environment probably left much to be desired: Students frequently had to squeeze into desks designed for schoolchildren, and classes were held mostly from 7 to 10 p.m., frequently leaving students to read by gaslight and skip dinner to arrive on time.[74]

They were accompanied in the move by Sam Reinstein, Harry and Ada's nephew. His name back in Russia was probably a variant of "Schmiel[75] Dreizenl" It's unclear why he decided to take his mother's maiden name in the voyage over, but it may have been part of some kind of scheme with Harry and Ada—when Sam arrived, he was detained, as Ada and the children had been. Again, Harry took a boat out to Ellis Island to pick up a new arrival, though he for some reason told officials Sam was his brother. (Harry had pulled a similar move the year before, when 17-year-old "Ruchel Reinstein" was picked up from detention by her "brother"—her actual identity is unknown, though she may have been one of Sam's actual siblings.)[76]

Bringing Sam into the city likely kicked off a flurry of activity. The community took seriously the task of bringing "greenhorns" up to speed, particularly *landslayt*, or natives of the same hometown as the new arrival. Their first stop was probably somewhere near Canal Street for Sam's first step in adjusting to the new world—making sure he had a fresh suit of American clothes.[77] One immigrant recalled later: "Everything had to be American. Clothes from home were defective, even if they were of good quality and well sewn. Going to the stores with the greenhorn was a joyful procedure."[78]

Sam lived with the family for eight years, including for a time after he was married. This doesn't appear to have been a particularly uncommon arrangement: A study on the Lower East Side done the year he arrived found that families relied on their teenagers for between 44 and 69 percent of their household income. When there weren't quite enough teenage siblings, cousins frequently picked up the slack.[79]

The familial nature of Jewish immigration was somewhat novel to begin with: Between 1899 and 1814, women accounted for 44 percent of Jewish immigrants, while the remaining groups of immigrants averaged about 30 percent women. Jewish children in particular were arriving at more than double the rate of any other group: 25 percent of Jewish immigrants were children younger than 14, while children made up only 11 percent of immigrants of other ethnicities.[80]

From what we can infer about the state of the Reinstein home, Ada's role running the household probably kept her busy almost around the clock. In addition to managing six children younger than 12, lack of refrigeration and unreliable food preservation meant trudging to marketplaces for food almost every day. One man described the same meal he ate daily while living as a boarder in a Jewish home: "The main meal in the evening always consisted of the same courses, namely a piece of herring or chopped liver, pea or barley soup, cooked meat, and cooked plums, always accompanied by a pickle[v,81] and a glass of beer."[82]

---

[v]Curiously, there isn't anything about a "kosher dill" pickle that is particularly kosher, as nothing about other pickles is non-kosher; they retained that name simply because that particular type of pickle, heavily seasoned with dill and garlic, was favored by the Jewish community.

Harry B. Reinstein (5-30), Ada Newman (5-31)

Tzvi Dov "Hersch" Reinstein was born possibly[vi] 31 May 1875[83] in Medzhybizh[84] (or *Mezhbizh*, in Yiddish), a small *shtetl* in the Pale of Settlement that had by then been a regional hub of Jewish culture for hundreds of years. Harry's gravestone and death certificate include a middle initial of "B,"[85] but what it stands for is not known for sure. His Hebrew name was *Tzvi Dov*, which may offer an explanation: The Hebrew word *tzvi* means "deer." The Yiddish word for "deer" is *hirsh*— the name Harry gave on arrival, later Americanized to "Harry." The Hebrew word *dov* means "bear," which in Yiddish is simply *ber*. The best guess, then, for Harry's middle name, is probably "Bear," or its Yiddish equivalent.

Edel[86] Newman was also a native of Medzhybizh, born abt 1876.[87] The couple married in abt 1896,[88] and immigrated to New York 8 years later: Harry, traveling under the name "Hersch Reinstein,"[89] went to Glasgow, Scotland and boarded the *Corinthian* 27 Feb 1904,[90] arriving at Ellis Island two weeks later, on 11 Mar 1904, with $2 and the address of a "cousin" he could stay with.[91] As far as we know, he was living on Hester Street,[92] at the center of the infamous tenements of New York's Lower East Side.

Figure 5.1: "Uncle Nat" Reinstein at the beach in the 1930s, from the collection of his niece, Ann Dondero 3-7.

[vi]Harry gave his birthday as 4 Jul 1874 in his application for U.S. citizenship, but as 31 May 1875 several years later when he registered for the World War I draft. Census records suggest his birthday could have been as early as 1871, but there is little in the way of confirmation.

Photojournalist Jacob Riis described the area in his 1890 study *How the Other Half Lives*: "The tenements grow taller, and the gaps in their ranks close up rapidly as we cross the Bowery and, leaving Chinatown and the Italians behind, invade the Hebrew quarter... No need of asking here where we are. The jargon of the street, the signs of the sidewalk, the manner and dress of the people... There is no mistaking it..."[93]

It was exceedingly common for immigrants in the garment industry to work from homes or tenement rooms converted into work areas, as Riis observed: "You are made fully aware of it before you have travelled the length of a single block in any of these East Side streets, by the whir of a thousand sewing-machines, worked at high pressure from earliest dawn till mind and muscle give out together. Every member of the family, from the youngest to the oldest, bears a hand, shut in the qualmy rooms... It is not unusual to find a dozen persons—men, women and children—at work in a single small room."[94]

Figure 5.2: Hester Street, where Harry Reinstein likely lived when he arrived in 1904.[95]

All documented evidence of Harry's occupation lists him as a tailor; it seems most likely that he, stumbling off the barges of Ellis Island without a job or any knowledge of English, likely ended up among those small rooms.

Riis explains how the tenements offered employers free rein to take advantage of their impoverished labor: "Ten hours is the legal work-day in the factories, and nine o'clock the closing hour at the latest. Forty-five minutes at least must be allowed for dinner, and children under sixteen must not be employed unless they can read and write English; none at all under fourteen. The very fact that such a law should stand on the statute book, shows how desperate the plight of these people. But the tenement has defeated its benevolent purpose. In it the child works unchallenged from the day he is old enough to pull a thread. There is no such thing as a dinner hour; men and women eat while they work, and the 'day' is lengthened at both ends far into the night."[96]

It was common for immigrant "trailblazers" such as Harry to take the cheapest lodgings they could find—for example, sleeping in a cramped basement corner—to better save money to send back home, or to purchase passage for other family members to come over.

Figure 5.3: The signature of Harry Reinstein 5-30 from his 1909 citizenship application. The document suggests he was unable to read the forms he was signing (in English), and that they had to be read to him.

Edel and the children arrived 3 Jul 1905. By 1910 they had adopted American names (Hersch became "Harry," Edel became "Ada" or "Ida")[97] and settled in Brooklyn, where four generations of the family would live. With them was Sam Reinstein,[98] their 18-year-old nephew who had arrived 24 Jun 1907 from Medzhybizh.[99] Sam (and, later, his wife[100] Dora)[101] lived with the family until about

1915,[vii] and they were close for decades after.[102]

Harry and Ada's grandson Jay Arbeiter remembers Sam and his brother Hyman:[viii] "When I was growing up, my grandmother was referred to as 'Saint Ida.' Whoever came over from the old country, they stayed with Ida. And Harry too, of course, but it's my understanding it was mostly her. They would feed them and clothe them. They slept on floors and couches—they were really very poor people themselves. His whole family told me, 'If it weren't for your grandmother, I wouldn't be here.' . . . I'd bet that most of the family of that time stayed with the Reinsteins when they came over," he said, in a 2017 interview. "She was supposedly a wonderful, wonderful woman."[103]

Harry and Ada had seven children:

- **Perl**[104] (possibly Perel); used the name "Pearl" in America. Born 24 Dec 1899 in Medzhybizh, Russia,[105] died 30 Nov 1964 in New York City.[106] Married Harry Gitlin (b. 13 Mar 1897 in Brooklyn,[107] d. 7 Feb 1979[108] in Miami, Florida).[109] Pearl was literally the "girl next door": Pearl's family moved to 82 Throop Avenue in probably 1907, and the Gitlin family ended up at 84 Throop between 1905[110] and 1910.[111] They married 10 years later, in 4 Jan 1920,[112] and had two children: Shirley and Saul.[113]
- **David**, b. 31 Oct 1900 in Medzhybizh,[114] d. 29 Aug 1971 in Virginia. Married Tillie Sovelove in 1922;[115] had two children: Jerome[116] ("Jerry")[117] and Marvin.[118] Moved to Richmond, Virginia, at some point before 1942[119] and separated from Tillie in 1958.[120] Before 1966, he (and likely at least his son Marvin)[121] moved to Crewe, Nottoway County, Va., to run a grocery

---

[vii]They appear together in the 1915 New York census, but Harry and Sam Reinstein list different addresses in their World War I draft registrations in 1918.

[viii]See the section for Zipre Reinstein *6-61* for more about them.

store.[122] Was killed in an armed robbery of his store
29 Aug 1971.[123] Rarely in contact with the other
Reinstein siblings—according to extant family stories, it was David's little sister Ruth whom his family
called when he died, and she was the only Reinstein
to attend his funeral.[124]

- **Chane**,[125] went by "Anna" in America, b. 18 Jan 1903[126]
  in Medzhybizh,[127] d. 6 May 1984 in Pinellas County,
  Florida.[128] Married Arthur Gladstone (b. 6 May 1895[129]
  in London, England,[130] d. Oct 1981);[131] had one son,
  Daniel.[132]

- **Nathan**, b. 23 Aug 1906 in Brooklyn, New York,[133]
  d. 26 Jan 1938 in Brooklyn. Worked as a chauffeur
  from about ages 21 to 31; contracted meningitis in
  abt November 1937; was hospitalized 20 Dec 1937,
  and died the following month.[134] Likely named after
  Nachman Reinstein *6-60*, his paternal grandfather.

- **CLARA** *4-15*, "Claire," b. 30 Mar 1908 in Brooklyn,[135] d. 5 Oct 1992.[136] Married Solomon Arbeiter
  4-14; see "Arbeiter" chapter for more.

- **Hyman**, "Herman," b. 21 Jul 1911 in Brooklyn, d.
  Feb 1972 in Brooklyn.[137] Married Lillian Feldman
  (b. November 1913,[138] d. 6 Nov 1982 in Florida);[139]
  had two children: Alice (married David Arlen) and
  Ned.

- **Ruth**, b. 14 Apr 1920 in Brooklyn, d. 9 Jun 1998.[140]
  Married Milton Kaufman (b. 28 Oct 1917, d. 7 Aug 1998)[141]
  on 10 Apr 1943; had one son, Peter.

Figure 5.4: The Reinstein family in abt 1909, from a photo long displayed in the home of Ann Dondero 3-7. L–R: David, Nathan, Harry, Pearl, Claire (front), Ada and Anna.[142]

Ruth was considerably younger than the other siblings— Ada and Harry were well into their 40s when she was born, and there was a 20-year gap between Ruth and her oldest sibling, Pearl. Ada was diagnosed with liver cancer when Ruth was 9, and died 18 Aug 1931, at the family's home at 441 Pine St.[143] She was buried in Mount Zion Cemetery in Queens, in a section run by the "Medgibosh Progressive Solidarity Society," a *landsmanshaft* social club and burial society made up of members from her and Harry's hometown of Medzhybizh.[ix]

Ruth, age 11, went to live with her older sister, Claire Arbeiter *4-15*,[144] who had already married and had a daughter, Ann *3-7*. Ruth had a sisterly relationship with Ann for the rest of her life.

Harry remarried[145] about two years after Ada's death,

[ix]In addition to social connections, *landsmanshaftn* acted as a form of amateur life insurance: Frequently, paying dues entitled members to a Jewish funeral (with guaranteed attendance), a lump-sum payout, plus money to make up for wages lost during the family's week sitting *shiva*.

on 18 Nov 1933, to Esther Siegel.[x,146] He died of lung cancer 6 Nov 1944, at their home at 853 Belmont Avenue.[147] He was buried the next day at Mount Zion Cemetery, in the same section as Ada *5-31*. Esther Reinstein most likely died 17 Apr 1950 at the age of 70.[148]

Harry and Ada were added in 2017 to the American Immigrant Wall of Honor, a sprawling memorial on Ellis Island containing the names of immigrants submitted by their descendants. They can be found on panel 763.

Figure 5.5: A modern photo of 441 Pine Street in Brooklyn, the house in which Ada Reinstein 5-31 died.[149]

---

[x]Esther is of no known relation to the other Siegels in Nancy Abdill's tree.

Figure 5.6: Clockwise from bottom-left: Jay Arbeiter, Claire Arbeiter 4-15, Anna Gladstone, Lillian Reinstein, Ruth Reinstein, Ann Arbeiter 3-7, Ned Reinstein. Claire, Anna and Ruth were sisters; Lillian was their sister-in-law, and the three children were Claire's and Lillian's.[150]

Figure 5.7: Col. Herman Reinstein (left) receiving a medal, likely during World War II. Ann Dondero 3-7 wrote on the photo that he was receiving the Croix de Guerre, a French medal for valor; while the man on the right is wearing what appears to be a French military hat, the unit insignia on his sleeve remains unidentified.[151]

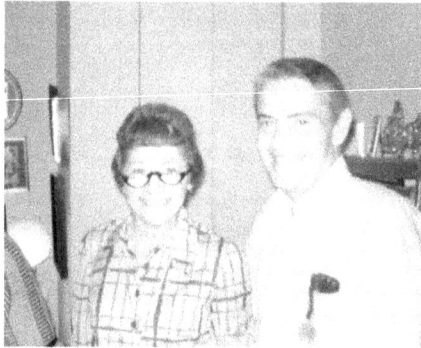

Figure 5.8: Ruth and Milton Kaufman.[152]

Nachman Reinstein (6-60),
Zipre (6-61)

Harry's father Nachman almost certainly never came to the United States—we can guess that he was born in the 1840s,[153] probably in Medzhybizh,[154] but the only known mention of his name is on Harry's tombstone.[155] Nachman died at some point before 1905, when Zipre *6-61* was recorded as a widow.[156]

Hebrew tombstones frequently mention the father of the deceased—in this case, Harry's stone says *Tzvi Dov ben Nachman HaLevi*—*Tzvi Dov* is Harry's original name, *ben* means "son of," and *Nachman HaLevi* means "Nachman the Levite." Levites are a Jewish caste traditionally assigned a set of religious responsibilities similar those of the *Kohanim* or priests, though a Levite was something closer to a priest's assistant. (By way of example, the gravestone of a kohen frequently features the image of two hands raised in a gesture of priestly blessing.[157] The gravestone of a Levite—including the one belonging to Harry—may include an engraving of a pitcher of water, which the Levite would have used to ritually cleanse the hands of the priest.)

Leviim are ostensibly the descendants of the "tribe of Levi," and inherit their tribal status patrilineally—so, at least according to tradition, Harry and Nachman should be able to trace their fathers' fathers back to Levi, the son of Jacob and Leah, and, depending on how closely one follows the biblical genealogies, back to Jacob's grandfather, Abraham, and backward from there, through Terah and eventually back to Shem, one of the three sons of Noah. What this information is worth is up to the discretion of the reader, but Noah's 8th great grandparents are claimed in scripture to be Adam and Eve. Though there are a few unknown generations in between Harry and Levi (around 180 generations, give or take), this would be our family's connection to the mythical beginning of mankind.

Even if we discard biblical literalism, there is ample evidence of a levitical lineage with surprising genealogical accuracy: A 2003 study in the *American Journal of Human Genetics* found significant evidence of genetically unique patterns among the males who identified as Ashkenazi Levites, including the conclusion that the "event" that yielded such observably different genetic patterns among Levites likely "involved very few, and possibly only one, founding father."[158] The time period and location of this "group" of founding fathers remains undetermined, but the point remains that it is entirely possible that many of the world's Levites actually are related to each other.

Harry's mother, Zipre, is only slightly less mysterious than Nachman: She was born abt 1851 in Russia[159] and was alive when the Reinstein family bought their ticket to America in 1905.[160] After she failed to make the trip with the others, there is no evidence she ever again attempted to travel to the United States.

Either Nachman or Zipre may have had a sibling—Harry said when he arrived in 1904 that he was staying with a cousin who was already in the U.S.,[161] though of the fibs we know Harry told at Ellis Island, this would probably have been the most mundane.

The graves of Zipre and Nachman are likely lost as well, assuming they died in Medzhybizh: Though there are two Jewish cemeteries in the town, one is disorganized and poorly maintained,[162] and the older one, which has burials dating back to at least 1555, was mostly destroyed in the 1940s when a German artillery battalion unlimbered atop the graves.[163]

The couple likely had at least two children:

- **Rachel**, b. maybe 1868 in Medzhybizh, d. probably after 1916 in Russia. Married Moshe Dreizen. See section below for details.
- **TZVI DOV** *5-30*, "Harry," b. abt 1875 in Medzhybizh, d. 6 Nov 1944 in New York City. Married Ada Newman. See preceding section for more.

Rachel Reinstein and Moshe Dreizen

We don't know when Nachman and Zipre's daughter Rachel was born, though her oldest child was 8 years older than Harry's, so we might guess that Rachel was 8 years older than Harry as well. However, this would mean a birth year of abt 1867—given what we know of Zipre's age, this would have made Zipre about 16 when Rachel was born, so we might add a year or two to the estimate. She was almost certainly born in Russia,[164] likely in Medzhybizh.

Rachel married Moshe[165] (or Moishe) Dreizen, whom their son indicated was deaf when he enlisted for the World War I draft.[166] Moshe died at some point after 1916;[167] according to descendants, he was killed by a horse.[168]

Rachel and Moshe had at least two children:

- **Shmuel**, b. maybe 25 Jul 1891 in Medzhybizh,[169] d. 1975 in New York.[170] Came to the U.S. aboard the *Livonia* 24 Jun 1907 and adopted the name "Sam Reinstein."[171] We have competing explanations for Sam's decision to adopt his mother's maiden name: According to Jay Arbeiter (son of Claire Arbeiter *4-15*), the family tale was "a screwup at Ellis Island,"[172] though we know now that immigrants spontaneously receiving a new name on arrival is a myth.[173] A more likely explanation is offered by the grandchildren

of Sam's brother Hyman, who say he changed his
name to better blend in with the family of Harry
5-30 and Ada Reinstein *5-31*, with whom he was
living.[174] (This also lines up with Harry's claim of
being Sam's brother when he was trying to fetch
him out of detention at Ellis Island.) Sam married
Dora Kohn[175] at some point before 1915;[176] had four
children: Selma, Sal, Shirley and Marilyn.[177]

- **Chaim**,[178] "Hymie,"[179] b. 10 Apr 1895 in Medzhybizh,[180] d. 20 Oct 1964 in New York City.[181] Arrived in New York 28 Jul 1913, where his name was
  recorded as "Chaim Renistein." Used the name "Hyman Dreizen" in America. Married Mary Isakoff
  (b. abt 1898 in Russia,[182] d. 9 Sep 1952),[183] had
  four daughters: Florence ("Flo"), Sylvia, Rae and
  Edith.[184]

- **Sonja**, of whom we have no documentation, but who
  is recorded by grandchildren of Chaim.[185]

- **Joseph**, undocumented like Sonja.[186]

Both Sam and Hyman, at least, came to the U.S. in the
early 1900s and are remembered vividly by living Reinstein
descendants; see the entry for Harry *5-30* and Ada *5-31*
for more.

It appears Rachel and Moshe never came to the U.S.;
Moshe, and possibly Rachel, were still alive in 1917, when
Hyman said he was supporting "parents in Russia" on his
draft registration.

Chapter 6

Newman

Daniel Newman (6-62), Susie Green (6-63)

Daniel and Susie are another set of ancestors we only know from their passing mention in other documents—their names are given as the parents of Ada (Newman) Reinstein *5-31* in her death certificate,[1] though that is the only mention we currently have of them. Both were born in Russia,[2] and we can guess that "Susie Green" was an anglicized name she received after coming to America, though we have no proof either ever did. In addition, "Newman" is probably not their "original" surname; something like "Nowak" or "Novak" is possible, in reference to the Polish term for "new one," or "new man [in town]."[3] The couple had one (known) child, **ADA** *5-31*, in abt 1877. Susie either died or the couple split up before abt 1896 when Daniel married a woman named Rose and had two more daughters with her:

- **Ray**, who was remembered clearly by Ann Dondero *3-7* but has not appeared in any documentation. Died sometime after February 1955.[4]

- **Golda**,[5] "Goldie," b. 1896[6] in what may now be Ukraine,[7] d. 24 Sep 1970.[8] Married Joseph Task (b. 8 Jan 1895 in Russia,[9] d. 3 Jul 1970 in New York)[10] on 28 Feb 1920;[11] had three children: Dorothy, Ethel and Martin.[12]

Daniel died at some point before 1925;[13] Rose lived with Goldie until Rose's death 25 Jul 1949.[14] It should be noted that while Rose was certainly in the U.S. and Daniel *may* have been, we have no documentation indicating he came here. There is also an apocryphal family story involving someone's wife "running off to Russia" to leave her husband. It's believed to be a reference to Susie, though no one familiar with the story actually knew her name, nor where she "ran off" from.

(b) Ray Newman (left), Harry Gitlin (married Ray's niece,

(a) Rose Newman, called "Bubbe Newman" by Ann Dondero 3-7, in an undated photo.[15]

Pearl Reinstein) and Ray's niece Claire Arbeiter 4-15 in Florida, February 1955.[16]

Chapter 7

Siegel

It was a beautiful[1] spring day when the S.S. *Birma* puttered out of New York Harbor into the Atlantic. By 1912, the *Birma* had been shuttling immigrants along the same route for three years—on one end was New York City, on the other, Libau, a port town in modern-day Latvia. At the time, however, it was in Russia, a valuable throughway on the Baltic, the only harbor the empire controlled that didn't freeze over in the winter.

It was a Thursday when the crew set sail. They expected to be gone for more than two weeks: The *Birma*, rated at 13 knots, was slow, one of the smaller ships run by the Russian East Asiatic Steamship Company. It had a single "funnel," or smokestack, painted a pale yellow; a persistent splotch of coal soot ringed the top. It had room for 300 first- and second-class passengers. Third class, or "steerage," could accommodate 1,150 souls, though the return trip to Libau was always a light one—in 1912, not many were interested in immigrating *into* Russia.

The steerage passengers are the ones depicted in the iconic photos of Ellis Island, crowded with tired-looking immigrants wearing huge coats, inscrutable notes pinned to their lapels. The upper-class passengers got to bypass the inspection ritual, which was reserved for the poorest passengers—when the ships arrived in Manhattan, U.S. inspectors came onto the boat and gave the more well-to-do immigrants a quick once-over before letting them loose in the city. It was at this point that those with cheaper third-class tickets were loaded onto barges and carted over to the processing center, where they would be poked and prodded and questioned about how they intended to support themselves in America and whether they harbored any "undesirable" opinions about life or liberty.

The *Birma* was headed east—after some time following the coast of Newfoundland, they would set their sights squarely on the English Channel. The ship would then follow the European coast for a stop at Rotterdam, in the Netherlands, then on to Libau. The bulk of the journey would be spent looking at nothing, just the vast, empty North Atlantic. Every evening, the monotony was broken when the nightly news briefing came clicking into the telegraph room, sent from a giant broadcasting station on Cape Cod. When there were passengers aboard, the report would be transcribed and distributed to those on the upper decks. Steerage didn't get copies of the news.

The ship had been following the eastern seaboard for three days, and it was approaching midnight on Sunday when the day's news update began. Unexpectedly, another broadcast cut in, from a boat this time. The unknown ship sent three letters: "CQD." It followed them with the new, international version of the phrase: "SOS," followed by a brief distress call. Someone, somewhere to the north, needed urgent help. The telegraph operator woke his colleague, and the two brought the message to the bridge, where Captain Ludwig Stulping set a course for the coordinates offered by the mystery boat. The captain woke up fifteen extra workers to stoke the furnaces and shovel coal. He cranked the engines to full throttle: 14.5 knots. They had 106 miles to go, and couldn't quite hit 17 miles per hour.

The unknown ship had signed its messages "MGY." The *Birma* had an identification book of ship callsigns, but there was no entry under that listing. Soon, the telegraph operators heard other nearby ships responding to the distress call as well. One, the S.S. *Frankfurt*, was about 100 miles behind the *Birma*. The operators asked the *Frankfurt* if they knew who "MGY" was. They responded soon after: "Titanic."

The operators wired back to the *Titanic* that they were on the way: "We are 100 miles from you, steaming 14 knots, be with you by 6.30." The response came back: "OK OM." The operator translated the Morse code shorthand: "All right, old man."[2]

The *Birma's* head steward called in his staff, who worked through the night baking as much bread as their ovens could hold. A joint statement from the crew afterward explained, "Food of every sort was prepared, stewards and stewardesses got ready rooms, couches, even blankets, in the saloons, for the reception of travellers in distress. Everywhere was activity, coupled with the intensest anxiety I have ever witnessed."

The boat continued on, dreading what they might find on arrival. The dispatches from *Titanic* were getting more dire: "SOS SOS CQD CQD - MGY. Sinking head down," they sent, "Come soon as possible." The last message the *Birma* noted was painfully simple: "Women and children in boats. Cannot last much longer - MGY." It was addressed to "CQ," a telegraph abbreviation for "Anyone who can hear us."

The *Birma* and multiple other ships arrived after 7 a.m. near the coordinates given by the *Titanic*, which ended up being woefully inaccurate. Another ship, the *Carpathia*, indicated that they were to the north, on the other side of an ice field. The *Birma* looped around the ice, eventually reaching the *Carpathia*, which was already headed the other way, toward Canada. The *Carpathia's* crew had unloaded what lifeboats there were, and pulled aboard the survivors they could find. The remainder, 1,513 passengers,[3] were in the water somewhere, dead.

The next day, headlines across the world blared: "TITANIC DISASTER; GREAT LOSS OF LIFE." The public was stunned by the scope of the calamity. The unsinkable! Why did the rescuers take so long to get there? How could they have ended up in the wrong spot? Shipping companies tried to defend themselves, putting out exacting statements in anticipation of a massive investigation. The world wanted to know—what happened to the *Titanic*?

In Libau, the Siegel family sat and waited. Their ship to America, the *Birma*, was going to be late.

A 9-year-old boy was with them; he would soon go by the name "Morris Siegel," but for now he was still Moische Sigalow, and he was probably very tired of traveling with his family. He had said goodbye to his father and older brother two years earlier, when they'd struck out for Hamburg, Germany, and from there to start a new life in New York City. Morris's father, Salman, worked as a locksmith; his brother Jakob was a joiner,[4] a skilled woodworker who frequently dealt with items such as furniture. It is not surprising that both of them were artisans, even in a region where people were frequently described as working in trades "not far removed from those of the middle ages of Western Europe."[5] Agriculture—and, in some areas, subsistence farming—was still the largest industry in Russia, but Jews were the exception in that, and almost every other, arena: While 61 percent of non-Jews had agricultural jobs, only 3 percent of Jews could say the same. By contrast, Jews made up only 12 percent of the working population in the Pale of Settlement but represented 77 percent of those working in commerce.[6] Of Jews engaged in manufacturing, most were craftsmen like Salman and Jakob.[7] However, they also followed another common Jewish trend in America—once they arrived, they became part of the two-thirds of Jewish immigrants who were forced to take jobs in occupations different from those they had performed at home.[8]

In spring 1912, the time had come for the rest of the family to join them, so Moische packed what little he had and set out for Libau with his mother Heni and four sisters, Basse, Brane, Czipe and Cziwi. The journey had started somewhere near Medvin, Russia, in the countryside south of Kiev. They had set off going north, across all of Belarus and Lithuania, to the Latvian port city called Liepaja (or its German name, Libau). Depending on the route they took, it's likely the family traveled more than 800 miles to the coast.

Kiev and Medvin are in Ukraine now, but in 1912, Ukraine, Belarus, Lithuania and Latvia were all simply, "Russia." The Sigalows may have come into town on the Libau–Romni Railway, which had been completed in 1874 and carted people and cargo across almost the entire length of the Pale of Settlement. (The train line is still in service today.)

Along the way, they would have needed to evade robbers, scammers, and swindlers of every persuasion: counterfeit tickets were sold to unwitting emigrants, or real tickets on boats that had no business traveling on the ocean.[9] Once in Libau, the family likely stayed in the newly built "Great Emigrants' House," a huge, red brick building near the water. It was built by the owners of the Russian–American Line, after years of legal trouble arising from immigrants rooming with the locals.

The Great Emigrants' House was a grand, stately building, with huge windows and three Russian flags flying on tall poles, one over each wing of the structure. Its ruins still sit in the town today, vines growing through empty window frames.[10] Libau was closer and simpler to get to than Hamburg, where Salman and Jakob had departed from, and did not require illegally crossing any borders to get there. However, Hamburg was run by foreign, German authorities without much interest in the fate of the migrants—Libau was full of Russian officials, who posed a much more direct threat to Russian men, particularly those old enough to be drafted into the czarist army.[11] This, plus the high costs for passports and legal immigration from Russia, may have motivated Salman and Jakob to find their alternate route.

Once the *Birma* finally arrived (the ship had made an unscheduled stop at Dover to give a defensive statement to the press),[12] the Sigalows boarded, climbed deep into the steerage compartments, and said goodbye to Russia forever. Ships only ran the New York–Libau route from 1906 to 1914, but during that time it's estimated at least half a million emigrants made their last footprints on Russian soil in the city's streets.[13][14]

Figure 7.1: An advertisement for the Russian–American Line, which operated the S.S. Birma. (The ship pictured is the S.S. Russia; the Birma was smaller, and only had one smokestack.)[15]

The boat traversed the southern edge of the Baltic Sea, then had to work its way west, through the North Sea and English Channel, and ultimately to the Atlantic Ocean. The problem, if one is trying to get between the North Sea and the Baltic, is Denmark: To put it simply, the whole country's in the way. The Jutland peninsula separates the two bodies of water, and going around it adds hundreds of miles to the journey and leaves the ship more exposed to danger. The Kiel Canal solves this problem beautifully— cutting across the entire peninsula on the German side, the 60-mile canal bypasses the rest of the North Sea plus the Danish straits.[16] It was the most useful shortcut on the whole trip.

Unfortunately, that the canal was on the German side ends up being relevant to the story in 1912: There was an unprecedented naval arms race in the first years of the 20th century, and the massive dreadnoughts of the German navy were larger, heavier and—of the least convenience— wider than the battleships of old. The Kiel Canal was too narrow to accommodate their passage, so Germany spent seven years enlarging the canal. When it was time for the Sigalows to pass through, it had already been closed for more than three years, adding still more time to their journey.

Interestingly, the Kiel Canal's closure may have played a significant role in saving the Sigalows from getting trapped in Europe during the first world war: As early as 1911, German military leaders were discussing the possibilities of an imminent war with England,[17] one that could easily expand into a much wider conflict with Russia. Several naval leaders saw the completion of the widened canal as a prerequisite for any armed conflict with Britain, and the work still had years to go. On 25 Jul 1914, the first modern German battleship passed through the Kiel Canal for the first time. Less than two weeks later, the world was at war.

In short, if the Sigalows had been able to use the Kiel Canal, then so would the German navy, which was itching for a fight that would likely have shut down most immigration altogether. At the time, however, all the family knew was that the trip was going to take ages. Of the two-dozen immigrants in Nancy Abdill's *2-3* family tree, Anna Siegel and her children spent the longest time aboard a boat, far longer even than Anna's husband and eldest son. They departed May 1, 1912, and didn't arrive at Ellis Island until May 19.[18]

Though their arrival at Ellis Island was supposed to be the end of the Siegels' ordeal, there was one more hurdle to clear: There was some issue with the paperwork for Basse Siegel, Moische's sister, and even as that was straightened out, the family was detained as part of the "special inquiry" process.[19] Anna and the five children were listed under code "LPC," indicating that inspectors thought them likely to become "public charges," or charity cases. It was relatively routine for authorities to detain mothers traveling without husbands, but the special inquiry process involved more than just being picked up by a relative; one's entrance at that point had to be approved by a panel of officials, which had the potential to take weeks without any guarantee of success. The family, however, was apparently able to do this quickly—while some *Birma* detainees were in custody for days, the Sigalows appear to have been held for an afternoon, fed lunch, and sent on their way. (Though it's likely the family was called before a board of special inquiry, an index of the Birma's collected documents shows no record of a transcript.)[20]

Martin Stanley Siegel (3-6),
Ann Etta Arbeiter (3-7)

Ann Arbeiter was born 8 Nov 1930, though she steadfastly refused to disclose the year to almost everyone until she was in her mid-80s.[i] She was born in the back of a taxi, according to family lore, on the way to a hospital in Queens. The mythical fur coat in which she was swaddled supposedly belonged to her aunt, Tillie Reinstein.[ii],[21]

Martin Stanley[22] Siegel, "Marty," was born 17 Apr 1929[23] in Brooklyn, New York,[24] to Morris and Helen Siegel. Morris died when Marty was a toddler, and Marty and Helen moved into an apartment with Helen's siblings. They are listed in the 1940 census living with Henry and Rose Steinman, and Helen's sister Adele lived next door with her husband, Frank Katz.[25]

Marty remained close with his unconventional family—while he was living at home, he shared a room with his uncle Henry, and he kept a photo of Frank and Adele Katz on his dresser for the rest of his life.[26]

He was estranged from his father's family, though it's unclear how the rift came about. Marty's father was described as "happy go [lucky], but the black sheep of the family," by other Siegel relatives,[27] and living cousins on that side knew little of his life and family—they didn't know Marty had children, for example, and Marty's children didn't know about them.

---

[i]Ann's daughter Nancy *2-3* thought Ann had gotten married at age 19; it wasn't until after Ann had died that Nancy realized Ann had actually been 21, and had been telling people she had been born in a later year.

[ii]Tillie Sovelove married David Reinstein, the brother of Claire Reinstein *4-15*.

Ann and Marty were married 1 Jun 1952[28] and had
two children:

- **Mark Robert**, b. 20 Apr 1955 in Brooklyn, New
  York. Married Denise Barbara Luftman (5 Sep 1955–
  19 Aug 2006)[29] on 24 Jun 1979;[30] divorced 1999.[31]
  They had one son, Adam Frank (b. 7 May 1982,
  married Bridget Henry). Lives in Florida. Named
  after Morris Siegel *4-12*.[32]
- **NANCY ELIZABETH** *2-3*, b. 4 Nov 1959 in
  Brooklyn.[33] Married Richard Abdill *2-2* on 6 Sep 1986;[34]
  three children: Richard *1-1* (b. 1 Nov 1989,[35] married Lauren Redding), Katie (b. 26 Feb 1992) and
  Claire (b. 22 Mar 1996). Lives in New Jersey.

Their daughter Nancy *2-3* said the couple met at some
kind of party or social, probably in late 1951, and were
married less than a year later.[36]

Ann and Marty divorced in November 1969;[37] Marty
never remarried, and after co-owning a jewelry store (Trin-
ity Jewelers, in Manhattan's financial district),[38] he started
selling windows and aluminum siding in the 1970s.[39] He
died probably 27 Sep 1995 in Manhattan, but the circumstances surrounding his death are still somewhat mysterious: Authorities discovered on 28 Sep 1995 that Marty
had died at home;[40] Nancy *2-3* says she talked to him on
the phone the evening of 26 Sep, which makes the most
likely date of death some time on the 27th. Both of Marty's
children expressed some skepticism about how he died, or
even whether he had died at all—Nancy says she was told
it was difficult to get a positive identification of the body,
even though he had only been dead perhaps 24 hours when
he was found, and neither Nancy nor Mark saw Marty's
body before he was buried.

In addition, Ann *3-7* said she was told by the Social
Security Administration in 2016 that they had no record

of Marty's death. A 2017 public records request by the author only further complicated matters: Two envelopes from Social Security arrived on the same day—in the first, a plain letter stating that the documents about Martin Siegel could not be released because they had no proof he had died. In the second envelope were all the requested documents.

Ann married Ronald Dondero on 21 May 1975.[41] They lived at 23 McCoy Ave. in Metuchen, New Jersey,[42] before moving to several other condominiums, then briefly to Delran, New Jersey, near the family of Nancy *2-3*. They moved permanently to St. Petersburg, Florida, in 2011,[43] where Ron died 23 Dec 2015. Ann died less than two years later, on 21 Apr 2017.

Dondero

Ron was born 15 May 1935[44] in Hoboken to John J. Dondero and Carmella DeMartino.[45] He was previously married while living in Lima, Ohio,[46] where he adopted a step-son, Mark,[47] and had one other son, John E. Dondero (b. 22 Feb 1963),[48] currently living in Florida. Ron moved back to New Jersey at some point before 1966,[49] and continued teaching high school English and drama until he became a vice principal, then retired around 1995.[50]

Ron's father, John Dondero, was born 31 Dec 1908[51] in Hoboken, New Jersey.[52] He was the youngest of eight:[53] his siblings were Joseph, Ernest, Tessie, Florence, Raymond, Madeline and Grace.[54] His father, also named John Dondero, was a Hoboken longshoreman born abt 1868 in Italy; he immigrated to the U.S. in abt 1878.[55] John's mother (Ron's paternal grandmother) was Angela[56] "Jennie" Garbarini, born in Italy abt 1871 and immigrated to America abt 1880.[57]

Ron's mother, Carmella DeMartino, was born 31 May 1911,[58] also in Hoboken. She and John married in 1932; John worked as a newspaper printer at the *Hudson Dispatch* in

Union City. The couple had three sons: John, Ron and
Raymond. The couple moved to Ohio later in life.

Carmella died 14 Sep 1976 in Toledo, Ohio,[59] where
John also died on 2 May 1980.[60]

Figure 7.2: Mark and Nancy at Nancy's wedding in 1986.[61]

Figure 7.3: Mark, Ann 3-7, Marty 3-6 and Nancy Siegel 2-3 at Mark's bar mitzvah celebration, 4 May 1968. Nancy said she could still remember how uncomfortable her pink shoes were almost 50 years later.[62]

(a) Mark and Nancy Siegel, circa 1963.[63]

(b) Ann 3-7 and Marty 3-6 at their wedding 1 Jun 1952.[64]

Figure 7.5: Ron Dondero and Ann 3-7 with Nancy's daughter Claire Abdill, named after Ann's mother.

Morris Siegel (4-12),
Helen Steinman (4-13)

Morris Siegel was born abt 1901[65] probably around Medvin, Russia.[66] Numerous documents (and current Siegel descendants) record the family's origins as being in "Kiev"—this is likely a reference to the Kiev gubernia (Киевская губерния), a region roughly equivalent to a state. Gubernias were broken down into *uyezd*, or districts; the Siegels were probably from the Kanev uyezd. Medvin was a *volost*, sub-district, of Kanev.[67]

Morris's birth name was "Moische Sigalow," (in Russian, something like "Моисей Сигалов"[68] and pronounced with a "v" sound at the end) and he immigrated to the U.S. with his family in 1912.[69] Helen and her siblings came to the United States in 1900; see the "Steinman" chapter for details.

It's difficult to nail down an exact birthday for Helen, though it's possible she didn't know either. She claimed to be 12 in 1905, for example, but said five years later that she was 15. No two documents suggest the same birth year: the 1905 census suggests the oldest (1893)[71] and her marriage certificate gives the youngest (1903);[72] everything else falls in between. We know the date on her marriage certificate is incorrect: She couldn't have been born in 1903 and also appeared as

Figure 7.6: Marty Siegel 3-6 and his mother Helen 4-13 in 1968.[70]

a 4-year-old in a ship manifest when her family arrived in New York in 1900. That manifest is probably our most

solid clue: Given the scrutiny her documentation would
have received on arrival, it's unlikely Helen would have
been of a dramatically different age than the age listed on
the manifest.

In 1920, Helen is listed as a clerk at a department store.[73] Helen and Morris married 24 Jun 1928,[74] when Morris was about 27 and Helen probably in her mid-30s. It's not clear who on the Siegel side, if anyone, knew her real age. The couple had one son,

Figure 7.7: The signature of Morris Siegel 4-12 the couple's 1928 marriage certificate.

MARTIN *3-6*, born 17 Apr 1929.[75] (See the previous
section for more about him.)

Morris died of complications from appendix surgery[76]
30 Mar 1932,[77] and Helen moved with Marty into a home
with her siblings Emma, Rose, Henry and Adele. At some
point before 1935, the family moved into an apartment at
3101 Avenue I in the Midwood neighborhood of Brooklyn.[78]
At some point before July 1943, they all moved to 180
Langham Street,[79] in the Manhattan Beach neighborhood,
where they spent the rest of their lives.

Sam Siegel (5-24), Anna Stein (5-25)

Sam Siegel was born abt 1875 in Medvin,[80] Russia.[81] Anna
was born probably abt 1873, also in Russia,[82] to Tzvi Stein
6-50 and Dora Cohen *6-51*.[83]

Sam and Anna had six children:

- **Jack**, b. 1895[84] in Russia,[85] d. 1987 in New York
  City.[86] Married Mary; had three children: George,
  Irene and Eugene.[87] Worked as an accountant.[88]

- **Bessie**, b. 1897[89] in Russia,[90] d. 1985.[91] Married Emanuel Weiss; later married Jack Sagerman.[92] Worked as a dentist.[93] Arrived under the name "Basse Sigalow."[94]
- **MORRIS** *4-12*,[95] b. abt 1903, d. abt 1931. Married Helen Steinman *4-13*. See entry above for more information.
- **Sophie**, b. abt 1907 in Russia,[96] d. 25 Feb 1920; living Siegel relatives say it was of rheumatic fever.[97] While her death certificate does not give a cause of death, her physician wrote that Sophie had "chronic cardiac valvular disease" for a year before her death,[98] a condition that was likely caused by rheumatic fever at some point. Arrived under the name "Czipe Sigalow."[99]
- **Berdie**, b. 17 Apr 1909 in Russia,[100] d. 10 Apr 1964.[101] Married first Joseph Boyer (b abt. 1902,[102] d. probably 11 Mar 1929 in Brooklyn),[103] had one daughter, Ann (b. 21 May 1928, d. 21 Oct 2015).[104] Remarried 25 Mar 1938[105] to Rubin D. Prussin (b. 20 Sep 1910 in New York[106] to David and Anna Prussin of Russia,[107] d. 20 Jul 2000 in Miami-Dade County, Florida).[108] Rubin had a son, Joseph (b. abt 1934 in New York), but it's unclear who Joseph's mother was.[109]
- **Sylvia**, b. 28 Feb 1909[110] around Medvin, d. 22 Jul 1986 in Dade County, Florida.[111] Married Max Chernow (b. 16 Apr 1898,[112] d. June 1981 in Dade County, Florida).[113] Had one son, Joseph Chernow.[114] Arrived under the name "Cziwi Sigalow."[115]

Sam *5-24* and Jack arrived in the U.S. on 28 Nov 1910 aboard the *Kaiserin Auguste Victoria*, under the names Salman and Jakob Sigal. Sam had two other children with him: Aron and Dwoire Sigal, who are listed as his children but are more likely to have been something closer

to a niece and nephew. (For a closer examination of the
Siegel immigration documents, see the "Siegel to Sigalow"
appendix.)

The family was reunited in Brooklyn about a year and
a half later, when Anna (under the name "Heni") and the
children arrived 1 May 1912 aboard the *Birma*. At some
point before 1920, the family moved to 310 Bedford Ave.,[116]
in the Williamsburg neighborhood of Brooklyn. Sam sold
fruits[117] and vegetables on Manhattan Avenue.[118] Next
to working in the garment industry, becoming a vendor or
peddler was one of the most common vocations picked up
by immigrants of the time—pushcarts could be rented for
a dime, and, though Italian and Greek immigrants were
known to be the primary peddlers of fruits and vegetables,
it would have cost only a few borrowed dollars to stock up
Sam's cart.[119] From there, the goal would likely have been
to save up enough to establish a storefront, though Sam's
venue of fruit selling is unknown.

Anna died 6 Oct 1924 of "general abdominal carcinoma."
Though her family did not know her birthday to include it
on the death certificate, it gives her age as 51.[120] (Anna
died at Mount Sinai Hospital, in Manhattan; 65 years later,
her great-great grandson, Richard Abdill *1-1*, was born
there.)

Relatives say Sam later married a woman named Rose
Kaufman,[121] though there is no known documentation of
this, and Sam's death certificate lists him as the widower of
Anna. A descendant says he remembers "playing ball with
grandfather Sam" in Brooklyn in the early 1940s. Sam was
hospitalized in late 1944 with stomach cancer, and died in
the early hours of 20 Dec 1944 at the Montefiore Hospital
for Chronic Diseases, in the Bronx.[iii,122]

[iii]The hospital is in the same place today, though the giant facility
is now known as the Montefiore Medical Center.

Schleme Sigalow (6-48),
Clara Green (6-49)

The only known documentation of Schleme and Clara is in the death certificate of their son, Samuel—it says they were born in Russia, and were living somewhere in the Kiev Governorate when Samuel was born abt 1874. Given his age, one might guess that they were born in the 1840s, though we don't know for sure.

Chapter 8

Steinman

The format of this section is slightly different from the others: While the siblings of ancestors are given a brief mention elsewhere in the series, the Steinmans all have biographies here. Basically, it's difficult to write about one without writing about the others—most of them lived together for their entire adult lives, and their journeys to America were closely intertwined.

Marcus Steinman (5-26), Sarah Borowski (5-27)

Sarah Borowski was born 10 Mar 1857[1] somewhere in the Russian empire[2] and arrived in the U.S. in 1900.[3] Unfortunately, we know little about her other than that: She lived with her children in Brooklyn, then died of arteriosclerosis on 30 Mar 1927.[4]

We know a surprising amount about Marcus (born "Zelig Mordechai"),[5] given his comparatively late arrival in America. According to his death certificate, he was born 30 Jun 1837 in Russia.[6] If the birthplace of his first children is any indication, he may have been born somewhere in what is now northeastern Poland. (Curiously, he, Sarah, and the children they arrived with in 1900 all told officials that their "mother tongue" was German.)[7]

His parents' names, according to his death certificate, were "Abraham Steinman" and "Lana Steinberg",[8] though this is almost certainly not accurate: "Steinman" wasn't Marcus's last name when he arrived here, and both of his parents were likely dead long before the family came here and adopted the name. In addition, Marcus's gravestone says his father's name is "Shmuel,"[9] though a name like "Shmuel Avraham" would not be out of the question. Given their son's date of birth, they may have been born some time in the 1810s, though all we know for sure is that their family said they were born in Russia.

Marcus gave the surname "Steinfirst" when he arrived in America,[10] though no available records show whether this was the surname he used in Europe; since he at some point moved from Poland to Prussia, it's possible "Steinfirst" is a more German-sounding name that he adopted when he immigrated there. As for his first name, he went by several "M" names in the U.S., including "Max"[11] and "Morris."[12] (His death certificate spells his name "Markus,"[13] but his tombstone says "Marcus."[14] All available marriage documents from his children use the latter spelling.)

Marcus married Sarah Lubitzky[15] at some point before abt 1866, when their first child was born.[16] The couple had two children that we are aware of:

- **Chaya Liba**,[17] "Lizzie,"[18] b. maybe June 1866,[19] died 14 Apr 1950.[20]
- **Aron Michel**, "Michael," b. 4 Aug 1867,[21] probably in Poland;[22] d. 15 Mar 1917 in Brooklyn.[23]

Lizzie's birthplace is recorded as "Ratzk, Russ Poland"[i] on her 1887 marriage certificate, which likely indicates

---

[i]See the "Shifting borders" appendix for more about Russian Poland.

the family was living in Raczki, a *shtetl* in the Suwalki Governorate of northeastern Poland. Her brother Michael's marriage certificate lists a similar name, "Ratzky, Russ. Pol."[24]

This is likely as close as we'll be able to get to guessing the birthplace of Marcus Steinman, as we have no mentions of the family's location before 1866. A Raczki taxpayer list from 1863 does not list anyone by the name of Steinfurst, Steinman or Lubitzky. Several other people on the tax list have been investigated, who have unrelated surnames but have first names starting with "M" that could have been Marcus—"Mejer Sjgatowicz," for example, and "Mowsza Sidorowski"—but other birth and residency records from the Suwalki Governorate don't line up with what we know of the family. There are several possible explanations for this—unfortunately, the most likely seems to be that the Steinmans went by yet another surname while in Poland.

Marcus remarried and had a child in 1877, so we can assume Sarah Lubitzky died sometime between 1866 and 1876.

At some point after her death, Marcus married Chaya Sarah Borowski *5-27*—Marcus would have been about 40, and Sarah was younger than 21.[ii]

We don't know for sure that Marcus and Sarah met in Prussia, as Sarah also oscillated between reporting that she was born in Germany or Russia: She told U.S. census-takers in 1910 that she was born in Germany, but "Russia" is listed as her birthplace in both the 1920 census and her 1927 death certificate. It's notable, however, that this answer flipped to "Russia" after the outbreak of World War I, when U.S. sentiment turned sharply against the "mad brute" of Germany, and German immigrants were targeted for heightened scrutiny and suspicion—Mark Siegel, the great-grandson of Marcus *5-26* and Sarah *5-27*, said Helen *4-13*

[ii]Sarah is recorded as having three different birth years in three censuses; the earliest year is 1855, the latest 1860.

and her siblings "were always concerned about downplaying
their German heritage," so, while it's possible Sarah's 1910
listing as German is a mistake, it is a tidy reversal to
observe at that particular time.

Marcus and Sarah had six children, all born in Schippenbeil, Germany:[iii]

- **Henry**, b. 20 Jan 1877,[25] d. Sep 1969.[26]
- **Emma**, b. abt 1884.[27] Died in Brooklyn, NY some
  time in the 1970s. Married Max Eisenstat (died
  maybe 14 May 1945)[28] on 19 May 1912.[29]
- **Rose**, b. abt 1888.[iv],[30] Never married; died in the
  1970s.
- **William**, b. 15 Jul 1889, d. October 1961.[31] Mar-
  ried Anna Friedman 1935.[32]
- **Adele**, b. abt 1891,[33] died abt January 1963.[34]
  Married Frank Katz 17 Jun 1931.[35]
- **HELEN** *4-13*, b. abt 1893. Married Morris Siegel
  4-12; see "Siegel" chapter for more.

How (and why) Marcus and Sarah ended up in Schippenbeil is unknown—it's about 100 miles west of Raczki,
but we can only guess about the impetus of their departure:
There was a cholera epidemic in the area in 1868,[36] and
a famine in the Suwalki Gubernia in 1868 and 1869 that
drove hundreds of Jews into Prussia.[37] Either of these
would also explain the untimely death of Marcus's first
wife.

The two oldest siblings, Michael and Lizzie, immigrated
to the U.S. in the 1880s—we have no idea when, or whom
they may have been meeting. Henry followed in 1892,[38]

[iii]For more information about Schippenbeil, now known as Sepopol, see the "Shifting borders" appendix.

[iv]Rose's birth year is given in documents as anywhere between
1880 and 1889. The majority of the dates are at the end of the
1880s.

then Rose in 1898[39] and the rest of the family in 1900. (See the following sections for details of their immigration.)

It would appear both sets of siblings were close after arriving in America, at least geographically: In 1900, Michael and his family[40] were living less than a half mile from the home of Michael's sister Lizzie, where their half-brother Henry was staying as well.[41] In 1910, there were three Steinman households (Michael's, Lizzie's, and their father Marcus's *5-26*),[42] all along the Bedford-Stuyvesant border: Three generations, at least 15 people in all,[v] lived on a 12-block stretch of Broadway in Brooklyn.

Marcus died two years later, on 11 Mar 1912, at the Bed-Stuy tenement where the family lived.[43] At some point before 1917,[44] Sarah and the children moved seven blocks south, to 285 Pulaski St.[45] Sarah died 30 Mar 1927 in Crown Heights, Brooklyn,[46] but it's not clear if the family was living there at the time.

Lizzie Steinfurst, Philip Simon

Lizzie was born probably in June 1866[47] and immigrated to New York in about 1880.[48] It is unknown whom the young teen may have been meeting in America, but we can guess that life was chaotic: At this point, her mother had died, her father had remarried to a woman who may have been 8 years older than Lizzie, and she got on a boat as a 15-year-old to land on the opposite side of an ocean as her remaining family.

She married Philip Simon 19 Jun 1887.[49] Philip was born probably in April 1863 in Poland; he came to the U.S. in about 1884.[50]

The couple had four children,[51] all born in New York:

- **Sarah**, b. Aug 1888,[52] died maybe in the mid-1960s.[53] Married Herman Barnett (b. abt 1885

---

[v]The 1910 location of Lizzie's son Norman is unknown.

in Russia)[54] between 1910 and 1913;[55] divorced before 1940,[56] likely before 1930.[57] Had two children: Norman and Harold.[58] Mark Siegel, a grandson of Lizzie's half-sister Helen *4-13*, says he can remember "Aunt Sarah" frequently visiting the other Steinman siblings;[59] she would have been Mark's father's first cousin.

- **Louis**, b. 27 Sep 1890,[60] date of death unknown, but was living with Philip and Lizzie, plus his sister Sarah and her two sons, in 1930.[61] Likely alive at least through the end of 1936.[62]
- **Norman**, b. April 1892;[63]
- A child who died at some point before 1900.[64] Lizzie reported having had four children in the 1900 census but only three who were living. We don't know the identity of the fourth, and unfortunately there are dozens of children in New York with the surname "Simon" who died between 1888 and 1900.[65]

Lizzie died 14 Apr 1950.[66] Philip died probably 25 Apr 1952[67] and, according to cemetery records, is buried next to Lizzie. For some reason, his half of the couple's gravestone was never engraved with his name.[68]

Michael Steinman, Rebecca Hoffman

Michael was born 4 Aug 1867;[69] he claimed in multiple documents to have been born in Germany, but it's likely that his older sister Lizzie was born in northeastern Poland the previous year, so his assertion is at least questionable. At different times, he was said to have immigrated to the United States in 1878, 1881[70] or 1885.[71] As with Lizzie, there is no known record of his arrival, but it appears he went by the name "Michael Stone" for a time.

Rebecca Hoffman was born 14 Jan 1872[72] in Russia;[73] it's unknown when she came to the United States, but she gave multiple years between 1885[74] and, impossibly,

1903.[75] (She may have been the "Riwke Hoffman" who arrived on the *Oder* 23 Mar 1885, but that person said she was born abt 1865.)[76]

Rebecca and Michael were married 1 Feb 1892, when a wedding between a "Rebecca Hoffman" and "Michael Stone" was recorded in Brooklyn.[77] While there is no other evidence that the "Stone" surname was used at any other point by Michael (or anyone in the Steinman family), other documents list their marriage as happening in 1892, and the names of Michael's parents *and* his place of birth line up exactly as expected, so it appears he used the name at least for a time. (In addition, the word "stone" in Yiddish is *shteyn*, giving the "American" surnames "Stein" and "Stone" a logical connection.)

The couple had four children:

- **Louis**, b. 1893[78] in Brooklyn; married Miriam Cohen in 1919,[79] one child: Barbara Jeanne Steinman (b. 19 Mar 1923, d. 17 May 2007).[80]
- **Sylvia**, b. 4 Aug 1894 in New York,[81] died possibly May 1974.[82] Married Irving Jacobson 25 Dec 1919; two sons:[83] Malcolm Arthur (b. 29 Sep 1920[84] in New York,[85] d. 15 May 2010 in Boynton Beach, Fla.)[86] and Jacques (b. abt 26 Nov 1925).[87]
- **Lena**, b. 30 Nov 1897,[88] d. 23 Jul 1898.[89] While we don't know for sure that Lena was the child of Michael and Rebecca, they reported in 1900 that they had four children, three of whom were still alive; Lena is the only "Steinman" child who was born and died in Brooklyn after their marriage.
- **Nettie**, b. abt March 1900.[90]

Michael died 15 Mar 1917, age 49, of complications from a gallbladder infection;[91] Rebecca lived another 20 years and died 1 Sep 1937. They are both[92] buried near Marcus *5-26* and Sarah *5-27*.[93]

Michael's death certificate lists his mother's maiden name as something like "Sarah Bawlsky," presumably a reference to the name of his father's second wife, Sarah Borowski. All evidence points to this being incorrect. Primarily, it's doubtful because Sarah Borowski was about 9 years old when Michael was born; in addition, his 1892 marriage certificate gives his mother's name as "Sarah Lubovsky," which matches Lizzie's mother's name. Given they were born about 14 months apart, it seems safe to say his death certificate is incorrect.

Henry Steinman

Henry was the oldest of the children of Marcus and Sarah, born 20 Jan 1877,[95] probably with the name "Heinrich."[96] He came to the U.S. 5 Dec 1892 aboard the *Scandia*, a steamship loaded with 501 passengers; he had no luggage.[97] He landed at the newly constructed Ellis Island immigration facility in New York Harbor. At age 15, he likely went to live with his half-sister Lizzie and her young family, with

Figure 8.1: Rose, Emma and Henry Steinman, with Helen's grandson Mark Siegel in 1968.[94]

whom he is recorded in the 1900 census.[98]

Interestingly, Henry was likely the only Steinman to travel through Ellis Island. His older siblings Michael and Lizzie arrived in the 1880s, before Ellis Island had been built and immigrants were instead processed at New

York's Castle Garden facility, located at the southern tip of Manhattan.

Henry arrived in 1892, the first year Ellis Island was open. In 1897 the entire complex burnt to the ground, forcing authorities to process immigrants through the "Barge Office" processing center in Manhattan for three years,[99] during which time all the other Steinmans arrived. The facility currently at Ellis Island was the (fire-resistant) replacement for the wooden structures where Henry was processed.

He got a job as an insurance agent in about 1894,[100] an industry he worked in until at least 1920.[101] It's likely his older half-brother, Michael, had a hand in this: Michael worked in the life insurance business for years,[102] and was in the industry as early as the 1900 census.[103] Having arrived perhaps 10 years ahead of Henry, Michael may have already had business connections in place.

Starting in 1930,[104] Henry's field is listed in documents only as "chemicals." In 1940, he is an "executive" in that industry;[105] surviving family who knew him have no idea what this might mean.

It appears he at least helped to sponsor the passage of his entire family to come to New York in 1900[106] with the exception of Rose, who had arrived two years earlier than the others.[107]

Henry became a U.S. citizen 7 Aug 1900.[108] Never married, and died in September 1969.[109]

Emma Steinman, Max Eisenstat

Emma was born abt 1884,[110] and immigrated to America 29 Aug 1900 aboard the *Kaiser Wilhelm der Grosse* out of Bremen, Germany.[111] She and Rose worked as equipment operators at a dress factory[112] starting at some point before 1905.[113]

She married Max Eisenstat 19 May 1912,[114] two months after her father's death. Max was born abt 1877 in Germany[115] to Moses and Jeanette (Grossman) Eisenstat.[116] He was working as a "window dresser" when he and Emma married in 1912,[117] and in 1915 is listed as a self-employed sign painter.[118] We have no evidence of their life together, other than that he probably died after 1940, when all of Emma's other siblings were living together, and definitely before the 1960s, when relatives remember Emma living with those siblings and not Max. She died in Brooklyn some time in the 1970s.

Rose Steinman

Rose was born some time around 1888 (or possibly several years earlier)[vi,120] and came to the U.S. under the name "Rosa Steinfurst."[121] The circumstances of her arrival in the U.S. are somewhat unclear: We know she landed at Ellis Island 20 Dec 1898 aboard the *Kaiser Wilhelm der Grosse*, but the ship manifest says her passage was paid for by her aunt, of whom we have no knowledge.

Figure 8.2: Emma and Rose Steinman, with Mark Siegel in 1968.[119]

Rose is listed next to two German women of about the same age, though their names are hard to read; the best guess of Ellis Island researchers is "Amalie and Martha Parkonsky," who both came from the same town ("Schippenbiel") as Rose and are listed as having their passage paid

---

[vi]Rose's birth year is given in documents as anywhere between 1880 and 1889. The majority of the dates are at the end of the 1880s.

by their aunt also. This seems to suggest that "Parkonsky" was either Sarah's *5-27* maiden name or the married name of Marcus or Sarah's sister, but their whereabouts are unknown, as is Rose's location in the 1900 census; it's likely she was staying with that family, as her brother Henry was staying with Lizzie.

Rose worked in the garment industry until some time between 1910 and 1920,[122] and died in the 1970s.

William G. Steinman, Anna Friedman

William was born 15 Jul 1889[123] and was listed upon his arrival in the U.S. as "Willy Steinfirst." He arrived on the *Trave*, out of Bremen, Germany, on 28 Dec 1900, along with his parents and his two younger sisters.[124]

He got a job as a stock clerk in the garment industry at some point before 1905,[125] a position he held until at least 1910.[126] By 1920, however, he'd started his own business manufacturing "ladies waists,"[127] according to that year's census. Eventually, the "William Steinman & Associates" dressmaking company would become hugely popular. He and Anna Friedman were married in summer 1935.[128]

Anna was born abt 1907 in New York.[129] The couple adopted[130] their daughter Sandra in abt 1940[131] and lived in Manhattan on the Upper East Side.[132] William died in October 1961;[133] Anna lived until approximately early 1996.[134]

Adele Steinman, Frank Katz

Adele was born abt 1891, probably as "Emilie," though the spelling given on the ship manifest when she came to America may be a corrupted anglicization of her name.[vii] While

---

[vii] In citizenship paperwork filed in 1928, Adele gave her birthday as 31 Oct 1900, which mean a child listed in the ship manifest as being 9 years old would have to have actually been a month old. We don't have much choice but to assume the year is a fabrication.

surviving relatives remember her as "Adele," it appears
she went by the name "Amelia"[135] until the late 1920s.[136]
She worked as a supervisor in an undergarment factory[137]
for more than 20 years.[138]

Adele married Frank Katz 17 Jun 1931.[139] Frank was
born 14 Feb 1893 in Budapest, Hungary,[140] and immigrated
to New York 24 Nov 1907 aboard the *Cambroman*.[141]

Figure 8.3: Frank Katz, from a 1920 passport application.[142]

Figure 8.4: The signature of Lizzie (Steinfurst) Simon from her 1887 marriage certificate.

Figure 8.5: The signature of Henry Steinman from his 1900 citizenship application.

Figure 8.6: The signature of William Steinman from his World War I draft registration in about 1917.

Figure 8.7: The signature of Adele Steinman from 1928 citizenship paperwork.

Figure 8.8: The signature of Helen (Steinman) Siegel from her 1928 marriage certificate.

Chapter 9

Borowski

Nochym Borowski (6-54),
Reuza Eufman (6-55)

All we know of the parents of Sarah (Borowski) Steinman *5-27* comes from the documentation of her death: Her death certificate says her parents' names were Samuel Borowski and Rosie Klein, both born in Russia,[1] though it's unlikely these obviously anglicized names were actually the names they went by. The Hebrew inscription on Sarah's tombstone says she is "Chaya Sarah, daughter of Nachum,"[2] which is likely a more faithful representation of her father's name.

Given that, the only probable guess to be made with available records comes from Rajgród, a town in the modern-day Podlaskie Voivodeship of northeastern Poland: There, we find the record of a marriage between Nochym Borowski and Reuza Eufman in 1844;[3] *Nochym* is an alternative transliteration of "Nachum," from Sarah's gravestone, and *Reuza* is strikingly close to "Rosie." They were married 13 years before Sarah's birth, in a town about 20 miles south of Raczki, the town in which Sarah's children were born. There are no records of the children of Nochym and Reuza, though if we accept these people as Sarah's parents, then it's likely she had multiple older siblings. As the marriage record of Nochym and Reuza also includes their parents, we may have the hint of another two (and a half) generations. On Nochym's side:

- **Nochym Borowski** *6-54*, b. abt 1821 in Rajgród, Poland.
- **Srol Borowski** *7-108*, father of Nochym.
- **Liba** *7-109*, mother of Nochym.
- **Idzko Borowski** *8-216*, father of Srol.

And the family of Reuza:

- **Reuza Eufman** *6-55*, b. abt 1819 in Rajgród; married Nochym Borowski, had at least one daughter, Chaya Sarah *5-27*, though records of her birth have not been found.
- **Srol Eufman** *7-110*, father of Reuza.
- **Fejga** *7-111*, mother of Reuza.
- **Judko Eufman** *8-220*, father of Srol *7-110*.

Chapter 10

Shifting borders

The story of Nancy Abdill's family includes broad strokes of daring aspiration in search of a better, safer life: Three of her four grandparents were born outside the United States, and her eight great-grandparents were all born abroad. Because of this, unravelling the ethnic and national questions of our origins gets complicated quickly. For example: Using the borders of the time, at least seven of her great-grandparents were born in Russia, and possibly one in Germany. Using the borders redrawn by the conflicts of the 20th century, however, that count becomes four in Ukraine, four in Poland—and none in Russia. (In addition, the cities that shifted from Russia to Ukraine were, until the late 1700s, actually also in Poland.)

This is further complicated by the complex questions of ethnicity that existed in these countries even while those ancestors were living there—for example, though our family could have been living in Poland for upwards of 600 years[i] at the time they left for America, they were not considered *Poles*—they were Jews. "Poles" are recognized as a Slavic

---

[i]Jews lived in Poland before the reign of King Casimir III, but he was the Polish ruler to codify their rights and allow more Jews to settle in the region.

ethnic group distinguished, in general terms, as Polish-speaking and broadly Roman Catholic. Ethnicity was a far more defining characteristic than nationality, particularly because the shapes of "nations" had a tendency to move around any time someone kicked off a war.

Wyszogród, Poland

In the time we know the Arbeiters lived in Wyszogród, about 40 miles upstream from Warsaw and just outside of Płock, Wyszogród was solidly within the Russian empire, through a circuitous route of 19th century European treaties.

Płock was a major city in the early Polish kingdom starting in about the 11th century. Jewish settlers arrived at some point in the 1500s, around the same time as the official founding of the Polish–Lithuanian Commonwealth, in which the king of Poland also served as the grand duke of Lithuania. (Nearby Wyszogród was of approximately equal age.)

A backlash against corruption and political power-grabs led the commonwealth's parliament (the "Great Sejm") to adopt a constitution of broad democratic reforms in 1791, making it the first codified constitution in Europe and the only in the world other than the U.S. constitution that had been adopted two years earlier. Complicated dynamics (including Russia considering Poland a "protectorate" in its domain) were exacerbated by the attempted changes, and in 1792 Russia invaded the commonwealth, in what became the Polish–Russian War of 1792. The conclusion of the three-month conflict left Poland utterly conquered, and the series of agreements to conclude the conflict resulted in the "Second Partition of Poland,"[ii] which split 118,500 square

---

[ii]The first, in 1772, resulted in the commonwealth losing 81,000 square miles of territory containing almost 4.5 million people, split between Prussia, Austria and Russia.

miles of territory between Russia, who had conquered the commonwealth, and Prussia, which had refused to help defend against the invasion.

Poland, as a state, was gone, and Płock was pulled into the Kingdom of Prussia—for a little while, at least. The War of the Fourth Coalition would change that: Fought in 1806 and 1807, the conflict got its name from the coalition of countries that had joined forces to fight the French military, which had plowed through Prussia, conquered Berlin and was making its way into Russian territory.

As far as we know, Abraham Arbeiter's great-grandparents, Szoel *8-226* and Ruchla Chrzanowski *8-227*, were living in Bieżuń at the time, which means they would have been present for the invasion of French dragoons in their town in December 1806. Several miles down-river, fighting was personally observed by Emperor Napoleon Bonaparte.

By the following spring, the French had single-handedly defeated the armies of Prussia, Saxony, Great Britain, Russia and Sweden, and in summer 1807 the parties signed the Treaties of Tilsit to bring most of the fighting to a close. Among other concessions, France was granted the lands that became the Duchy of Warsaw, a French-controlled area that some hoped could eventually form the nucleus of a re-formed Polish nation. Just a few miles up-river from the city of Warsaw itself, Wyszogród and Płock were under the thumb of France. That, too, would not last long.

The Congress of Vienna began in late 1814: The War of the Sixth Coalition had concluded with France's defeat, Napoleon had been exiled to Elba, and the states of Europe convened to redraw the map, rolling back the Napoleonic conquests and resizing the nations of the continent to ensure a more stable balance of power. The result for Płock was another reorganization, into "Congress Poland" under Russian rule. At first, the Polish state was relatively autonomous, though the tsar of Russia also acted as the king of the "new" Poland. After the November Uprising in 1830 and 1831, however, much of this autonomy was confiscated: The Polish parliament was abolished, and the country was pulled into a much closer, "real" union with the Russian empire.

Abraham's parents, Davis *6-56* and Annie *6-57*, were in their late teens at the time of the January Uprising, a two-year rebellion that started in early 1863 in response to Russian conscription efforts. The first armed conflict of the uprising happened less than nine miles northeast of Płock, where rebels in a village now called Ciółkowo attacked Russian troops armed only with swords and pikes.

Płock was chosen to be the "headquarters" of the uprising, but rebels were unable to capture the city from the Russians.[1] About 200,000 Poles are estimated to have participated in the two-year conflict. When the Russians were finally able to regain control, they responded with heavy action: Thousands were exiled to Siberia, dramatic tax penalties were levied throughout the region, and the last remnants of Polish self-rule were destroyed. Abe Arbeiter's 1878 Polish birth certificate is written in Russian.

This state of affairs would continue through the first world war, after which Poland was once again granted national sovereignty. U.S. President Woodrow Wilson famously publicized the "Fourteen Points" that America was pursuing in the World War I peace process; the independence of Poland was point 13.

November 11, the anniversary of the ceasefire, was celebrated in the United States as Armistice Day, now known as Veterans Day—in Poland, it is celebrated as Independence Day.

Sepopol, Poland (Schippenbeil)

The Steinman family consistently reported they had emigrated from Schippenbeil, an East Prussian town that was part of the German Empire. Marcus Steinman *5-26* lived in Raczki, Poland in the 1860s, and may have been born there—our best guess for the family's move to Schippenbeil is at some point in the late 1860s.[iii]

When the Steinmans arrived in Schippenbeil, East Prussia had been involved in decades of conflict and political reorganization: The lands had been part of the Holy Roman Empire for 1,000 years, until it was dissolved in 1806 following Napoleon's conquests in Europe. The Kingdom of Prussia would operate separately from the newly formed German Confederation until about 1867, when almost two dozen German "states" were pulled together into the North German Confederation, likely the state that the Steinmans moved to.

In the closing act of the Franco–Prussian War, the "unification of Germany" in 1871 brought together most of central Europe under the umbrella of the German Empire. (When Nazi Germany described itself as the "Third Reich," it was with the understanding that this unified Germany was the second one.)

Though the Steinmans' government then included regions such as Bavaria and Saxony, it almost certainly didn't have any appreciable effect on their lives; Prussia was by far the largest kingdom in the empire and exerted the lion's share of political influence. The region experienced a seismic shift, however, in the aftermath of World War II, when Schippenbeil was confiscated from Germany and pulled into the reorganized country of Poland. Its German residents were expelled and the town's name was changed from the German "Schippenbeil" to the Polish "Sepopol," the name by which it is known today.

[iii]See the "Steinman" chapter for more about this move.

Die Stadt Schippenbeil. 1872.

Nach der Natur aufgenommen von Frau Pfarrer Gregorovius.

Figure 10.1: An engraving from an 1874 book. Its caption reads, roughly: "The city of Schippenbeil, 1872. Image taken from nature[2] by Frau Pfarrer Gregorovius,[3] (wife of Pastor Gregorovius)."[4]

Medzhybizh, Ukraine

Medzhybizh was already a centuries-old town when Harry *5-30* and Ada Reinstein *5-31* were born there in the mid-1800s. Because of its central location between the heart of Russia and the larger powers of Eastern Europe, Ukraine had been a part of a half-dozen long-dissolved nation states before it was pulled into the Russian empire.

Its modern history might start in the 1700s, when the town grew to be a large and influential area in the Polish–Lithuanian Commonwealth. As with Płock to the west, Medzhybizh was deeply affected by the Second Partition of Poland in 1793, when it too was pulled into the Russian empire.

The Ukrainian War of Independence overlapped with both World War I and Russia's February Revolution, and the period after World War I was chaos for Ukrainian governance. The war in Ukraine was fought between multiple countries *and* multiple factions within Ukraine itself—at various points, control of the region was being pursued by (among others) Germany, the Bolsheviks (the "Red Army"), anti-communists (the "White Russians"), and a band of anarchists who wanted to form a stateless society in lands formerly governed as Ukraine. The fight over Ukrainian independence in the Bolshevik revolution is particularly complicated—a loose analogy might be if the American Civil War had been fought between the Union and the Confederacy, but halfway through both armies left to fight in a separate war already happening in Texas.

Starting in 1922, the government of the Ukrainian Soviet Socialist Republic became one of the member states of the USSR, second in population and land mass only to the Russian Federation. The area was conquered by Nazi Germany in 1941, but was returned to Soviet control after the end of World War II. Like the other Soviet states, Ukraine gained its independence in 1991 when the Soviet Union was dissolved.

Figure 10.2: A 1935 photograph of the "Bach Synagogue," built in Medzhybizh in the 1600s and named in honor of Joel Sirkis (a rabbi also known as "the Bach"), who had recently completed a turn as rabbi in the town.[5]

Medvin, Ukraine

The birthplace of the Siegel (or Sigalow) family, Medvin's fate follows the historical fortunes of "Right-Bank Ukraine," the region of Ukraine west of the Dnieper River. Like Medzhybizh, it was pulled from the Polish–Lithuanian Commonwealth in 1793 and put under Russian control, where it officially became part of the conceptual region known as "Little Russia."

The "Little Russian" identity became entangled in the centuries-old ethnic disputes in the area—before the Siegels and Reinsteins left for America, its use had come to compete with the concept of a "Ukrainian" identity. Many Ukrainians saw the concept of "Little Russia" as an attempt to undermine their sovereignty, seeing it as an unsubtle implication that Ukraine was a piece of Russia that happened to occasionally be a part of other countries. (Incidentally, that is also why referring to the area as "The Ukraine," rather than "Ukraine," has fallen out of favor: The argument is that the phrase "the Ukraine" is an attempt to make the country sound like more of a region—such as "the borderlands" or "the Midwest"—than a state.) There were countless other concepts tied to ethnicity and nationhood at play there in the 19th and 20th centuries—for example, debates even today about the status of the "Rusyn" minority, which rejects attempts to classify members as ethnic Ukrainians—but all of them specifically excluded the Jews, who were seen as an alien influence even in relation to the nascent Polish presence left over from the 1793 partition.

Medvin's legal and governmental fate in the 20th century mirrors that of Medzhybizh, and it is currently part of the Kiev Oblast of Ukraine.

Chapter 11

Wyszogród memories

This section contains two essays written after World War II by former residents of Wyszogród, the hometown of the Biłgoraj and Arbeiter (Arbajter) families. The first paints an impressionistic picture of life before the war, small snapshots of a fondly remembered town that now exists only in those memories.

The second essay tells of the destruction of the Jewish presence in Wyszogród, both the people and their works. It should be pointed out that the essay describes events that happened after Abraham Arbeiter *5-28* and his family had been in America for more than 30 years—it is included here as a means to answer those who would visit now, looking for evidence of our family. Finding nothing, the inevitable question is, "What happened?" The answer is ugly, and readers should be forewarned of its graphic nature—it is not a quiet business when half a town is melted down for parts.

The essays were compiled in a 1971 publication called *Book to the martyrs of Wyszogrod Poland*, edited by Haim Rabin. It is part of a genre of *yizkor books*, published after various calamities throughout history as a way to preserve communal memories. The yizkor book saw a tragically widespread resurgence after the Holocaust, compiled from various locations and organized mostly based on stories from a particular town.[i]

The editors of *From a Ruined Garden*, a book examining the phenomenon of post-war memorial books, call the form "the single most important act of commemorating the dead on the part of Jewish survivors."[1] You'll notice, even in just the two essays presented here, that the writing has an exaggerated attention to detail, a focus on capturing glimpses of characters even at the fringes of the story. The authors are incapable of writing, "And ten of us collected to pray," without following it immediately by a roster of names and relations. It makes for choppy reading, but to a family for whom it is the only hint of a relative's fate in the *Shoah*, graceful narrative flow is not likely to be the primary concern. Yizkor books were a gesture of defiance, a triumph over Nazi attempts to erase not only the Jews, but the Jewish story stretching backward through the ages. Survivors authored hundreds of yizkor books, first-hand accounts of a lost world, a history that refused to be buried.

From a Ruined Garden observes several categories of memorial books, based on key words in their Hebrew titles. The Wyszogród book is titled *Wyszogrod, sefer zikaron le'kedoshei*; "sefer"—literally, "book"—is explained to indicate that the work is intended to be a holy text, a "book" in the same sense as a book of the Bible or a volume of rabbinic commentary. "Le'kedoshei" indicates that the collection was dedicated to the town's martyrs killed in the Holocaust.[2] "Zikaron" is simply a word for solemn remembrance.[3] Gerontologist Marc Kaminsky explained the form in (among many other places) a 1988 article: "They contained chronicles of vanished communities, portraits of outstanding individuals—rabbis, philanthropists, artists,

---

[i]According to the Holtzman translation, the assistant editor was A Felz. The editorial board is listed as N. Daicz, B. Gutman née Zawierucha, VA, Felz H., H. Levine, P. Melineck, M. Walfish.

political leaders—and also of memorable characters—a traveling tailor, a blind cantor, a coachwoman. They included diagrams of former homes, street maps, anecdotes, poems, photographs—nothing that bore witness to the life of the vanished community was excluded. All surviving documents and reminiscences were in-gathered here, since each, as symbol and as information, counteracted the death of dead relatives and neighbors, and of the lost public world the living had shared with the dead."[4]

In the mid-1990s, members and administrators of the JewishGen email listserv began an effort to track, catalog and translate about 1,200 yizkor books, an ongoing effort that can be found today on their website at `JewishGen.org`. Though much of the Wyszogród book remains only in Hebrew, JewishGen volunteer Ada Holtzman translated and compiled the names of more than 1,500 residents included in the book's necrology list, plus the table of contents and captions of photographs. In addition, the organization (and its lawyers) tried to find the organization that had published the book and anyone who may have been involved, in an effort to solicit their input about the obvious copyright concerns. Unfortunately, by the time the JewishGen project started looking, the group (The Former Residents of Vishogrod Organisation) no longer existed, and no one connected to the project could be found.[5] So, it would seem JewishGen and this book had similar rationales for including the work here without an explicit license from its authors—primarily, because the book wasn't intended to be a lucrative money-maker; it was, like so many of the other yizkor projects, an effort to preserve the community's stories in a form that could be literally handed down between generations. In that way, all of these projects had an identical aim: As JewishGen's Joyce Field put it, "to unlock the histories of these towns and the sufferings and joys of their former inhabitants—so that the world would learn and never forget."[6]

Even then, though, JewishGen ran into issues: "Seemingly, the writers and editors of the books were writing for each other and never expected that their efforts would be translated and put on the Internet. At the beginning, as the translation project sought permission from the *landsman-schaftn* [social organizations based mostly on the hometown of immigrants now living elsewhere], there was great difficulty explaining what the Internet was and convincing them that others—most of whom were English-speakers—were interested in the contents of the yizkor books. It took their children and grandchildren to explain the digital revolution to the survivors at that time. The initial reluctance of the survivors to trust others with their memories has faded, to be replaced with satisfaction and pride that their memories are being honored and validated."

The Wyszogród book includes a section at the back written entirely in English, a startling rarity among *yizker bikher*.[7] It is from this section that the following two essays were initially printed; they have been transcribed directly from the copy that was digitized by the New York Public Library.[ii,8] This book is the only known anthologization of any of the Wyszogród yizkor book's content outside of its original format.[9]

[ii]Typographical and spelling errors have been preserved as they were in the original; to avoid disrupting the flow of the narrative, this transcription omits the "*Sic*" notations acknowledging them.

I Remember...

By Bella Zawierucha-Gutman

I see you in all the glory and richness of my earliest youth.

Here you are, stretching alongside the Vistula river, on which we look down from our town-on-the-hill. The long way up from the Vistula leads to the rectangular market-place. From there extend all the side-streets, large and small. For me all of it is unique, more beautiful, more friendly, more joyful than anything else; the houses and cottages, the shops of different size and cellars, and the shopkeepers, men and women. I see each baker and his family, each tradesman, each storekeeper and villagebuyer, each orchardist and watercarrier, all the members of the community and the notables.

All, all of them were upright, decent people, high-minded, possessed of the Jewish "over-soul."

Broad is the flow of our Vistula, where it converges with the Bzura. It rushes noisily, carrying with it, every now and then, fragments of the bank belonging to the town or to the castlehill that rises aloof, by itself, and about which we have so many tales and dreams...

The castlehill is very high, and we look up to it, and see in it more and more the enchanted castle of the King Casimir the Great, with his—our—Esther'ke.

137

It's a long time, nothing has remained of the castle, but it's so good to spin out the legends; everybody likes the legendary and fanciful.

In wintertime, the Vistula is locked in by the frost and waits silently for the spring, when we will wonder at its surging up, when the ice-floes begin to stir more and more, noisier, quicker, and the flow carries away trees, bridges and huts.

Uphill from the Vistula, you can reach the shoamekers' street,[iii] so near to my aunt Hendel's, my uncle Shiye's and my cousins Moshe and Israel.

The small street continues to the Rembova street, ending in a row of woodem, red-daubed huts, bordering on the big deep "parowes" (ravines) that follow the whole width of the town, far away, to the Vistula, in one direction, and in the other one, farther still, up to the "stegenes" (uphill paths), this magnificent walk alongside the Vistula.

Because of those deep big ravines that cut the town in two, two streets are connected by a bridge. It seems to us so natural, such a stone bridge in the heart of a small town. We think, sure all small towns are built like that.

One can also ascend from the Vistula to the town center by stairs, leading to the synagogue, close to the house where we are living, and to the house of Sara-Toibele, Ya'acov Moshe Goldman's wife.

This is the home of several families; each one in its inherited quarters, together with the married children. There was the drygoods store of Goldman-Selman, and the hardware store of Lipman, and the button factory of Maisdorf-Popowski. About this house alone you could write a history book of human energy, wisdom, piousness, kindness, and progress.

Our window facing the synagogue was occupied on all Sabbat days and holidays by my friends: Mania and Sala Weingart, Henele Rotbart, Hadaske Baum, Sara Malka

---

[iii]A typo referencing the "shoemaker's" street.

Kirshenbaum, Eta Lichtenstein, Sima Gmach, Haya Libe Gutfarb, Eidel Krongrad, Also kept company with us Tove Ides and Blime Lea Goldman. We liked them very much and welcomed them gladly.

We look out at the synagogue. The stout thick walls, the large green double door and tall windows, looked all week long like an enchanted castle, fast asleep. On Sabbat[iv] and holiday the synagogue came alive. It was full with people, and round it colorful children with their parents in Sabbat finery; everybody moved towards the synagogue.

From outside the synagogue did not look very tall, because it was [s]quare, big, with a roof with cupolas; but whoever entered it was wonder-struck with its height. (People said that it had been built deep under ground level, because it was forbidden for a synagogue to be higher than a church). Therefore you had to go down from the entrance by stairs. And then you saw a magnificent, great work of art, an object of wonder and interest to everybody: The Eastern wall, large, marvelously carved, the great pictures on the side walls; on the entrance wall, the lions, one of them being so lifelike, that it seemed to look at you from any direction.

The center of the ceiling looked like open heaven, with Shor-Habor and the Leviathan round it. From both sides stairs led up to carved balconies, where we used to stand to hear the shophar blowing. In the large entrance halls, on three sides, there were spiral stairs up to the women's part of the synagogue. Near them, there were small rooms for those coming to pray early. In the middle entrance hall there was still the pillory chain, of the "kuna."[v]

[iv]This unconventional spelling, which looks like a combination of "Shabbat" and "Sabbath," appears numerous times in the text.

[v]Curiously, "kuna" is a Polish word approximately translated as "pillory." Though they are described mostly as a feature of Christian houses of worship, it would appear the Wyszogród synagogue also had one, in which someone would be attached to the wall by the neck and wrists.

Each time I was standing on the balcony to hear the shophar blowing, I used to wish to see that lion, that used in former days to hand out the tora scrolls from the Holy Ark and let hear such a lifelike deep roar, it scared pregnant women. It proved necessary to take out the contraption which constituted its life. In my time, it was, unfortunately, dead.

Between the synagogue and the bes-midrash[vi] there was a large square, where we, our crowd, used to play on workdays and set free our energy and skill. Two gates were leading from the square into the yards of Weingart's and Rotbart's. There was the bakery, and Henele let us perform plays on the oven platform. Our first rehearsals were held there, and later on Sabbat afternoon we played in the Rotbarts' drawingroom, before the whole family and guests, with great success.

We used to be much scared in the evenings when we were obliged to cross the dark house and the dark yard, where Gedalia Moshe, son of Yohere of the dairy, a handsome, tall, sturdy man, with magnificent black eyes, was standing quiet, deep in his thoughts, and from time to time let out with his loud, beautiful voice: —I am Bar-Kochba, where is Shulamit?[10]

Every day at the same hour, the three roads to the Vistula come alive: the ship is coming, the only means of communication in the summertime of the Płock–Warsaw route. On the landing pier, it grows lively with the arrival of the ship. Moshe Zlotnik gets busy. Porters get ready to earn a little money. Guests arrive and leave. Merchants bring goods from Warsaw. People see off guests.

On one of those beautiful summer days, when the ship was at the pier and some passengers on deck were poking fun at Jews, their joking wound up in betting, who of them

---

[vi] A *besmedresh* (in Yiddish) or *bet midrash* (in Hebrew) was a public institute for Jewish study. Students sometimes spent so much time there that some slept there at night.

would have the closest aim, with an apple, at a porter on the shore. And before long there is a tumult, loud shouting: the thrown apple has hit the broad-boned porter Yitzhak Okovietz Rudlak. His broad, gray beard is covered with blood from his plucked-olut eye.[vii] Even before the German Nazis there were Polish hooligans.

In town itself, Jews and non-Jews live in peace side by side. Koblinski the Gentile says in Yiddish: —God save me from Gentile hands and Jewish heads. He also was rather inclined to go to law before a Jewish religious court than before a civil court.

The town draws its livelihood from the surrounding villages. At dawn, the village buyers, men and women, go out to the villages, in pursuit of their living. They buy up fowls, fodder, eggs, calves, cows. At nightfall they are seen coming back, tired, exhausted, one with a bundle, another driving a calf, another disappointed, emptyhanded...

There are some who do not go afoot; they have horse and wagon, and drive around like gentlemen-farmers. Such one, for instance, was Izie Lisser, son-in-law to aunt Malka— his whole appearance, too, was like a country-gentleman's. Izie and Hana had three beautiful sons, and like all parents, they very much wanted them not to follow their parents' profession, and wanted to push them further, out of the limited parochial possibilities.

On market days, Tuesday and Friday, the farmers used to come to town and bring with them product for sale: fowls, fodder, eggs, fruits, calves, cows, horses, grain, hogs. There was a noisy commotion, of human voices, sounds of beasts; they are buying and selling, bargaining, running about. After the sale, each farmer made his own purchases, in turn: working and cooking utensils, foodstuffs, cloth, clothes. These are the important days providing the living for the whole week.

[vii]A typo that is probably supposed to read "plucked-out," unbelievable as it is.

The Rembova street goes from the market place, continues out of town up to the highway, the Warsaw route turn, where Leibbish Gmach is living. Here one goes for a walk on Sabbat evenings. Here live my aunt Malka and my uncle Itzhak. The whole large family gathers there for Sabbat tea: Zeinvel the son and wife, Hershl the son with wife Beile of the Kirshenshtein family and two children, daughter Feige with her husband Baruch-David Wisenberg, daughter Hana with her husband Ize Lisser and three sons, another son and daughter, aunt Hendel, uncle Shiye, Moshe and Israel, uncle Yiki with wife Malka.

❧

My parents, Avraham and Yocheved Zawierucha, and the little children, none of them are left alive, all of them found their death as martyrs of Hitler's horrid mechanism.

Hershl Futerman was the victim of the earliest bombardment of the town; together with Menashe Grosdorf (Diabel's son), they sought shelter in a building, a burning bomb fell there, and they were both burned alive.

Some of the youth of the Lisser-Futerman family were martyrized in Nowy Dwor, the rest in the gas chambers.

We recall them, as they were in life. But we must also remember them, after they are dead.

From the diary

By Nathan Daicz

On Friday the 1st of September 1939, at 6 o'clock in the morning, the Nazis started bombing the Western parts of Poland. We were then in the orchard, 10 km from Vishogrod. We reported immediately in Vishogrod, to enlist in the army, in order to fight the Nazis. We were four brothers: Nathan-Leib, Yitzhak-Ya'acov, Shmuel, Michal. On Friday nothing happened in our town. We were busy gluing paper strips over the cracks to prevent gas seeping. (They did use gas, but, to our sorrow, to kill 6 million Jewish martyrs.)

On Sunday, the 3rd of September, Vishogrod was bombed for the first time. Bombs fell into the Vistula, opposite the firemen's hall. Panic broke out, and 60–70% of the Jews fled from town.

Monday the 4th of September 1939: All the authorities fled away and the town was left in anarchy. The vice-mayor Leibish Gemach together with the firemen put up a militia force to keep order.

Sabbat, the 9th of September 1939—another heavy bombardment, and Vishogrod was occupied. The houses from Kaminski's up to Mendel Firsht's were bombed. The first victims were Menashe Grosdorf's son, Hershl Lisser,

Baruch Mordechai Kobelniker, Puterman, and the son of
Yoshua Plum's. At the termination of Sabbat the German
murderers fulfilled the Scripture of the Ki Tavo'u Section:
"Thy ox is slain before thine eyes and thou shall not eat
thereof. Thy ass is taken away from thee and shall not
be returned to thee. Thy sons and daughters are given
to thy foe into slavery for scorn and derision and there is
no savior. A shameless people is upon thee that will not
respect the old and will not have mercy upon children."
All the evil and distress unmentioned in the Book befell
us, to our great sorrow. We were like slaves. We spent our
strength to the utmost, just to survive. (Later, we were
driven afoot to the crematory, to be gassed and burned.)

I and my family, my father and two sons and a daughter, my uncle Zacaria Natan with his family, my brother
Yitzhak Ya'acov with his wife, and Shmuel Moshe, and
Leibl Kopenhagen, all of us spent the first weeks of the war
in the village Stare Wody near Mlodziszyn. We were there
till Tuesday after New Year. Two days before Atonement
Day we came to Vishogrod.[viii] I took at once the Tora
scroll of Zeirei Agudas Israel to my house. We read from
it all the time we were in the ghetto. We were soon taken
to all kinds of filthy work, accompanied by blows. We also
worked repairing the bridge.

On Yom Kippur[ix] part of us prayed in private homes,
part in the synagogue. Amidst the prayer at the synagogue,
the Gestapo came, drove people out to work and beat them
to death.

The day after Yom Kippur a goose disappeared at
neighbor Shpitulski's, the manager of the landing pier.
Police came and took ten Jews to shoot them: 1. Raphael

[viii] "Atonement Day" is a reference to Yom Kippur.
[ix] In that year, Yom Kippur was on 23 Sep.

Mordechai Dziedzic; 2. his son; 3. the present writer; 4. Yitzhak Ya'acov Daicz; 5. Michal Daicz; 6. Saul Rosenfeld; 7. Moshe Meilech Rosenfeld; 8. Nachman Daicz; 9. Tovia Rosenfeld. I do not remember who was the tenth man. It was a miracle the goose was found on the Vistula, and the Jews escaped death.

Sukkot—part of the Jews erected a sukka,[x] but they had to be guarded, like in the days of the Spanish inquisition.

When the Germans occupied the village Sladow eight Jews were found in a cellar: 1. Mates Sheinblum; 2. Pinhas Sheinblum; 3. Wolf Zlotnik; 4. Moshe Mendel Shlosberg; 5. Yosel Holender; 6. A'ron Hosman and his two children. They were shot. Pinhas Sheinblum was lying wounded among the dead for some hours. Then he felt he was alive. At night he came to Vishogrod and told the tale.

Hol-Homoëd of Sukkot[xi] all stores were plundered, and the goods were relinquished. After Sukkot Mendel Firsht was arrested and deported to Dachau. Some time later the Germans brought a box with his ashes. They asked several hundred marks for it of the family. It was buried at the cemetery.

Jews were compelled to wear a yellow patch, to take off their hat to every German. Part of the youth escaped to Russia. The rich fled to Warsaw. All businesses were liquidated. Workmen still had something to do. People sold household goods to buy food. Goods were expensive: They had to be smuggled from Warsaw, and therefore the prices rose. Two farm laborers from Grutkowa informed the commissar they had paid fifty marks for a pair of boots, and four men were arrested: Moshe Lipski, Ya'acov Shtern, Shimon Zayonc and his son Asher. They were held in priosn

---

[x] Part of the observance of Sukkot—literally meaning "booths"— involves building small structures in which to eat and socialize, reminiscent of the portable shelters used during the biblical 40 years of wandering under Moses.

[xi] *Chol Hamoed* simply refers to the middle days of the multi-day festival.

in Plock, until all the Jews of the district were deported, it was made "judenrein." Then they went together with me and another 39 Jews to Auschwitz.

The last session with our Rabbi

Soon after Sukkot 1939[xii] there arrived money from America for needy people. The Rabbi R'Naphtali Spivak of blessed memory called a meeting: R' David Hirsh Lubin of blessed memory, R'Pinhas Gorbarz, Avraham Grywacz, A'ron Zelig Holender, Israel Gedalia Daicz, Moshe Lipski, Yoshua Sokolov, Pinhas Kostas, Meilech Gemach, Baruch Mordechai Skszydlo, Tovia Goldman, Faivel Meir Lichtenshtein, Yasichek Diamand, Natan Leib Daicz.

The Rabbi of blessed memory said: Brothers Jews, we are in a time of dire stress. We shall be able to ease our situation somewhat only if we help each other without any haughtiness. When two small points are at the same height, like this "it is: God's name; when two small points are one above the other, like this: then—God forbid!—it means sof posuk, the end has come."

These words had their influence upon our town. We may be proud—the Vishogrod people have followed his words.

The first Jewish Council (Judenrat) was asked to put up a list of people to be sent to Belsk.[xiii] They did not do it. Thereupon the prominent Jews in town and part of the Judenrat were taken. The Gestapo demanded a list of 200 Jews to be deported to Slopie Nowa.[xiv]

[xii]Sukkot in Hebrew year 5700 was 28 Sep through 4 Oct 1939.

[xiii]It's unclear what "Belsk" could be a reference to; there is an area called *Bielsk* in northeastern Poland, but at this point in the war it was under Soviet control.

[xiv]This could indicate the village of Nowa Słupia, though it's unclear why residents would have been deported there.

The destruction of our ornate synagogue

At Hanukka time[xv] Jews were driven into the synagogue. The Gestapo beat with whips and rifle butts and compelled Jews to pull down the beautiful Eastern Wall and all wooden benches. The Gentiles got this wood to use as fuel.

Till Passover the whole synagogue was pulled down, to its foundations. The source was closed up.

On the 8th of May 1940 all the houses below the castle-hill were destroyed, from Reuben Haim Lebenzki's to Meir Yente's. Afterwards all Jewish houses in Shoemakers' street were pulled down, from the butchers' shops to Avraham Stoliarz', on both sides of the street. Then the old cemetery was desecrated, the tombstones broken, the place levelled, and the bones thrown into the Vistula. By means of a big bribe to the overseers the bones could be gathered and buried at the new cemetery.

❧

The 9th of Av 1940[xvi] the Belsk camp was established. 120 Vishogroders were there, until the camp was liquidated.

On the 6th of March 1941 700 Jews were deported to Slopie Nowa, and an open ghetto was established: from the market place by Kobilinsky monastery street from the left hand; from the Plock street to Yasieczek's and the place of R'Binyamin, with Moshe Hmiel's house from behind.

On the 9th of Av 1941 the ghetto was close up, fenced in with barbed wire, and an order was issued, whoever would be caught outside the ghetto without a permit would be

---

[xv] December 6–14, 1939.

[xvi] "Av" is a month in the Hebrew calendar. *Tisha B'Av*—literally, "the ninth of Av"—is a fast day of mourning; in 1940, it fell on August 13. According to tradition, it is the date on which both temples in Jerusalem were destroyed 500 years apart.

shot. 3–4 families were herded in one room. Life became hell.

In summer 1941 groups of one hundred people were taken out to rid them of lice. The people were driven to the electricity plant of Wita. There was a water tank, 100 m. farther there was a building. The Germans beat them terribly. And they were compelled to take their clothes off, men and women together, and run stark naked those 100 m. The Polish inhabitants of the neighborhood peeked and looked. So we were humiliated. Such was Nazi culture. A physician had been brought over from Plock to direct the delousing. On the third day Yitzhak Bohl, the chairman of the Judenrat, managed to bribe the physician with a big sum to annihilate this decree.

In August 1941, many refugees return to Vishogrod from Warsaw and from Slopie Nowa.

On a beautiful morning people were driven out in the street. 120 were loaded on 3 tracks, taken away, and nobody knows till this day were their bones lie. 50 other Jews were driven to the Vistula, put on rafts, beaten up terribly, part of them thrown into the water, part driven to Warsaw.

Jewishness in the Ghetto

In spite of all the persecutions, Jews in the ghetto preserved their Jewishness. There were several prayer congregations. I put set up a minyan in David Meir's storeroom. We put there the Tora scroll from Ze'irei Agudas Israel. Every now and then Jews were caught praying, were driven out into the street, and made fun of and put to shame. But we did not desist, we prayed in congregation each Sabbat and holiday. On Yom-Kippur there was a great minyan in the yard of Meilech, where Kohn had his sugar magazine. Avraham Yizraelovitz the cantor said the Kol Nidrei and Mussaf; Neila—Meir Shochet; morning prayer—the present writer.

🐦

On Thursday Parashat Vayetze all people from the Belsk camp were brought. On Friday it was already known that on Sabbat all would be deported from Vishogrod. At midnight a guard drew up at the ghetto. People started wailing, crying, saying good-bye to each other.

On Sabbat p. Vayetze all were driven to the market place. 600 Jews were sent to Czerwinsk on farmers' carts; 1200 persons were herded on trucks. They were beaten, the knapsacks were cut off. A great part of them were left without anything, emptyhanded. In the early afternoon we arrived in Nowy Dwor ghetto, broken, humiliated. We were crammed into the small ghetto, 3–4 families in one room. We slept on the hard floor. A committee of three was appointed: Leizer Rotbart, Yoel Lipa Kroy, Yoel Bohm. People were registered, got ration cards. The rations were very small. A soup kitchen was organized to distribute a little soup. A Vishogrod Jew, Hershel Fuks, was cook; he is living now in Israel.

Owing to overcrowding, filth and bad food an epidemic of typhoid broke out. Several hundred Vishogrod Jews died of typhoid in the ghetto of Nowy Dwor.

Life was very hard. We sold our last belongings to keep living. Each day 300 hundred Jews were driven to the river port to work. Overseers were war invalids. They shouted Jews were responsible for the war and for their having become invalids. They took revenge on us, beating and killing. We were compelled to roll the barbed wire rolls like a ball. Blood streamed like from a fountain. Men came home from work completely incapacitated. It was forced labor, unpaid.

Jews smuggled for a livelihood. Whoever was caught, was hanged. Once 7 Jews were hanged, among them a son of Wolf Levin's, a 16-year old boy. They were left hanging in the ghetto for 24 hours. All Jews were obliged to be

present at the execution and to look at it. There were
many such executions.

❧

Jews created congregations and prayed under danger
of life. There was one minyan at the Lanziner Rabbi's of
blessed memory; another one at the ritual slaughterer's
of Zakrocim. In the little ghetto there was a minyan at
Shimshon Silberboim's, Avraham Grzywacz had a shophar,
and on New Year he went from minyan to minyan to blow
it.

Before Passover the Rabbi ordered baking mazzos of the
dark flour we received. I and Avraham Grzywacz showed
them how to bake the mazzos in the kitchen.

After Passover people were deported to the camps. An
order was issued to hand over money and rings. Should
something be found with anybody, he would be shot.

In the month of November 1942 all Jews from Czerwinsk
ghetto were brought over. 20–30 persons were herded in
one room. They started sending transports to Auschwitz.
On a certain day 40 persons were wanted to fill up the
quota; militia arrived and seized forty. Eleven of them
succeeded in getting away. The remaining 29 were taken to
a certain place to work. After work, they were ordered to
dig a ditch, they were butchered and buried half-alive. Two
men from Vishogrod were among them: Shlomo Buchner
and Moshe Puterman. At night, when the eleven returned
to the ghetto, there was a great tumult there.

❧

On the 12th of December 1942 the last transport was
sent to Auschwitz, in the morning. In the afternoon, the
6th of Tevet,[xvii] our nearest and dearest, fathers, mothers,

---

[xvii] "Tevet" is another month in the Hebrew calendar; in this year,
6*th* of Tevet was 14 Dec.

wives, children, sisters, brothers, were gassed and burned in Birkenau. May the Lord revenge their blood. May their memory live in eternity.

The Hell

We were picked, 600 able-bodied men; we were told to take off our clothes, and they sheared us from head to feet, 10 men at one time, all hidden spots of the body, tearing pieces of flesh in the process. We were given each a pair of trousers, a shirt, a coat. He were taken to sleep in a horse stable, 6 men in one stall; it was freezing cold. We were so tired, we managed to sleep. In the morning the numbers were tattooed on our arms. Mine was 83059. In the middle of the week we were given other clothes, striped ones. A transport of 30 men went to Bona. We were kept in a 3-week quarantine.

There was money found with me and with my brothers. They kept asking for more money and jewelery, which we did not have.

On Sunday the 18th of January, in the morning all our bloc, 200 men, were ordered out. My brothers and I were ordered to make penal exercises—running, falling down, knee-bending, for an hour. Afterwards we were taken to the bloc. They put all people in and put in a gallows. I and my brother were stood against the wall. The elder of the bloc said: Now the Daicz brothers will be hanged. You, the eldest dog—he said to me—shall hang first. I was ordered to take off the shoes and mount the hanging stool. I said the Confession prayer. They bound my hands behind me, I gave a last look at my brothers and my friends, and called out loudly Sh'ma Israel. The rope was put, not around my neck, but my hands. The stool was pushed away. I was hanging for 15 minutes, suffering tortures worse than death. The bloc elder asked me every now and then where I had hidden the jewelery. After 15 minutes my hands were freed,

and he said that he was sure now that the Daicz brothers
had no more money. He shouted, all prisoners with whom
money should be found, would be executed in this way.

❧

After 3 weeks in quarantine, I was transported in a labor
camp. We worked on hard jobs. Each day the "reserve" of
150–200 men were sent to the gas chambers.

Up to June 1943 my three brothers were destroyed,
among the others. A small number of Vishogrod men was
left; the rest had died of hunger and overwork.

In June 1943, by a miraculous stroke of luck, I was
detached to the shoemakers' shop. That meant sufficient
food, and even taking some for the hungry in camp. At that
time I became aware that all the women of our transport
had been destroyed on the 6th Tevet 1942; not a single
woman had escaped. All the people who had been taken
in reserve had been destroyed, so I had no relations left. I
was in utter despair. I was together with Hershel Naiman.
We comforted each other, we must live to see the fall of
Nazism, and take revenge.

Yet another thing that kept us up was our religious
life. When somebody's relative's death anniversary came
round, Kaddish was recited. In High Holidays season we
organized prayer congregations in the wash-room. We
prayed in the morning before work. A men named Radzik,
an electrician, who had a shed at his disposal, had a pair
of phylacteries.[xviii] We hurried there every now and then,
put on the phylacteries and said Sh'ma Israel.

Before Passover 1944 we began to take counsel about
mazzos and holding Seder. I had some connections with
the kapu of the kitchen: I obtained some flour. I spoke with
Ephraim Buchner (from Vishogrod, now in America), who

[xviii]Phylacteries are small leather boxes containing hand-written
quotes from scripture; they are used as part of prayer mostly in
Orthodox communities.

was servant and cook of the workleader at the Commander's post. I gave him instructions, and he baked mazzos, under risk of life, and thus 200 Jews were able to fulfill the religious commandment.

We held Seder in the Bona-Auschwitz camp in the year of 1944. We demonstrated and proved that we could be crushed in body, but not in spirit, and on the threshold of the crematory we did not lose faith in The Lord Blessed be He. I am thankful, too, to the elder of the bloc, Bernard Strauss, a Jew from Tchekia, who allowed to hold the seder in his bloc No. 60. I celebrated the Seder with tears and a bleeding heart; I prayed "This year slaves, next year free men" "This years slaves, next year in the Land of Israel." I think it a great merit to me, to my family and the town of Vishogrod, that Ephraim Buchner and the present writer were the initiators of this Seder.

❧

At the end of 1944 many were executed who tried to flee and escape the Nazi murderers. Most of them were caught, brought into camp and hanged, before the eyes of all, to put fear into our hearts.

On the 18th of January 1945 the camp was evacuated, and we were driven to Gleiwitz. On the way 50% of the prisoners were shot dead, after they had survived the years in camp. Zecharia Roch met a violent death. Yosua Lichtenshtein tried tu run away, and was shot.

From Gleiwitz Hershl Naiman and I were taken to Buchenwald, into Grauwinkel camp. This was a horrible concentration camp. We slept in airless underground bunkers, without drinkwater. At four o'clock in the morning we got up for roll-call.

❧

Hershel Naiman and I were freed in Theresienstadt in Tchekia. On the 20th of May 1945, we came to Warsaw, on the 22th—to Vishogrod. We found there Yoske Levin and his wife Marysia, the late Yitzhak Pasterniak, Ephraim Buchner, Israel Shvarzbart.

I married my present wife, established a new family.

The little town was empty without the Jews. In the morning I used to go to the foundations of the destroyed synagogue, prayed, and had a good spell of weeping. Each other day I used to go to the destroyed cemetery—there was no trace left of it, there was a coppice—asked forgiveness of the souls of our martyrs, recited Kaddish, and my wife said Amen.

After 5 months we left Vishogrod for ever, and went to Germany. We were there some time, and then we went home, to Israel, to the Jewish State, to stay here. We arrived in Israel on the 11th of May 1949.

Chapter 12

HaShoah

A brief note: Shoah, *a Hebrew word for destruction, was a term adopted before the conclusion of World War II to describe the mass murder of Jews by Nazi Germany. "Holocaust," a term that came into use over the following decade, is disfavored when discussing the attempted extermination of the Jewish people for two primary reasons: Firstly, it is a word that has its roots in the religious description of a burnt offering, which some find distasteful; in addition, groups such as Yad Vashem observe that "The Holocaust" has come to refer to the broader genocide perpetrated by the Nazis, targeting many different groups. The more precise term has been adopted here.*[1]

No direct ancestors of Nancy Abdill *2-3* were killed in the Shoah—all had either died or left Europe by the time the Nazis came to power. However, as we discover more branches of the family tree and get a clearer picture of the family's cousins, we get closer to encountering defined personal connections to the worst genocide in world history. Abe Arbeiter *5-28*, for example, had a first cousin, Haim Aron Biłgoraj,[i] whose family was killed in the Shoah: Though Haim Aron died in 1914,[2] his wife Brucha and three

---

[i]Haim Aron was the nephew of Hannah Arbeiter *6-56*.

of their children[ii] are included in the list below because of testimony offered to Yad Vashem specifically stating they were murdered.[iii] Israel, Haja Rykla, and Surah Biłgoraj were the second cousins of Solomon Arbeiter *4-14*.

Learning about the family's geographic origins inevitably conjures images of grand excursions to visit the homes of yore, to connect with far-flung relations still walking the streets of our ancestors. The most succinct way to describe the effects of the Shoah is simply to point out that none of these relations exist: All eight of Nancy's great-grandparents were born in cities later taken over by Nazi Germany; all eight have last names that appear in the rolls of the murdered. What follows is a brief examination of the influence of World War II on the homelands of the Siegel/Arbeiter lines— while our relationship to many of the victims listed below is unclear, the aim was to compile a list of possible relatives among the known martyrs in the areas where our family originated.

Figure 12.1: An undated photograph of Surah Biłgoraj, killed in the Shoah. She would have been about 29 at the start of the war, so it seems more likely that she is the younger woman on the left.[3]

[ii]Two other children, Michał and Szia, died young.

[iii]Yad Vashem is the Israeli Holocaust memorial, a large facility and museum that also hosts a wide range of historical scholarship and documentation.

(A brief note: In almost every case, names are presented below exactly as they have been recorded by the organizations keeping the records, many of which rely on reports in multiple languages from all over the world. Because of this, the English spelling of names can be inconsistent— "Chana" and "Khana," for example, both start with the same Hebrew letter, *chaf*, but can be transliterated differently. "Aaron" was probably spelled more like "Aharon," in Hebrew, and names with a *j* sound, such as "Joseph," may appear below as starting with an *I* or *Y*.)

Medzhybizh

The hometown of the earliest known members of the Reinstein and Newman families, in central Ukraine. It was one of the first stops of Operation Barbarossa, the German army's invasion of the Soviet Union that began in late June 1941. On 8 Jul 1941, the German army occupied the area, destroyed Jewish landmarks and established a strictly enforced ghetto. The following year, about 1,000 Jews were killed in ravines outside of town, probably on 21 Sep 1942, Yom Kippur.[4]

Since we only know two American surnames of Medzhybizh relatives, our knowledge of anyone affected is limited. Four victims from Medzhybizh have surnames from which "Reinstein" is a possible derivative:

- **Avadya Veinshtein**, b. 1886. Husband of Reizl. Murdered in 1941, per testimony of their son Meir Veinshtein.[5]
- **Reizl Veinshtein**, b. 1891. Wife of Avadya. Murdered in 1941, per testimony of their son.[6]
- **Evede Vaynshteyn**, murdered, per a report from the Soviet Extraordinary State Commission, 20 Jun 1944.[7]
- **Gregory Veinshtein**, b. 1928. Murdered in 1942, per testimony of his sister, Sheva Teper.[8]

Figure 12.2: One of the mass graves outside of Medzhybizh.
The area's Jews were killed in three locations to the west[9] of
town; the areas were later identified and covered in concrete.
Photo credit Yad Vashem.[10]

Figure 12.3: Brucha Biłgoraj, the mother of Surah. She was
married to the first cousin of Abe Arbeiter 5-28[11] and was killed
in the Shoah.

Płock

A ghetto was established in Płock in 1941; the Wyszogród synagogue, standing for almost 200 years, was destroyed in 1939;[12] on 22 Sep 1941, the Jews of the region who hadn't been killed already were deported. Our direct Arbeiter ancestors were in Wyszogród, but others were scattered throughout the Płock area; names from nearby are included below, even if we are unaware of their exact relation.[iv]

- **Alek Arbajter**, Płock. Murdered, per testimony of researcher Xavier Messalati.[13]
- **Hirsz Iccak Arbajter**, Płock. Murdered, per testimony of researcher Xavier Messalati.[14]
- **Hagar Arbajter**, Płock. Murdered, per testimony of researcher Xavier Messalati.[15]
- **Joseph Arbajter**, Płock. Murdered, per testimony of researcher Xavier Messalati.[16]
- **Yitzchak Arbeiter**, Płock. Spouse of Hungara. Sent to Soldau concentration camp in 1940, then the Starachowice labor camp; murdered at Treblinka in 1942, per testimony of researcher Ashley Proulx Gould.[17]
- **Hungara (Malenka) Arbeiter**, Płock. Spouse of Yitzchak. Murdered at Treblinka in 1942, per testimony of researcher Ashley Proulx Gould.[18]
  - **Elek Arbeiter**, Płock. Teenage son of Yitzchak and Hungara. Disappeared in 1940; presumed murdered, per testimony of researcher Ashley Proulx Gould.[19]
  - **Josek Arbeiter**, Płock. Murdered at Treblinka in 1942, per statements by his brother, Israel.[20]
- **Ihezkel Arbeiter**, Wyszogród. Spouse of Lea. Murdered, per testimony of relative Aizik Chapnik.[21]

[iv]There are other Arbajter victims listed in the comparatively close ghettos in Warsaw and Łódź; they have been omitted here because of the reduced likelihood that they are related to the Płock Arbajters within a reasonable time frame.

- **Lea Arbeiter**, Wyszogród. Spouse of Ihezkel. Murdered, per testimony of relative Aizik Chapnik.[22]
- **Mordekhai Arbeiter**, Płock. Born 1922. Inmate at the Mauthausen concentration camp; fate unconfirmed.[23]
- **Aaron Arbeiter**, Płock. Born 1925. Inmate at the Flossenbürg concentration camp; fate unconfirmed.[24]
- **Ziskind Arbeiter**, Sierpc. Spouse of Khana. Murdered, per the Memorial Book of Kehilat Sierpc.[25]
- **Khana (Khazan) Arbeiter**, Sierpc. Spouse of Ziskind. Murdered, per testimony of niece Khana Perl Morgenshtern Eizner Naparstek.[26]
- **Khaim David Arbeiter**, Sierpc. Murdered, per the Memorial Book of Kehilat Sierpc.[27]
- **Khava (Arbeiter) Florman**, Sierpc. Born 1903. Spouse of Moshe Florman. Held in the Warsaw Ghetto with her family, then murdered in the Treblinka concentration camp in 1942, per testimony of her brother-in-law, Tzadok Tzvi Florman.[28]
- **Moshe Florman**, Sierpc. Born 1901. Spouse of Khava Arbeiter. Murdered in the Warsaw Ghetto in 1943, per testimony of his brother, Tzadok Tzvi Florman.[29]
  - **Itka Florman**, Sierpc. Daughter of Khava and Moshe, born 1929. Held in the Warsaw Ghetto, murdered in the Treblinka concentration camp in 1942, per testimony of her uncle, Tzadok Tzvi Florman.[30]
  - **Israel Florman**, Sierpc. Son of Khava and Moshe, born 1933. Held in the Warsaw Ghetto, murdered in the Treblinka concentration camp in 1942, per testimony of his uncle, Tzadok Tzvi Florman.[31]
- **Jacob Bilgora**, Wyszogród. Born 1901. Murdered in the Auschwitz concentration camp, per the Auschwitz Death Registers.[32]
- **Brucha (Poznanski) Biłgoraj**, Wyszogród. Spouse

of Haim Aron Biłgoraj,[v] married 1900.[33] Murdered, per the testimony of niece Helen Masowicki Posnansky.[34]

- **Haja Rykla Biłgoraj**, Wyszogród. Daughter of Haim Aron and Brucha, born 1905.[35] Murdered.[36]
- **Israel Biłgoraj**, Wyszogród. Son of Haim Aron and Brucha, born 18 Aug 1909.[37] Murdered.[38]
- **Surah Biłgoraj**, Wyszogród. Daughter of Haim Aron and Brucha, born abt 1910.[39] Murdered.[40]

Wyszogród residents listed as martyrs in the town yizkor (memorial) book:[41]

- **Abram Biłgoraj**
- **Abram Jecheskel Biłgoraj**
- **Abramele Biłgoraj**
- **Bracha Biłgoraj** and her daughter
- **Chaim Biłgoraj**
- **Chana Biłgoraj**
- **Chunes Biłgoraj** and his wife and children
- **Dwora Biłgoraj** and her 4 children
- **Efrat Biłgoraj**
- **Jacob Biłgoraj**
- **Jankele Biłgoraj**
- **Jehudit Biłgoraj**
- **Malka Biłgoraj**, her husband and children
- **Miriam Biłgoraj** and her 2 daughters
- **Moishe Biłgoraj**
- **Nache Biłgoraj**
- **Rachel Lea Biłgoraj** and her 5 children
- **Ryfka Biłgoraj**
- **Sara Biłgoraj**
- **Sara Brejna Biłgoraj**
- **Sime Biłgoraj**
- **Szalom Biłgoraj** and his wife and 4 children

---

[v] See "Biłgoraj" chapter for more about Haim Aron.

- **Szlomo Zalman Biłgoraj**
- **Szmuel Biłgoraj** and his wife and 5 children
- **Tuwia Biłgoraj** and his wife and 2 children
- **Zecharia Biłgoraj**
- **Zysel Biłgoraj**

Israel Arbeiter

Israel "Izzy" Arbeiter was born in Płock 25 Apr 1925.[42]
His parents, Yitzchak and Hungara Arbeiter, are in the
list above, as are two of his brothers. They were killed at
Treblinka, but Israel and his remaining two brothers, Motek
and Aron, were kept on as slave labor at the Starachowice
concentration camp. All three survived the war[43] and eventually came to America—Israel became a vocal survivors'
advocate and ran several Holocaust memorial organizations. He appeared in a 2013 documentary, *A Promise to
My Father*, in which he returned to Płock and made trips
to Treblinka and Auschwitz. His exact relationship to the
Arbeiters described in this book is unclear, though we have
several clues about the ancestry of his father, Yitzchak: In
a 2017 interview with the author, Izzy explained what little
he knew of his grandparents, whom he never met: "The
Arbeiter family comes from Wyszogród," he said. "My
paternal grandfather passed away before I was born... so
the only thing I know about him was what my father used
to say... One of my brothers was named after my paternal
grandfather, that I know for sure."[44]

This may give us the exact foothold we need: While
Yitzchak Arbeiter and his family lived in Płock, the others
were in Wyszogród, where we have a much more compre-
hensive understanding of who is related to whom. Israel
was one of five brothers:

- Elek, presumed dead in the Shoah.
- Motek, went by "Mack" in America.
- Israel, worked as a tailor with Mack.

- Aaron, started a plumbing business in California.
- Josek, the youngest, also killed during the war.

Given the evidence available, our best guess for the identity of Israel's grandfather is Josek Arbajter, born 1 Oct 1863 in Wyszogród. Josek's parents were Mosek Arbajter and Łaja Ficman,[45] making Josek the first cousin of Dawid Arbajter *6-56*. (Mosek's parents were Berek *8-224* and Ruchla Arbajter *8-225*; see their biography in the "Arbeiter" chapter for more about them and Mosek's family.) That would mean Josek's (hypothetical) son, Yitzchak Arbajter, was the second cousin of Abraham Arbeiter *5-28*, and Israel Arbeiter and his siblings the third cousins of Solomon Arbeiter *4-14*.

It should be noted that this is not based on any direct evidence of the parentage of Yitzchak Arbajter—while it's likely that Yitzchak's birth was documented somewhere, the author was not able to find it. However, Josek's name does coincide with one of Israel's brothers, as he said it did, and his year of birth (1863) lines up without issue for someone whose grandchildren were born around the 1920s. (This also lines up with a genetic match between Nancy Abdill *2-3* and a descendant of Aaron Arbeiter, Izzy's brother. See the following chapter for details.)

Figure 12.4: A Schutzstaffel soldier oversees the deportation of Jews from the Płock ghetto in 1941. The eagle emblem on his sleeve indicates his membership in the dreaded "SS" paramilitary organization operating under the Nazi Party. Photo credit Yad Vashem.[46]

Figure 12.5: Residents of the Płock ghetto being loaded into rail cars for deportation. Note the white armbands identifying them as Jews. Photo credit Yad Vashem.[47]

Medvin

It appears the Sigalow clan (some of whom became the
Siegels, of chapter 7) had a substantial presence in Medvin
going into World War II. In addition to the old Jewish
cemetery, there are two mass graves outside the town where
more than 200 Jews were buried in 1941.[48]

- **Sizel (Sigalov) Shubinskaya**, b. 1879. Murdered,
  per testimony of her son.[49]
- **Matvey Sigalov**, b. 1897 in Medvin. Lived in Kiev;
  murdered in the Babi Yar Massacre of September
  1941, per testimony of his granddaughter, Marina
  Kalyuzhnaya Sigalova.[50]
- **Iosiph Sigalov**, b. 1859. Murdered in 1941, per
  testimony of his son,[51] also probably the testimony
  of researcher Ilia Levitas.[52]
    - **Freida Sigalov**, b. 1896. Daughter of Ioseph.
      Murdered with three of her children in 1941, per
      testimony of her sister.[53]
- **Braina (Geller) Sigalova**, b. 1898; murdered in
  1941 along with four children, per the testimony of
  her sister.[54]
    - **Ben Sigalov**. Son of Braina. Murdered in 1941,
      per testimony of researcher Ilia Levitas.[55]

Researcher Ilia Levitas has spent decades working from
Kiev to chronicle the history of the Jews of Ukraine.[56] He
is responsible for the documentation of most of the Medvin
Sigalows killed in the Shoah, all in 1941:

- **Aryl Sigalov**[57]
- **Duved Sigalov**[58]
- **Zus Sigalov**, a teacher.[59]
- **Kutz Sigalov**, b. 1917.[60]
- **Leyba Sigalov**[61]
- **Nusik Sigalov**[62]
- **Moshko Sigalov**[63]
- **Osvey Sigalov**[64]
- **Srul Sigalov**, b. 1911.[65]

- **Yakov Sigalov**, a hairdresser.[66]
- **unknown Sigalov**, wife of Yakov.[67]
- **Pyrlya Sigalova**[68]
- **Sophia Sigalova**, a teacher.[69]
- **Khava Sigalova**[70]

Raczki

The first known home of Marcus Steinman *5-26* was occupied by Russian troops in 1939, though they abandoned the town weeks later—the town's official history attributes this to an agreement with the German government.[71] Soon afterward, the entire area was occupied by German forces; Jewish residents were forcibly relocated to Suwalki, a nearby city, and then to Lithuania, where an unparalleled extermination effort took place over the following five years. Since we don't know the surname Marcus had when he was born, it's difficult to compile a list of possible relatives; the same goes for Schippenbeil, the town the family lived in before moving to New York.

Chapter 13

Genetic testing

Depending on how you interpret the results, there are between three and five distant cousins of Nancy Abdill *2-3* whose DNA helps us confirm several pieces of the family tree. Their names have been mostly excluded here, out of respect for their privacy.

How it works

At its simplest, the AncestryDNA project is just a program that compares the DNA of all its participants to give them a list of their relatives. Based on information extracted from a saliva sample, Ancestry gives you a list of users who have also taken the test and whose genetic data shows that they are related to you. This alone is fascinating, but the most powerful part takes advantage of Ancestry.com's oldest feature: family trees.

Based on DNA alone, all Ancestry tells you is whether someone is related to you, nothing more. You can estimate how closely the relation is based on how similar the samples are (you probably have more of your mother's DNA than your third cousin's), but there isn't any way to determine for sure. However, because many participants in the AncestryDNA program have built their family trees on the website, Ancestry.com uses that data to determine *how* you are mostly likely to be related: Once you are "matched" with another user, the website will compare your family tree to theirs to find where the common ancestor is. The result is a list of people that have traced their family lines back to an intersection somewhere in your tree.

This is powerful information for multiple reasons. Mainly, it is a form of loose validation that your connection to that ancestor is correct: If DNA data says I am related to Person X, and we both have family trees that list Zipre Reinstein as a great-great-great grandmother, that goes a long way to validating that we are both legitimately connected to Zipre Reinstein (and that Person X is my fourth cousin).

There are, however, multiple important caveats with this conclusion: For starters, there isn't actually any evidence that either I or Person X are *actually related to Zipre Reinstein*: Zipre's DNA wasn't tested, so we can't draw any concrete conclusions.[i] What we learn from a match with Person X is:

1. I am related to Person X, and have enough DNA in common to suggest a relationship of fourth cousins.
2. Both I and Person X have included Zipre Reinstein in our family trees.

So, it's entirely possible that Person X and I are related in an entirely different way, and one (or both) of us is incorrect about being related to the person we think is our "common" ancestor. This uncertainty grows exponentially with each generation: If someone is your second cousin, that means you share one (or two) of your great-grandparents. You only have eight great-grandparents, so there's relatively little space for mistakes. But what if someone is, say, an eighth cousin? That means you share a pair of 7th

---

[i]There are two exceptions to this uncertainty: Two ancestors of the author—Sally (Stone) Abdill *3-5* and Nancy Abdill *2-2—did* take the AncestryDNA test, and results reflect that they are both related to their common ancestor, Richard Abdill *1-1*.

great grandparents—you probably have more than 500 of those, so the odds are higher that at least one of you misidentified an ancestor that also happens to appear in the other person's tree. Still, the odds are low enough that even a coincidence can give us a solid lead.

In addition to the author's results, Nancy (Siegel) Abdill *2-3* also participated in the AncestryDNA project. This produced much more productive results, in short, because she has more of her ancestors' DNA than the author does— being a generation older, somewhere around twice as much. For this reason, she has far more matches than Richard Abdill *1-1* in this line.

Despite the uncertainty of the results, it is still a boost to be able to say two cousins independently tracked their ancestry back to the same person, coincidence or not. Richard Abdill *1-1* and Nancy (Siegel) Abdill's *2-3* known matches are listed below.

The results

Five AncestryDNA matches support Nancy Abdill's relationship to two different pairs of her ancestors. The names of the matches have been excluded to protect the privacy of living descendants.

Sam Siegel (5-24), Anna Stein (5-25)

We were able to contact an AncestryDNA user who is linked to the results for both Richard *1-1* and Nancy *2-3* in July 2017—he is a grandson of Berdie Siegel, whom the author had guessed was a sibling of Morris Siegel *4-12* and the match was able to confirm. The match, and several of their cousins, were able to provide vital information about the Siegel family that is now included in their chapter.

Nachman Reinstein (6-60), Zipre (6-61)

There are four different AncestryDNA users who are both a match to Nancy *and* include Reinsteins in their family tree. Again, this doesn't conclusively prove that this relationship is correct, but for it to be wrong, two of Nancy's cousins would need to have mistakenly traced their lineages back to the Reinsteins.

The most clear link is between Nancy and a family in which three generations of Reinstein descendants have taken the AncestryDNA test: Nancy is linked to a woman plus her daughter and granddaughter, all of whom, unsurprisingly, appear to be from the same family. This is why the number of matches depends on your interpretation—since we have a connection to one person, it tells us nothing new that we are also connected to two descendants of that person.

In any case, the eldest match in that line is a grand-daughter of Hyman Dreizen and Mary Isakoff. Hyman's mother was Rachel (Reinstein) Dreizen, the sister of Harry Reinstein *5-30*. The common ancestors, therefore, are Harry and Rachel's parents, Nachman *6-60* and Zipre Reinstein *6-61*. Given that, we can determine that the eldest match is the third cousin of Nancy *2-3*: The match's great-grandmother, Rachel, and Nancy's great-grandfather, Harry, were siblings.

There is another match on this side of the tree, but no communication has been established with him. It appears he is a grandson of Sam Reinstein, the brother of Hyman Dreizen,[ii] which would make the final match another third cousin of Nancy and the second cousin of the Dreizen match.

[ii]See the "Reinstein" chapter for more about why their surnames are different.

Berek Arbajter *8-224*,
Ruchla *8-225*

This connection is more speculative than the others—at the conclusion of the previous chapter, a theory was explained about the connection between "our" Arbeiter family and Israel Arbeiter, an activist and Auschwitz survivor currently living in Massachusetts. One of Nancy Abdill's AncestryDNA matches was with a descendant of Izzy's brother Aaron that Ancestry.com estimates them to be between fifth cousins and eighth cousins, meaning their common ancestors are somewhere about as far back as a great-great-great-great grandparent. Given the presented hypothesis for his ancestry, this would be their common set of ancestors.

Szymon Biłgoraj (8-228),
Rasza (8-229)

Mitch Gordon, one of Nancy's AncestryDNA matches, had traced his ancestry back to Szymon *8-228* and Rasza Biłgoraj *8-229*—he is a descendant of their son Lajzer, and Nancy's family is descended from their other son, Szulim Haim Biłgoraj *7-114*. Though their common ancestors lived in Poland in the early 19th century, Richard and Mitch discovered they lived about 20 minutes apart in Minnesota, and that Mitch's brother Scott (another fifth cousin, once removed) worked seven blocks from Richard's house.

The three met up in September 2017 to compare notes, and Mitch helped review a draft of this book.

*Figure 13.1: Baruch Dziedzic (1858–1949), a great-great grand-
father of Scott and Mitch Gordon.   His first wife, Estera
Biłgoraj (1858–1889), was the first cousin of Abraham Arbeiter
5-28.*[1]

*Figure 13.2: Rich Abdill 1-1 (left), Scott Gordon and Mitch
Gordon in St. Paul.*[2]

Appendix A

Translated documents

The foreign-language documents used in the research for this book were only accessible because of the hard work of translators converting four different languages into English: Polish, Russian, Hebrew and Yiddish. Polish records were written in the Polish language before 1868, but in that year the Russian empire began exerting considerably more influence over local administration,[i] and all records shifted into Russian, using the Cyrillic alphabet.

The Polish documents were translated by Dr. Dorota Rzymska of the American Translators Association. Russian documents were translated by Maria Nikolskaya of Moscow.

They are presented in chronological order. You'll note that several of these records use "double-dating," in which an event is recorded as happening on some date such as the "eleventh/twenty-third day of July." These refer to the same day, but on two different calendars: The Russian empire (and the Russian Orthodox Church) was still using the Julian calendar at this time, but the Poles had already converted to the Gregorian calendar in use today. If there are two dates given, the later one is the Gregorian date. (Russia didn't switch to the Gregorian calendar until 1918.)

---

[i]See the "Shifting borders" appendix for more.

Marriage certificate, Zelman and Ryfka Arbayter

The 1843 marriage record for Zelman Arbayter 7-96 and Ryfka Chrzanowska 7-97 was found in records of the town of Bieżuń and contains the four oldest known signatures in the family of Nancy Abdill 2-3; Zelman and Ryfka's parents, who had to sign the document, are her fourth-great grandparents, born in the late 1700s.[1]

This event took place in Bieżuń on the third/fifteenth day of February eighteen hundred forty-three at three p.m.

David Bimberg, of the Orthodox faith, the local rabbi in the presence of **Zelman Arbayter**, of the Orthodox faith, bachelor, twenty-three years of age, residing in the city of Wyszogród with his parents of the Orthodox faith, Berek and Ruchla, the Arbiters, and **Ryfka Chrzanowska**, of the Orthodox faith, maiden, twenty years of age, residing in Bieżuń with her parents of the Orthodox faith Szol and Ruchla, the Chrzanowskis, and witnesses: Lachman Lachmanowicz Gertman, the synagogue's sexton, seventy-three years of age and Zyskinder Krywiec, haberdasher, eighty-three years of age, both residing in Bieżuń, and declared that in his presence on this day between **Zelman Arbayter**, of the Orthodox faith and **Ryfka Chrzanowska**, of the Orthodox faith, the religious marriage was contracted.

The marriage was preceded by three readings of the banns which were announced in the synagogues of Bieżuń and Wyszogród: the first on the second/fourteenth day of January, the second on the ninth-twenty-first day of January, the third on the sixteenth/twenty-eighth day of January of this year.

This marriage was allowed by the oral agreement of the parents of the groom and the bride who were present [at the ceremony] and no one was opposed to the marriage. The newlyweds testified that no premarital agreement had been

made between them. This act was read to the appearing
parties and witnesses and signed by the authorized parties.
Signed:

- Szol Chrzanowski
- Dawid Bimberg [in Yiddish]
- Ruchla Chrzanowska [in Yiddish
- Berek Arbayter [in Yiddish]
- Ruchla Arbayter [in Yiddish]
- Lachman Gertman [in Yiddish]
- Zyskinder Krzywiec [in Yiddish]
- Civil Register

Birth record, Hana Itta Biłgoraj

*Hana Itta Biłgoraj 6-49, the mother of Abraham Arbeiter
5-24, was born in Wyszogród, the same town in which all
of her children would grow up.*[2]

This event took place in the city of Wyszogród in the
eleventh/twenty-third day of July eighteen hundred forty-
six at two p.m.

Szulim Chaim Biłgoray, of the Orthodox faith, a
butcher, twenty-three years of age, personally appeared
[before us], in the presence of witnesses, Szaia Skórka, of the
Orthodox faith, a synagogue watchman, forty-nine years
of age and Lewek Akawicz, of the Orthodox faith, a night
guard, forty-five years of age, all residing in Wyszogród and
presented us with an infant of the female sex declaring that
she was born in Wyszogród on the fifteenth day of July of
this year at ten p.m., [the daughter] of his wife **Sura [nee]
Abram**, twenty years of age, and who [the daughter] was
given the name **Chana Ita**. This record was read to the
appearing father and the witnesses and signed by them.

Marked by: Szulim Chaim Biłgoray, stated that he is
unable to write; Szaia Skórka; Lewek Akawicz—unable to
write

Death record, Szymon Biłgoraj

Szymon Biłgoraj 8-196 is the oldest known ancestor in the Biłgoraj line; he is the grandfather of Hana Itta Biłgoraj 6-49, the mother of Abraham Arbeiter 5-24.[3]
This event took place in the city of Wyszogród on the fourth/fourteenth day of December eighteen hundred forty-six at 10 a.m.

Lewek Akawicz, of the Orthodox faith, a night guard, forty-five years of age and Markus Lewek Ayzenberg, of the Orthodox faith, [profession illegible], forty-seven years of age, both residing in Wyszogród, personally appeared [before us] and stated that yesterday in this month and this year, at 10 p.m., in Wyszogród, **Szymon Biłgoraj**, of the Orthodox faith, a butcher, seventy-four years of age, residing in Wyszogród, died.

He left his widowed wife, **Basza** [?] **Biłgoraj** and four children: 1. **Szulim Chaim**, 2. **Layzer**, the sons; 3. **Dwoyra Fayga**, 4. **Sura**, the daughters, all residents of Wyszogród. There was no estate left [by the decedent].

After establishing the death of the decedent, this death record, which I executed, was read by the appearing parties and was signed by them.

Marked by:
• Lewek Akawicz
• Markus Lewek Ayzenberg

Death record, Berek Arbajter

Berek Arbajter 8-224 was the grandfather of Davis Arbeiter, and the great-grandfather of Abraham Arbeiter 5-28.[4]
This event took place in the city of Wyszogród on the seventeenth/twenty-ninth day of April eighteen hundred fifty-five[5] at ten a.m.

Israel Szyngel, of the Orthodox faith, a night guard, seventy-one years of age and Markus Lewek Ayzenberg, of the Orthodox faith, sixty-five years of age, sexton of the synagogue, both residing in Wyszogród, personally appeared [before us] and stated as witnesses that yesterday, in this month and this year, at ten p.m., in Wyszogród, **Berek Arbejter**, of the Orthodox faith, a butcher, sixty years of age, residing in Wyszogród, died.

He left his widowed wife, **Ruchla**, sixty years of age, and two children: **Myndla**, twenty years of age and **Mordka**, thirteen years of age.

After establishing the death of the decedent, this death record, which I executed, was read to the appearing parties and was signed by them.

[Note: The documented children of Berek and Ruchla are two sons, Zelman 7-96 and Mosek, both of whom would have been in their late 20s when their father died. Dr. Rzymska stated that there was nothing in the document specifically indicating that Myndla and Mordka were the couple's only children, so we can assume, if this is the correct person, that it only lists those under 21 years old.]

Marriage certificate, Davis and Hannah Arbeiter

The 1864 marriage record for Dawid Arbajter 6-56 and Hana Itta Biłgoraj 6-57.[6]

This event took place in Wyszogród on the twenty-fourth day of August eighteen hundred sixty-four.

We hereby declare that in the presence of the witnesses, David Jakób Lesser, of the Orthodox faith, age eighty-one, and Markus Lewek Ejzenberg, of the Orthodox faith, age seventy-three, both sextons of the synagogue, residents of Wyszogród, a religious marriage was contracted on this day between **Dawid Berkowicz Arbajter**, of the Orthodox faith, bachelor, Born in Bieżuń, the administrative district of Mława, twenty years of age, son of Zelman and Ryfka nee Chrzanowska, the Berkowitz Arbajters residing in Bieżuń, and **Chana Ita Biłgoraj**, of the Orthodox faith, maiden, born in Wyszogród, daughter of **Chaim Szulim** and **Sura Ester nee Abram**, the Biłgorags, eighteen years of age, residing with her parents in Wyszogród.

This marriage was allowed by the oral agreement of the parents of the newlyweds. The newlyweds testified that no premarital agreement had been made between them. This act was read to the appearing parties and signed by the witnesses and the Assistant Rabbi. The newlyweds and their parents stated that they were illiterate.

Signed: Mayer Zienkowicz; Icek Frydman, Assistant Rabbi

Birth record, Abraham Arbeiter

The recording of the birth of Abram Arbajter (known later as Abraham Arbeiter 5-28) is the first in this collection to have been recorded in Russian rather than Polish; it and the following entries were translated by Ma Nikolskaya.[7]

Held in the city of Wyszogrod on January 31, 1878. At 3 o'clock in the afternoon **Dawid Arbajter** personally appeared, a tailor or a tavern keeper, 36 years old, a resident of the city of Wyszogrod; and in the presence of witnesses Moshka Gersh Meinwald, 48 years old, and Pinkus Lisser, 56 years old, both synagogue watchers living in the city of Wyszogrod, he introduced us a male child; announced that he was born in the city of Wyszogrod on January 22 of this year at 5 o'clock in the morning from his legal wife **Hana Itta Bilgoraj**, 33 years old. At circumcision the child was given the name **Abram**.

Birth record, Nauma Arbeiter

Nauma "Nelly" Arbeiter was the sister of Abraham Arbeiter 5-28 and the daughter of Davis 6-56 and Hannah Arbeiter 6-57.[8]

Held in the city of Wyszogrod on January 18, 1881. The Jew **Dawid Arbajter** personally appeared, a merchant of 45 years old living in Wyszogrod, in the presence of witnesses Moshka Gersh Meinwald, 53 years old, and Pinkus Lisser, 60 years old, synagogue watchers living in Wyszogrod, introduced us a female child, announced that she was born in Wyszogrod on January 11 at 6 o'clock in the morning, this year, from his legal wife, **Hana Itta Bilgoraj**, 45 years old. At the closure of the rite the child was given the name **Nauma**.

Birth record, Jacob Arbeiter

Jacob Arbeiter was the son of Davis 6-56 *and Hannah Arbeiter* 6-57.[9]

Held in the city of Wyszogrod on July 8, 1883, at 11 o'clock in the morning. The Jew **Dawid Arbajter** personally appeared, tavern keeper of 40 years old, resident of Wyszogrod city, in the presence of witnesses Moshka Gersh Meinwald of 55 years old and Pinkus Lisser of 62 years old, synagogue watchers living in Wyszogrod city, introduced us a male child, announced that he was born in Wyszogrod city on July 1 of this year at 1 o'clock in the afternoon, from his lawful wife **Hana Itta**, born Bilgoraj, 37 years old, living with her husband. In the religious rite the child was given the name **Jacob**.

Appendix B

Arrivals

"The day of an immigrant's arrival in his new home is like a birthday to him. Indeed, it is more apt to claim his attention and to warm his heart than his real birthday. Some of our immigrants do not even know their birthday. But they all know the day when they came to America."
—Abraham Cahan[1]

5 Dec 1892, S.S. *Scandia* from Cuxhaven, Germany:[2]
• Henry Steinman (as "Heinrich Steinfurst")

20 Dec 1898, S.S. *Kaiser Wilhelm der Grosse* from Bremen, Germany:[3]
• Rose Steinman (as "Rosa Steinfurst")

29 Aug 1900, S.S. *Kaiser Wilhelm der Grosse* from Bremen, Germany:[4]
• Emma Steinman (as "Emma Steinfurst")

28 Dec 1900, S.S. *Trave* from Bremen, Germany:[5]
• **Marcus Steinman** *5-26* (as "Marcus Steinfurst")
• **Sarah (Borowski) Steinman** *5-27*
• William Steinman (as "Willy")
• Adele Steinman (as "Emilie")
• **Helen** *4-13* (as "Helene")

11 Mar 1904, S.S. *Corinthian* from Glasgow, Scotland:[6]
- **Harry Reinstein** *5-30* (as "Hersch")

3 Jul 1905, S.S. *Astoria* from Glasgow, Scotland:[7]
- **Ada (Newman) Reinstein** *5-31* (as "Edel")
- Pearl Reinstein (as "Perl")
- David Reinstein
- Anna Reinstein (as "Chane")

27 May 1907, S.S. *Celtic* from Southampton, England:[8]
- **Abraham Arbeiter** *5-28*

23 Jun 1907, S.S. *Livonia* from Rotterdam, Holland:[9]
- Sam Reinstein, nephew of Harry and Ada Reinstein (as "Schmiel")

17 Nov 1907, S.S. *St. Paul* from Southampton, England:[10]
- **Sarah (Jacobs) Arbeiter** *6-57*
- **Solomon Arbeiter** *5-28*
- Betty Arbeiter (as "Rebecca")
- Benjamin Arbeiter (as "Benny")

18 Nov 1910, S.S. *Kaiserin Auguste Victoria* from Hamburg, Germany:[11]
- **Sam Siegel** *5-24* (as "Salman Sigal")
- Jack Siegel (as "Jakob Sigal")

19 May 1912, S.S. *Birma* from Libau, Russia:[12]
- **Anna (Stein) Siegel** *5-25* (as "Hene Sigalow")
- Bessie Siegel (as "Basse")
- **Morris Siegel** *4-12* (as "Moische")
- Berdie Siegel (as "Brane")
- Sophie Siegel (as "Czipe")
- Sylvia Siegel (as "Cziwi")

29 Jul 1913, S.S. *Gothland* from Antwerp, Belgium:[13]
- Hyman Dreizen, nephew of Harry and Ada Reinstein (as "Chaim Renistein")

Appendix C

Burials

New York

Mount Zion Cemetery

59–63 54th Ave., Maspeth, NY. 718-335-2500.[1]

- **Harry Reinstein** *5-30*: row 11L, gate 5. Entering the main gates on 54th Avenue, you'll encounter a fork in the road immediately after the office (on your right). Take the left path, and follow it until you find a metal sign on the right side for "Path 11." Turn right onto Path 11, and continue until you find a gate between two stone pillars with the numeral *5* painted in yellow toward the bottom of the right pillar. The gate should be marked "Medgibosh Prog. Solidarity Society."[i] Facing this gate (but staying on the main path), look three headstones to the left; this is Harry's.[2]

- **Ada (Newman) Reinstein** *5-31*: Row 11L, gate 5. Follow the directions as above.[3]

---

[i]See the "Reinstein" chapter for an explanation of this.

Mount Hebron Cemetery

130-04 Horace Harding Expy., Flushing, NY. 718-939-9405.[4]

- **Morris Siegel** *4-12*, father of Marty Siegel *3-6*: Block 16, section H, line 1, grave 2.[5] Entering at the main gate, you will pass the main office on the right side. Just past the office, there is a fork with three choices—take the middle road and follow it until it ends at a four-way intersection that it approaches from an angle. Bear slightly to the right, then take your third left. At this point, block 8 should be on your left, and block 7 on your right. Continue on this road; after four potential left turns, block 16 will be on your left.

- **Sam Siegel** *5-24*, father of Morris: Block 16, section H, line 14, grave 10.[6]

- **Abraham Arbeiter** *5-28*: Block 74, section H, lot 10, grave 6.[7] Entering at the main gate, you will pass the main office on the right side. Stay on the far-right road at the three-way fork immediately after the office; stop after passing three left turns; block 74 is on your left. Row H is toward the back of the section, near the curving road that provides the block's back border.

- Blanche (Friedman) Arbeiter, wife of Abraham: Block 74, section H, lot 10, grave 5.[8]

- Sylvia Arbeiter, daughter of Claire *4-15* and Sol Arbeiter *4-14*: Block 19, reference 22, section L, line A, grave 3.[9]

- Louis Buchalter, husband of Betty Arbeiter: Block 74, section H, lot 1/2 7 & 9, grave 3.[10] See above directions for Abraham and Blanche Arbeiter.

Mount Carmel Cemetery

83-45 Cypress Hills St., Glendale, NY. 718-366-5900.[11]

- **Marcus Steinman** *5-26*: section 1, block E, line 5, grave 11.[12] Section 1 is the "Old" Mt. Carmel Cemetery; the entrance is on Cypress Hills Street. Once going through the main gate, turn right and follow the main road—block E wraps around the perimeter of almost the entire cemetery, so all the graves on the right side of the road are block E. Line 5 is in the northernmost section of the cemetery, on the exact opposite side from the entrance.
- **Sarah (Borowski) Steinman** *5-27*: section 1, block E, line 7, grave 31. Standing with your back to the entrance of the cemetery, line 7 is to the right of line 5, where Marcus *5-26* is buried.[13]
- Michael Steinman, son of Marcus *5-26* and Sarah Lubitzky: section 1, block E, line 9, grave 13.[14]
- Rebecca (Hoffman) Steinman, wife of Michael: section 1, block E, line 11, grave 1.[15]
- Lizzie (Steinman) Simon, daughter of Marcus and Sarah Lubitzky: section 1, block E, line 6, grave 5.[16]
- Philip Simon, husband of Lizzie: section 1, block E, line 6, grave 4. Note: This grave appears to be unmarked; the other half of the "Simon" gravestone is blank, but cemetery records indicate Philip is here.[17]
- Potentially of interest: Mt. Carmel is also home to the grave of Sholem Aleichem, the Yiddish author whose stories of Tevye the Dairyman became the basis for the musical *Fiddler on the Roof.*

Montefiore Cemetery

121-83 Springfield Blvd., Jamaica, NY. 718-528-1700.[18]

- Esther (Siegel) Reinstein, second wife of Harry Reinstein *5-30*: Gate 5/S OPP. 90, block 97, row 009L, grave 8. Entering the main gates, make your second

left, just beyond the main building. Take this road to
the end, where it meets "Abraham Avenue." Esther
is buried in the area in front of you and to the right,
in the area between Abraham Avenue and the houses
behind the trees.[19]

- Hyman Dreizen, nephew of Harry *5-30* and Ada
  Reinstein *5-29*: Gate 5/S OPP. 90, block 97, row
  009L, grave 2.[20]
- Montefiore is also the final resting place of Jacob
  "Gurrah" Shapiro, the partner of Louis "Lepke" Buchalter.[ii] It is in section 406—if you follow the above
  instructions to Esther's grave, instead of making the
  final turn in front of you and to the *right*, it's the
  section to your left.

Beth David Cemetery

300 Elmont Rd., Elmont, NY, 11003. 516-328-1300.[21]

- Nathan Reinstein, son of Harry *5-30* and Ada Rein-
  stein *5-31*.[22] Likely section H-9.[23]
- Berdie (Siegel) Prussin, daughter of Sam *5-24* and
  Anna Siegel*5-25*.[24]
- Sam Reinstein, cousin of Claire Reinstein *4-15*. Sec-
  tion H-9.[25]

Washington Cemetery

5820 Bay Pkwy., Brooklyn, NY, 11230. 718-377-8690.[26]

- **Anna Siegel** *5-25*: cemetery 3, post 245, row 1,
  grave 29.[27]
- Sophie Siegel, daughter of Samuel *5-24* and Anna
  Siegel *5-25*. Cemetery 3, post 245, row 1, grave 23.[28]
- Pearl (Reinstein) Gitlin, daughter of Harry *5-30* and
  Ada Reinstein *5-31*.[29]
- Harry Gitlin, husband of Pearl.[30]

[ii]See the "Arbeiter" chapter for details.

Mount Ararat Cemetery

1165 Route 109, Lindenhurst, NY 11757. 631-957-2277.[31]
- Goldie (Newman) Task, daughter of Daniel Newman *6-62* and half-sister of Ada (Newman) Reinstein *5-31*: Section 48, range H, lot 2.[32]
- Joseph Task, husband of Goldie: Section 48, range H, lot 2.[33]
- Rose Newman, mother of Goldie Task and wife of Daniel Newman: Section 48, range H, lot 1.[34]

Wellwood Cemetery

1400 Wellwood Ave., Wyandanch, NY. 631-249-2300.[35]
- **Martin Siegel** *3-6*[36]
- **Helen (Steinman) Siegel** *4-13*
- Hyman Reinstein, sibling of Claire (Reinstein) Arbeiter *4-15*.[37]
- Lillian (Feldman) Reinstein, wife of Hyman.
- Henry Steinman, sibling of Helen.
- Emma (Steinman) Eisenstadt, sibling of Helen.
- Rose Steinman, sibling of Helen.
- William Steinman, sibling of Helen.
- Ann (Friedman) Steinman
- Adele (Steinman) Katz, sibling of Helen.
- Frank Katz, husband of Adele.

Congregation Agudas Israel Cemetery

290 North Street, Newburgh, NY. 845-562-5604.[38]
- **Sarah (Jacobs) Finkel** *5-29*, mother of Solomon Arbeiter *4-14*.[39]
- Samuel Finkel, second husband of Sarah.[40]

New Jersey

Beth Israel Cemetery

US Highway 1 North, Woodbridge, NJ. 732-201-3509.[41]
- **Claire (Reinstein) Arbeiter** *4-15*
- **Ann (Arbeiter) Dondero** *3-7*
- Ruth (Reinstein) Kaufman, sister of Claire *4-15*
- Milton Kaufman, husband of Ruth

Florida

Forest Lawn Cemetery

2401 SW 64th Ave, Fort Lauderdale, Fla. 954-792-9360.[42]
- **Solomon Arbeiter** *4-14*[43]

Temple Beth El Memorial Gardens

4900 Griffin Road, Davie, Fla. 954-584-7151.[44]
- Betty (Arbeiter) Jarwood, daughter of Abraham *5-28* and Sarah Arbeiter *5-29*.[45]

Sylvan Abbey Memorial Park

2860 Sunset Point Road, Clearwater, Fla. 727-796-1992.[46]
- Anna (Reinstein) Gladstone, sibling of Claire (Reinstein) Arbeiter *4-15*. Sunrise Garden area, section 11, row K, grave 2.[47]
- Arthur Gladstone, husband of Anna. Sunrise Garden area, section 11, row K, grave 1.[48]

Virginia

Temple Emanuel Cemetery

Just north of 2838 Orange Ave NE, Roanoke, VA. 540-342-3378.[49]

- David Reinstein, son of Harry *5-30* and Ada Reinstein *5-31*.[50]

England

East Ham Jewish Cemetery

Marlow Road, East Ham, London E6 3QG, United Kingdom. +44 20 8950 7767.[51]

- **Davis Arbeiter** *6-56*, father of Abraham Arbeiter *5-28*: Section G, row 15, plot 24. (Inscription spells name "Davis Arbiter.")[52]
- **Hannah (Biłgoraj) Arbeiter** *6-57*, mother of Abraham Arbeiter: Section G, row 15, plot 23. (Inscription lists name as "Annie.")[53], entry for Hannah Yetta Arbiter; East Ham Cemetery.
- Isaac Arbiter, son of Davis and Hannah Arbeiter: Section H, row 5, plot 18.[54]

Poland

Note: There are no gravestones at these locations, which were desecrated during World War II. See the "Arbeiter" chapter for details.

Wyszogród (new) Jewish cemetery

At the intersection of Pokoju and Niepodleglosci; gate on Pokoju.

- Ryfka Arbajter,[55] daughter of Davis *6-56* and Hannah Arbeiter *6-57*
- **Szulim Haim Biłgoraj** *7-114*[56]
- **Sura Ester (Wejs) Biłgoraj** *7-115*[57]
- **Szymon Biłgoraj** *8-228*[58]
- **Rasza Biłgoraj** *8-229*[59]
- **Berek Arbajter** *8-224*[60]

Bieżuń Jewish cemetery

Unmarked; believed to be along Leśna Street, just northwest of its intersection with Borek.[61]

- **Jakób Szoel Chrzanowski** *8-226*[62]
- Ester Chrzanowska, daughter of Szoel *8-226* and Ruchla Chrzanowski *8-227*, age 2.[63]
- Chaim Chrzanowski, son of Szoel *8-226* and Ruchla Chrzanowski *8-227*, age 1.[64]

Figure C.1: Gravestone of Milton and Ruth (Reinstein) Kaufman in 2017. The symbol of the hands indicates Milton was a kohen, a hereditary member of the priestly Jewish caste. See the "Reinstein" chapter for an explanation of Leviim and kohanim.[65]

Figure C.2:   The gravestone of Harry Reinstein 5-30.   The marker was almost entirely covered in ivy when it was found in 2017 by Kevin LaCherra, who cleared it before taking this photo.   The pitcher at the top is the symbol of a Levite (explained in the "Reinstein" chapter); the Hebrew on the stone (which includes several abbreviations) reads, "Here is buried Tzvi Dov, son of Nachman the Levite, died 20 Cheshvan 5705. May his soul be bound in the bonds of eternal life."

Appendix D

Finding the Steinmans

The origins of the Steinman family almost went undiscovered, were it not for a chance finding of a distant cousin's Social Security record. For the curious, here are the steps taken to determine that the Steinmans from Germany were actually the Steinfursts from Poland:

1. The entire Steinman family (as was known) appear in the 1905 New York census. Marcus (as "Max") and Sarah say they are from Russia, but that all the children were born in Germany. All said they arrived in the U.S. around 1900, but there is an exception: It says Henry Steinman, an insurance agent, has been in America for 15 years.[1]

2. This leads to a search for Henry's presence in the 1900 federal census. Eventually, he turns up living with the Simon family: his name is correct, his age lines up with the later census, his birthplace is listed as "Germany," and his occupation is "insurance agent."[2] The odds of this being a different Henry seem slim.

3. Later, another entry in the Simon family's record becomes obvious: Henry Steinman is listed as the brother-in-law of the head of the household, Philip Simon. This could indicate three possibilities: Henry could be the brother of Lizzie Simon, Philip's wife. Alternatively, Henry could be

married to one of Philip's sisters. Third, the entry could
be wrong, and he could actually just be boarding with the
Simons. Because Henry is listed in 1900 as being unmar-
ried,[3] research went forward assuming everything was as
reported, and Lizzie Simon was actually the sister of Henry
Steinman.

4. Assuming this to be true, the need arose to get
more information about the family of Lizzie Simon. Census records going through 1930 indicate the couple had
three grown children: Sarah, Louis and Norman.[4] Various
records were accumulated for each of Lizzie and Philip's
children (and grandchildren).

5. A collection of applications to the Social Security
Administration contains an entry for Louis Simon. It gives
his parents' names as Philip Simon and *Lizzie Steinfurst*.[5]
This was a promising lead, but it was still undetermined
whether this was accurate, and if it was, if it would be
helpful finding details about the other Steinmans.

6. New York City immigration records for millions of
names have been made available by the Statue of Liberty–
Ellis Island Foundation; a search of their database yields
multiple Steinfursts, but one, aboard the ship *Trave*, landing 28 Dec 1900, was of particular interest: A German
family of "Steinfirsts" was on board, hailing from "Schup-
penheil": Their names are listed as Marcus, Sarah, Willy,
Emilie and Helene.[6] The names map closely to the anglicized we are already familiar with—this, combined with the
family's ages closely resembling the established timeline,
provided significant corroboration of the theory that the
Steinmans had gone by this alternative surname on arrival.

7. There was still room for more data, however—only
three of the six Steinman siblings were accounted for on
the *Trave*. Further searching turned up a record for a
German 11-year-old named Rosa Steinfurst who arrived
two years earlier; it says her ticket was paid for by her
brother.[7] The same goes for 18-year-old Emma Steinfurst,
who arrived in summer 1900.[8] That's five of the six siblings

now, with the brother in both cases presumably being Henry Steinman, who was at this point still missing from immigration records.

8. Ellis Island returns no records of either a "Henry Steinman" or "Henry Steinfurst." The search is gradually widened until there are about 3,000 names similar to Henry's—last names such as "Steinburg," "Reinfurst" and so on. Eventually, a name indexed by Ellis Island researchers as "Himr Stenifurst"[i,9] appears, a 15-year-old Prussian from Schippenbeil.[10] The last Steinman sibling was found, with all of them—plus a half-sister—having entries under "Steinfurst" that correlate with their ages.

9. The last, unanticipated step came later: Upon finding the gravesites of Marcus *5-26* and Sarah Steinman *5-27*, cemetery records showed they were buried in a section of the cemetery administered by the "Heinrich Heine Lodge," a New York burial society.[11] There are two other Steinmans buried by that society in the same cemetery: Michael[12] and Rebecca.[13] Michael doesn't appear in any documentation with the rest of his family and was unknown to surviving relatives, but the Hebrew inscription on Marcus's gravestone reads, "Zelig Mordechai, son of Shmuel."[14] The one on Michael's identifies him as "Aron Michel, son of Zelig Mordechai,"[15] so the relationship was verified with a single line on an otherwise unnoticed tombstone. From there, it was just a matter of tracing Michael's arrival in America to find that Rebecca Steinman was his wife.

[i]While it's unclear what "Himr" means, researchers at the Castle Garden website interpret it as "Heinrich," *not* "Henry," presumably out of a pattern they observed with the abbreviation of German names.

Appendix E

Siegel to Sigalow, a proof argument

Please be aware going into this section: It is very boring. I'm the protagonist *and wrote the thing*, and even I think it's boring. It's included here, and goes into careful detail about individual documents, for anyone interested in the research done into the Siegels of America and the Sigalow immigrants to whom they have been linked. It has been written for future researchers and the exceptionally curious, with an eye to the Genealogical Proof Standard put forward by the Board for Certification of Genealogists, in case someone decides one day that they are skeptical that the Siegels and Sigalows are the same people. If you want the short version, skip down to the "Conclusion" section at the end, though I promise I will not be offended if you skip it altogether.

It's not a sure thing that I'm correct, but this report was prepared as a means to examine and present the evidence available, and to force me to validate that I am as correct as possible given the resources at hand. These conclusions were drawn from a mesh of records, gravestones and things people told me on the telephone. All are explained below.

The family, and the question

The documentation of the Siegel family in America is sparse. Evidence we do have paints a relatively consistent picture, though several people quickly disappear from the known paper trail. Living relatives in the same generation as Marty Siegel *3-6* and Nancy (Siegel) Abdill *2-3* are able to provide invaluable context: They have direct knowledge of many of the people in the tree that were unknown to Marty's side of the family and can help fill out the remainder of the tree going forward from those born in the 20th century.

The challenge is in going backward: When did the Siegels come here, and where was it they came from? What—and whom—were they leaving behind? Easy answers are not forthcoming: A Siegel descendant reported the family came here in 1912, but there are no Siegels that look like ours in the Ellis Island ship manifests recorded in that year.

Based on those living in the Siegel household in the 1920 census, the people we are looking for are:

- **Samuel** *5-24*, born abt 1872.[1] The father of the immigrant family in question. Spent decades as a fruit vendor in Brooklyn, according to family stories[2] and census records.[3]
- **Anna** *5-25*, born abt 1872.[4] Mother of the Siegels.
- **Jack**, born 1895,[5] the oldest known child.
- **Bessie**, born 1897.[6]
- **Morris**, born abt 1901.[7]
- **Sophie**, born abt 1907.[8]
- **Berdie**, born 17 Apr 1909.[9]
- **Sylvia**, born 1 May 1911.[10]

This list also conforms to the list of children known to living descendants. An assumption here is that a family of (at least) eight people would be overwhelmingly likely to appear in government immigration records. If that is true, the question is simple: Where are they?

Finding a year

The 1920 census lists all the Siegels as having arrived in 1912. However, the other information in the family's entry raises questions: For starters, the whole family is listed as Polish, which disagrees with all other available documentation of their origins. It also says they speak Polish, when it would have been much more likely for them to have spoken Yiddish. (There is no actual evidence to contradict the questionable language entries.) Anna's name is also recorded as "Hannah," which is inconsistent with other documents but may not be incorrect, as further explanation will show.[11]

The point of this is just to suggest that the data in the family's 1920 entry may not be entirely reliable. Many of these answers change in the 1930 census, though less of the family is living together, and Anna had died. The family is listed as coming from Russia in that year's records, rather than Poland, and their language is given as Yiddish. Most notably, Berdie and Sylvia, the only two children still living at home, are listed as arriving in 1912, while Samuel's entry just above them says he arrived in 1910. Basically, at least *one* of the censuses have to be incorrect on several counts.[12]

Given the commonality of 1912 between family stories and both census records, it seems a good place to start looking. So far, we have reviewed a set of names, an approximate year of arrival, and the general ages of everyone in the family. In practice, the only other searchable characteristic remaining is a town of origin.

Finding a town, and Morris

Family lore gives us an origin for the family: Kiev, which was in Russia at the time but is now the capital of Ukraine. This conforms with the 1930 census listing the family as

Russian, but there is no documentation specifically listing Kiev as the family's hometown.

Luckily, there is a lead in the probable documentation of Morris's untimely death in 1932, though that, too, has concerning contradictions. In that year, a 30-year-old Morris Siegel died in Rockaway, Queens of "epidemic cerebrospinal meningitis." This matches the story known to Nancy Abdill *2-3* that Morris died when her father, Marty *3-6*, was about two years old. The death certificate spells Morris's last name "Seigel," which doesn't match, and says his father's name is Jacob, not Sam. His mother's name, however, is recorded as "Anna Stern," remarkably close to "Anna Stein," the name recorded elsewhere as Anna's maiden name. It says Morris had been in the U.S. for 18 years, putting his approximate date of immigration at 1914. His occupation is listed as "fruit store clerk," and his wife's name is given as "Helen." [13]

So we have a certificate with a name that matches our Morris, except for a weird spelling change in the surname. His age lines up approximately with his age on his marriage certificate, and his occupation selling fruit matches Sam's— certainly a plausible answer, albeit in a far-flung borough. His wife's name matches the one we have confirmed, Helen (Steinman) Siegel *4-13*, and his mother's name is one letter off.[14] Given how closely it matches existing stories, it seems very difficult to rule out "Morris Seigel" as our Morris— there are just too many coincidences for it to be a different person, particularly because his age makes the number of possibilities far smaller. It seems safe, however, to be leery of taking some of the answers as gospel.

The reason Morris's death certificate is getting such annoyingly close scrutiny is because it is the single document that links us to the family's hometown. The certificate itself simply says he and his parents are all from Russia (another match with known information). However, it also says he was buried at Mt. Hebron Cemetery, in Queens—cemetery records there do indeed show a "Morris Seigel" buried there

30 Mar 1932,[15] which matches the death certificate exactly but repeats the misspelling. The burial society that oversaw his plot is listed as the Medwin Benevolent Association, a society incorporated in 1918 by residents of the town of Medvin, Russia.[16]

Medvin in the early 1900s was a tiny town, likely of less than 500 people,[17] sitting among the forests at the heart of what is now Ukraine. Russia at the time was broken up into governorates, somewhat analogous to a U.S. state. The most relevant fact about Medvin is that it was part of the *Kiev Governorate.*

So, the assertion that the family had come "from Kiev"[18] would technically be true, but something of a misdirection, given the notoriety of the city of Kiev. (Amusingly enough, there is a direct comparison to New York City and New York state—someone from another country is far more likely to be aware of the huge city, so hearing someone was "from New York" probably wouldn't inspire considerations of a suburb of Ithaca being a possibility.)

In summary, if we accept that the 30-year-old fruit vendor Morris Seigel is also Morris Siegel *4-12*, son of Sam the fruit vendor and Anna, then we know the town from which the Siegels came.

Anna and the kids

So now, we have the people we're looking for, the town they're from, and the year we can guess they arrived. A shallow search for the family's American names in 1912 yields no results, but we can guess at the Yiddish origins of several of the names: "Samuel" could have arrived as "Schmiel," for example, and "Jack" could be "Jacob," "Jakov," or possibly "Yitzchok," though none of those possibilities yield any tempting results in 1912. The most probable translation, however, is for Morris: Though "Moishe" was a popular name overseas, its English equivalent, "Moses," was not—a study found that 78 percent of immigrants arriving as "Moishe" (or a variant of it) ended up instead changing their name to "Morris."[19]

Unfortunately, the only match for that name between 1910 and 1914 is a child recorded as "Mojsche Siegel," who arrived in December 1913 at the age of two, putting his date of birth much too distant from the 1901 estimate we get from his death certificate and the 1920 census. Expanding the search to more creative variants of the family's surname—"Siegal," "Segal," "Dziegel," and so on—doesn't give us anything else of interest.

Results increase markedly when searching instead for surnames that *start* with a given string of letters, rather than those that are just similar: In searches using that option, for example, a search for the last name "John" would also return results for people named "Johnson." Within those results, a match eventually surfaced for a "Moische Sigalow," who arrived 19 May 1912 aboard the S.S. *Birma*. His age is 11, which matches our guess of a 1901 birth. He is listed as arriving with five people: his mother and four sisters, the Sigalow family.[20] If we arrange the listed siblings by age, their names line up plausibly well, as do their ages. Only Berdie appears to be out of order:

Siegel		Sigalow	
Anna	1872	Heni	1872
Bessie	1897	Basse	1898
Morris	1901	Moische	1901
Berdie	1909	Brane	1903
Sophie	1907	Czipe	1906
Sylvia	1911	Cziwi[i]	1909

Not a perfect match, to be sure, though for a group of six people, the resemblance is remarkable. In addition, it appears to be a uniquely suitable set of arrivals—searching for the children individually yields a few possibilities, but none nearly as well-fitting. For example, a "Pesse Segall," born 1898, arrived in 1913, but she was accompanied by three brothers and a mother who was 14 years older than the one we're looking for.

The town recorded as the birthplace of the entire family is of little help—it's in Russia, but the entry is mostly illegible. It appears it could be something like "Trotzk," which doesn't match any current maps. That town is mentioned in an 1845 encyclopedia as one of "the principal towns on the Russian borders," but it's not clear which border.[21] It also appears on at least one endorsement of early airmail envelopes: Somewhere in Russia, a "Trotzk" postmark ended up on an envelope in 1926 that was put up for auction in 2008 and sold for $45,000;[22] it offers even less clarity than the encyclopedia.

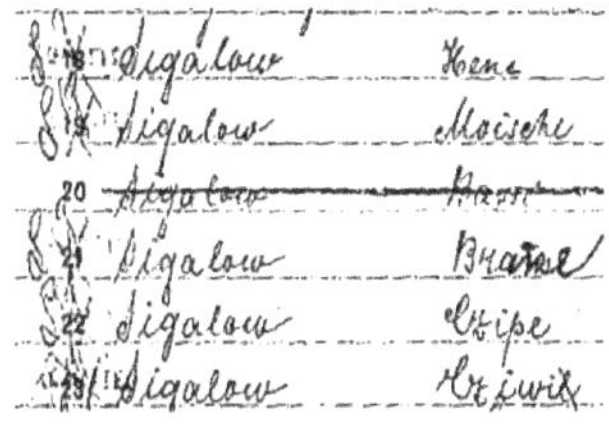

Figure E.1: The Sigalow family's entry in the ship manifest from their 1912 arrival.

Corroborating the Sigalow entries, finding Anna

There are several reasons to be optimistic about the entry, however. First, officials in the early 1900s began asking immigrants for the contact information of the "nearest relative or friend in country whence alien came." The entry for the Sigalows appears to be a sister or sister-in-law whose address is given as "Korni, Gub. Kiew." Korni, too, is not a current town, but it was apparently in the Kiev Governorate. ("Gub" is an abbreviation for *guberniya*.) Korni is also given as the last home of the Sigalows, meaning the six suspected Siegels are from the same area as the ones we're looking for.

The other main clue is that they said they were arriving

to meet their husband and father, "S. Sigalow," which could well have been a reference to Sam Siegel *5-24*. That would also line up with the possibility put forward in the 1930 census that he arrived before 1912. We might also consider that S. Sigalow is listed as living at "360 Madison St.," on the manifest, an address in Brooklyn. We know the Siegels were living in Brooklyn in 1920,[23] though they were about 2.5 miles north of that address.[ii]

There is another bit of corroborating evidence in favor of the Sigalow entries, though the way there winds around a bit. The grave and death records of Anna (Stein) Siegel *5-25* were difficult to locate—the only clue was that she appeared in the 1920 census but was nowhere to be found in the one for 1930. Unfortunately, "Anna Siegel" was a very common name, and dozens of possible candidates came up in searches of city death indices. The list can get whittled down to about eight entries if one is picky about the possible birth years, but it's still a much broader list than would be helpful. The list was finally narrowed to one candidate based on the guess that Anna may have been buried in the same cemetery as other Siegels.

Sophie Siegel died 25 Feb 1920, at age 14.[iii] Her death certificate states that she was buried at Washington Cemetery,[24] an assertion confirmed by the cemetery's records.[25]

The area in which she is buried was administered by a mix of two different burial societies:[26] Congregation Ahavath Jeshurun and the Independent Orler Benevolent Society.[iv] It appears to be a somewhat confusing arrangement, but, unless another 14-year-old Sophie Siegel died on the exact same day, we know that Sophie is the one we're looking for; her death certificate lists the family's house on Bedford Avenue as her home, and her parents are listed as

---

[ii]Their address in the 1920 census was 310 Bedford Ave., in the Williamsburg neighborhood.

[iii]For more about Sophie's illness, see the "Siegel" chapter.

[iv]The Orler society is a Polish organization, so it's probable the Siegels were associated with Ahavath Jeshurun.

Samuel Siegel and Anna Stein, so this is one of the more concrete facts we can use.

The reason this is helpful is because, in the same section, six graves away,[27] is one of the possible Anna Siegels. According to the gravestone, she was born about 1872 and died 6 Oct 1924,[28] dates that line up on both counts.[29] In addition, the stone is inscribed, "In memory of my beloved wife and our devoted mother," implying her husband was still alive, as Sam was—though, to be fair, at age 52 it doesn't seem unreasonable for many husbands to still be alive.

So, of all the Anna Siegels who died in New York City in the 1920s, one of them, born in the same year as "our" Anna, is buried six graves away from Sophie Siegel, who would be her daughter. If we accept that this is the correct Anna, then we have another clue pointing to the Sigalows: The translation of the Hebrew inscription on her gravestone gives her name as "Sarah Hene, daughter of Tzvi." Not only does the Yiddish name "Hene" (or "Hena") seem like a reasonable source of the anglicized name "Anna," but it also matches the name of the mother of our hypothetical immigrant family, recorded in two places as either "Hene" or "Heni."

Finding Sam and Jack

Even if we accept that the Sigalows described above are our Siegels, there are still two known family members absent from the documents: Sam 5-24 and Jack, the oldest child. No one in 1912 appears to match their description, so the next most likely place to search in 1910, the year given for Sam's immigration in the 1930 census. A search for Sigalow immigrants in that year brings up a Schlome Sigalow arriving 2 Aug 1910—however, his birth year is given as about 1890, which, if he were our Sam, would mean he had his first child at age 7. (Since Heni Sigalow was listed as being born in abt 1872, it also makes it very unlikely that Schlome is the "S. Sigalow" she lists as her husband.)

We know for sure that Sam eventually adopted the name "Siegel," if it wasn't his surname to begin with. A search for male immigrants with surnames similar to "Siegel" with first names that start with "S" yields a few possibilities: There are dozens of results, but many are young children or teenagers—by 1910, our Sam would have been in his late 30s at least. In addition to conforming to the documents we *do* have about him, his oldest child would have been 13 in 1910, so it seems unlikely he would have been younger than 30. Trimming those results out, the list (at least according to existing indices) falls to less than two dozen candidates in 1910. One is immediately drawn to a 40-year-old arriving 20 Sep 1910—his name is "Sam Siegel," and he is from Russia. It also says his "calling or occupation" is "merchant," which lines up with our Sam's later profession. His contact in his previous country of residence is given as his wife, whose name is partially illegible but is something resembling "Ger—del Siegel," which doesn't line up very well with "Anna." Importantly, it also doesn't line up with "Sarah Hene," the Hebrew/Yiddish name we know belongs to our Anna either. In addition, it says she lives in the Grodno Governorate, which was a 500-mile journey northwest from Medvin (and is currently in the northwest corner of Belarus).

One connection *may* support the family living in Grodno rather than Kiev—the Sigalows departed from Libau, a port on the Baltic Sea. Grodno is about 300 miles from Libau, while Medvin is an 800-mile journey. This seems unlikely to be a factor: To favor Grodno over Medvin—especially when Medvin and the Kiev Governorate have other supporting documentation—implies that those in the area would have had a better alternative than to leave via the Baltic. They could have in theory traveled to a port on the Mediterranean, but there is no evidence they did.

Mediterranean departures of Medvin residents

A quick survey reinforces the unlikelihood of Medvin residents having a better alternative to the Baltic or North Seas as a route to the Atlantic: If we look at immigrants to the U.S. from Medvin between 1906 (when the Russian–American Line began transporting passengers from Libau) and the start of World War I, we find 186 people listed from eight ports,[30] some of which may not have been their original point of departure. (For example, someone leaving from Liverpool, England, would have needed to take a boat to Liverpool in the first place. Either that or swim the English Channel.)

Hamburg	60
Rotterdam	34
Liverpool	34
Antwerp	23
Libau	22
Bremen	21
Havana	1
Trieste	1

While it's not a particularly large sample (and one that doesn't include the Sigalows), it seems relevant that out of 186 entries, only two—Havana, Cuba, and Trieste, Italy—don't specifically rule out the possibility that the emigrant left from a port on the Baltic or North Seas. Just under 12 percent of reported Medvin emigrants left via Libau, and another 18 percent left from Rotterdam, which was the stop after Libau on the way to New York for passengers on the Russian–American Line. While 12 percent isn't an overwhelming number of people leaving from Libau, the finding that almost a third of Medvin residents left via Hamburg illustrates an important point even more effectively: It's almost 1,100 miles from Medvin to Hamburg, so proximity to the Sigalows' port of departure should not be used as a gauge for the plausibility of a candidate for which immigrant is our Sam Siegel.

A locksmith and some strangers

So, in the search for Sam and Jack, it seems reasonable to at least discount the possibility that our Sam was the one who lived in Grodno with a spouse named "Ger—del." However, another Siegel immigrant presents interesting possibilities: Salman Sigal, who arrived on the S.S. *Kaiserin Auguste Victoria* on 28 Nov 1910. The last name is phonetically identical to "Siegel," and "Salman" presents at least a passing resemblance to "Samuel." More intriguing, he is listed as a life-long resident of Medvin, bound for New York City. When asked for a contact back home in Russia, he gave the name of his wife: "Heni Sigal."

In these regards, Salman matches our Sam exactly as one might expect—his hometown, Medvin, matches the burial society of his son Morris, his wife's name, Heni, matches the Hebrew name on Anna's gravestone, and his approximate year of birth, 1870, is within about two years of our other guesses. The theory is further strengthened by his traveling companion: Salman's son Jakob, born abt 1892.[31]

However, there are several confusing discrepancies: A relatively minor inconsistency is that Jakob is listed as several years older than we believe Jack to have been. His occupation is also listed as a "joiner," a woodworking trade for which we have no corroboration in documentation about Jack, who eventually became an accountant. In addition, they are listed as meeting Salman's brother-in-law in America; this person is unknown to existing family, and has not been found in other documentation.

Salman's occupation is also not familiar: He is listed in the ship manifest as a locksmith, which is a long way to go from fruit vendor. It's possible that Sam, unable to find work as a locksmith, took an opportunity to become a merchant instead, but it is the widest distance between Salman and Sam that we have.

This can be mitigated somewhat, however, by looking for evidence of this Salman in the following census, in 1920. 10 years is a long time, but it's the first set of records we can confidently link to the Siegel family we know about.

In that year, there were two Siegal locksmiths in New York:

- **Adolf Segal**, born in Russia in about 1863. He is living by himself and listed as "single," both of which are at least improbable given the Salman in question arrived with a son and provided the name of his spouse. In addition, Adolf reported arriving in 1895, far earlier than Salman and before the birth of almost all of Sam's children.
- **Max Siegel**, a Russian-born boarder born abt 1884 who is living alone but listed as "married." This is a closer match to Salman, except "Max" is still a drastically different name, he reported arriving in 1912, and he is more than a decade younger than we are expecting (plus only about 11 years older than Jack).

Leaving out the locksmith trade, there is only one "Salmon Siegel" readily located in the 1920 census at all, a carpenter living hundreds of miles west in Buffalo. His wife's name is "Annie," which is, as we've seen, a close match for the "Heni" given in the 1910 manifest, but this Salmon reported arriving in 1904 with his wife and the oldest daughter still living there in 1920. There are at least four others in New York City under the name "Solomon," though all four arrived decades before the Salman in question and none are locksmiths.

At the very least, it seems we can conclude the Salman Sigal arriving in 1910, if he had stayed within New York state, was probably not working as a locksmith 10 years later.

The biggest inconsistency with Salman's manifest entry is that he is traveling with three children, not just one— Jakob, age 18, lines up somewhat with our knowledge of Jack Siegel (and accounts for where he was in the Siegel's immigration journey), but there are two others: Aron, age 15, and Dwoire, age 16, both (allegedly) tailors. There is no indication of the presence of either of these people in the lives of the Siegel family we're looking for, which is concerning. However, it's possible Salman and Jakob were simply lying about their relationships with the other two Sigals they were accompanying, maybe in hopes of improving the teens' chances of being allowed in.

We have evidence that this happened on another side of the family tree, with the Reinsteins: We've established that Harry Reinstein *5-30* arrived in 1904, and the rest of the Reinsteins joined him in 1905. In 1907, Sam Reinstein, his sister's teenage son, came to New York and stayed with the family for at least a decade. When he arrived, however, he was detained at Ellis Island, where he was held until Harry attested that he was a relative; rather than saying he was Sam's uncle, however, Harry said he was Sam's brother.[32]

It had also happened the year before, when a Ruchel Reinstein arrived from Medzhybizh, the Reinsteins' home-town: The 17-year-old was also detained, and was picked up later by Harry, who, again, said he was her brother.[33]

Granted, these are both examples of falsifications made to Ellis Island officials by someone already in the United States, but the point remains, it's possible that Aron and Dwoire are not related to Salman and Jakob the way they claim to be. More information about the two of them was pursued to determine whether any other details might shed more light on the situation. Given the comparative difficulty in determining the "American" name Dwoire would have adopted—it could be "Dora," but there are far more possibilities than there are for Aron, who in all likelihood simply became "Aaron." The most likely candidate for the Aron Sigal arriving with Salman is living in Hartford, Connecticut in 1920: He says he was born in about 1890, which is close to the age given on the manifest. In addition, his birthplace in that year's census is given as "Kiev, Russia," an unusually specific answer that happens to conform to Aron's claim to have been born in Medvin.

The main problem with this Aaron's listing is that he is married to a woman named Fannie, also from Kiev, who is recorded as immigrating to the U.S. in 1912, the same year listed for Aaron. That they (allegedly) arrived in the same year from the same place would suggest they arrived together, though it's possible someone else incorrectly guessed the dates. It's tempting to keep an eye on this listing, however, because of the occupation listed: The Aron from the manifest is listed as a tailor, but the Aaron in Connecticut is listed as a salesman at a fruit store. Both Sam *5-24* and Morris Siegel *4-12* worked as fruit vendors, so this is a remarkable coincidence, albeit one that isn't particularly helpful in ironing out which person is related to which.

Siegel, Sigal, Sigalow

The introduction to this report originally included a line that said drawing definitive conclusions was difficult because there is no one document that states, "And then Salman Sigal changed his name to Samuel Siegel and started selling fruit." An exciting development late in the process changed that immediately: The key to the history of the Siegels lies with Sophie.

When Sophie Siegel died of rheumatic fever in 1920, her tombstone was engraved with the Hebrew names of Sophie and her father, creating the only overlap between all three surnames currently in question. Her epitaph reads, "Here is buried the maiden Tsippe, daughter of Zalman, died 6 Adar

5680."[34] This name, "Tsippe," is a direct transliteration of the name given at the hypothesized arrival of Sophie in 1912, Czipe Sigalow. Her father's name, "Zalman," is another almost one-for-one equivalent for the name given at the probable 1910 arrival of Sam Siegel, Salman Sigal. Sophie's death certificate, in conjunction with family stories, makes it a near certainty that she is the daughter of Sam *5-24* and Anna Siegel *5-25*. Her gravestone connects her to names in both groups of suspected immigrants, which means the marker at post 245, row 1, grave 23 is as close as we could get to a Rosetta Stone of the family's various ambiguously translated Russo-Yiddish surnames.

With this extra bit of identifying information, we can go back and look for other, more likely candidates for the arrival of Sam (Salman) Siegel in America. If we restrict the search to males with names similar to "Salman Sigal," born between 1860 and 1880, and arriving between 1905 and 1912, we only get seven results; not only is the previously identified Salman the only one from Medvin, he is the only one from Russia.

There is one tempting entry: Salomon Segal, arriving 4 Apr 1906. He said he was meeting his brother-in-law, whose name he gave as "Samuel Stein," which is the maiden name we have for Anna Siegel *5-25*. However, this immigrant is listed as Hungarian, and his brother-in-law lived in Boston. In addition, he would have arrived years before the birth of the family's youngest two children.

Conclusion

There are two ships carrying the immigrants believed to be the Siegels. The first arrived in 1910, carrying Salman and Jakob Sigal, posited above to be Sam *5-24* and Jack Siegel because their ages match within a few years of expectations, and because they were traveling together from the town of Medvin, in the Kiev Governorate of Russia. This is of

particular interest because the gravesite of Morris Siegel
4-12 was administered by the Medvin Benevolent Society, a
strong suggestion that this was the family's hometown. In
addition, Salman Sigal's entry in the ship manifest lists a
contact back in Russia as "Heni Sigal," his wife in Medvin.

We have established the location of the grave of Anna
Siegel *5-25* in Brooklyn's Washington Cemetery, at which
her gravestone gives her Hebrew name as "Sarah Hene,"
an almost direct match to the wife of "Salman" he gave
upon entering the U.S. The year of his arrival also matches
exactly the date Sam listed in the 1930 census for the year
of his immigration. In addition, the grave of Anna and
Sam's daughter Sophie lists her Hebrew name as "Tsippe,
daughter of Zalman," connecting a definite Siegel to both
boats of suspected family.

The second ship arrived in 1912 carrying six people
that are likely the remaining members of the family: Their
ages line up approximately with other evidence of the
Siegel children's ages, and the anglicized versions of their
names bear some resemblance to the ones given on the ship
manifest. A 1912 arrival also conforms to the years given
for the family in the 1920 and 1930 censuses.

The surname of the immigrants is given as "Sigalow,"
which is different from "Siegel" but certainly a potential
origin for the American version of the name. Though several of the children's birth years appear to be questionably
different from other estimates, none are out of the question. In addition to the family's claim to be from the
Kiev Governorate (where we believe the Siegels to have
been from as well), the main attribute in support of this
being "our" group of Siegels is that they all appear together: Independently, each of these entries would be a
reasonable guess at an immigrant who later changed their
name to one recognizable as a member of the Siegel family;
together, it seems an extremely improbable coincidence
for the names and births of two separate Siegel families
to match so closely in so many regards. The last fact of

interest with the second boat of Siegels is that the Sigalow
family said they were coming to meet their husband and
father, whose name is given as "S. Sigalow," which doesn't
rule out either "Salman" or "Sam" Siegel as the person
waiting for them.

If we combine the information from both manifests and
compare it to our best guesses for the ages of the Siegel
family, the comparison is impossible to ignore:

Siegel		Sigal/Sigalow	
Anna	1872	Heni	1872
Sam	1872	Salman	1870
Jack	1895	Jakob	1892
Bessie	1897	Basse	1898
Morris	1901	Moische	1901
Berdie	1909	Brane	1903
Sophie	1907	Czipe	1906
Sylvia	1911	Cziwi	1909

There are no plausible alternatives that have been found
to explain alternate arrivals for the Siegel children, particularly the youngest ones, so the hypothesis regarding
the arrival of Anna and the family's five youngest children
is presented with considerable confidence. There are two
main concerns with the suspected arrival of Sam and Jack:
First, Sam is listed as a locksmith by trade, which has
nothing in common with the occupation we know he held
in the U.S. selling fruits and vegetables. Primarily, however,
the concern is essentially that he arrived with too many
children: In addition to Jakob, Salman Sigal arrived with
two younger children, Aron and Dwoire, whose ages would
make them older than all the Siegel children except Jack.

While it's possible there were other, unknown Siegel
children who arrived in America and were then separated
from the rest of the family, it would seem the more likely
explanation is that Aron and Dwoire are the nephew and
niece of Sam *5-24* and Anna Siegel *5-25* but were described

as children in an effort to get them into the country. No one has been identified in later records as the Aron and Dwoire who arrived in 1910, though an "Aaron Siegel" was recorded as a fruit vendor in Connecticut in 1920.

The other details line up too well to disqualify that first group of immigrants as the Siegels: We were looking for a Sam and Jack Siegel from Medvin, Russia, arriving in New York in 1910. We instead found a Salman and Jakob Sigal from Medvin, arriving in that port in that year, and with given ages that almost identically match the ages given in later records we know are our Siegels.

The evidence we have for the Siegels' arrival in America is not an open-and-shut case. However, there are compelling similarities between the Siegels, Sigals and Sigalows to believe they are all the same people we are looking for. This information, when considered alongside American documentation of the Siegels—death records, cemetery information, census entries and gravestones—points strongly toward the conclusion that the Siegels arrived from Medvin, Kiev, Russia in 1910 and 1912, under the surnames Sigal and Sigalow. That there are no known, reasonable alternatives to this story lends more confidence to this solution as well.

Appendix F

Rasza's father

We have no direct documentation of the parents of Rasza *8-229*, who married Szymon Biłgoraj *8-228*[1] and was the great-grandmother of Abraham Arbeiter *5-28*. However, there are multiple reasons to believe her father's name was Icek, giving us the name of the person in the tree with Ahnentafel number *9-458*.

Primarily, the use of "patronyms"—names indicating one's father—was widespread in the region, particularly before 1821, when many in the Jewish community did not have official surnames. There is an example of this in the generation after Rasza's in the tree: Rasza and Szymon's son Szulim Haim Biłgoraj *7-114* married a woman named Sura Ester Wejs *7-115*,[2] whose parents are identified in the Wyszogród books of residence as Abram *8-330* and Ryfka *8-331*.[3] However, when Szulim Haim and Sura Ester had a daughter, the birth certificate lists Sura's name as "Sura [nee] Abram."[4] When that daughter (Hana Itta Biłgoraj *6-57*) got married, her mother's name was then listed as "Sura Ester nee Abram,"[5] giving at least one concrete example of a woman's surname being listed in multiple places as her father's given name, even decades after the official adoption of Jewish surnames.

In addition, Rasza and Szymon had a grandson named "Icek,"[6] indicating the likelihood that the name was at least considered a first name and not strictly a surname. The family's naming patterns show clear adherence to the Ashkenazi tradition of naming children after deceased relatives, particularly grandparents, suggesting "Icek" was the name of a relation of either Szymon or Rasza. A few examples from consecutive generations in the tree:

- Szymon Biłgoraj *8-228* died in 1846.[7] Two years later, his son Szulim Haim *7-114* had a son, and named him Szymon.[8]
- Szulim Haim's daughter Hana Itta *6-57* named her son Abram,[9] which was the name of her maternal grandfather, Abram Wejs *8-330*.
- Hana Itta gave birth to twin girls in 1886—she named them Ryfka[10] and Rasza,[11] the names of both of her grandmothers, Ryfka Wejs *8-331* and Rasza Biłgoraj *8-229*.
- Hana Itta's son Abram *5-28* named his first two children Solomon[12] and Rebecca,[13] the English variants of his (paternal) grandparents, Zelman *7-112* and Ryfka Arbajter *7-113*.
- Abram's son Solomon *4-14* named his son "Jay David," which lines up with the name of Solomon's paternal grandfather, Dawid Arbajter *6-56*.
- Solomon's daughter was named Ann Etta Arbeiter *3-7*, a close Americanization of his paternal grandmother's name, Hana Itta *6-57*, who in England went by the name "Annie."[14]
- Ann's daughter Nancy named her second daughter "Claire," after her grandmother Claire (Reinstein) Arbeiter *4-15*.

So, we have four consecutive generations in which there are multiple examples of people naming their children after their own grandparents (or, in Szulim Haim's case, a recently deceased parent). Given this pattern, if Rasza's father was named Icek, we might expect an "Icek" to ap-

pear two generations later. Indeed, that's exactly where
he does appear: Szulim Haim *7-114* named his youngest
son Icek, the suspected name of his grandfather.

There is one final notion supporting this possibility:
Szulim Haim was born in 1821, so Szymon and Rasza must
have gotten married at some point before that, probably
in the late 1810s—which means Rasza may not have had
a surname *at all* until after she was married, and at that
point it would have matched her husband's. That doesn't
rule out that "Icek" couldn't be the patronymic of someone
else in the family, but if she had to retroactively decide on
a "maiden name," it would seem a standard patronymic to
be the simplest solution.

Acknowledgments

The content of this book relies heavily on guidance and materials supplied by family members flung everywhere from Texas to England. I consider myself very lucky to have so many people to thank, but a single line in the back of an unpopular book is an embarrassingly inadequate expression of my thanks—I have tried to honor their contributions by presenting them in the preceding pages as well as I could.

Ann (Arbeiter) Dondero, the "Nana" of the dedication page, offered stories of her grandparents and memories of her childhood in Brooklyn; her 110-year photo collection has provided images scattered throughout the book, including on the cover. Her brother, Jay Arbeiter, spent hours discussing his aunts and uncles, which grandparents lived where and who ended up feuding with whom. The 20th century information in the "Reinstein" and "Arbeiter" chapters owes much to his insights.

The 19th century data in the "Arbeiter" and "Biłgoraj" chapters was driven mostly by the "Jewish Records Indexing - Poland" project, a nonprofit that has indexed more than 5 million vital records of Jewish communities in the present and former lands of Poland. Finding their collection of documents from the Płock Governorate is the only time research has left me breathless.

My mom, Nancy (Siegel) Abdill, spent countless phone conversations going over the memories of her childhood and the locations of far-flung aunts and uncles. (She was not aware the book would have her name on the cover until the first proof had been mailed to my house.) Likewise, her brother, Mark Siegel, contributed valuable information, particularly to the "Steinman" chapter. Both have a preternatural memory for dates, a never-ending gift for a flustered genealogist.

Steve Ginsburg and Joe Chernow are two new names in our family tree—both offered invaluable insight for the "Siegel" chapter. Data from Steve (a second cousin of Nancy) holds up the entire section about Sam and Anna Siegel. Joe, a first cousin of Marty Siegel, augmented this with the more recent developments of the Siegel descendants.

Regarding the actual production of the book, my dad, Richard Abdill (*2-2*), was once again a diligent and generous proofreader, albeit one with a tendency to write corny jokes in the margins. Three close friends were also of great help: Kevin LaCherra hiked to Queens to get information from headstones and spent months listening to hare-brained theories.[i] Anna Gindes created yet another beautiful cover, accepting only alcohol and Mexican food as payment. The third and closest friend on the list is Lauren Abdill, my wife, who provided thoughtful feedback and unflinching tolerance for my months of typing and fretting. I could write another few pages about how wonderful she is, but I promised to clean the litter box three months ago and still haven't done it—at this point, I think that will be more meaningful than extra adjectives.

Anyway, those were the acknowledgments. Yes, my name does show up on the front of the book, but these are the people who helped it come together, who offered their knowledge (and gasoline) to help nudge our family's history a little more into focus. You have my gratitude.

—Rich

---

[i]Unfortunately, my hypothesis that all barbers in the East End of London were related only partially panned out.

Endnotes

Chapter 1 Arbeiter

[1]Manifest, S.S. *Celtic*, 27 May 1907, stamped p. 94, index number 17, Abraham Arbeiter; *Passenger and Crew Lists of Vessels Arriving at New York , NY, 1897-1957*, microfilm publication T715, (Washington: National Archives and Records Service), roll 905, frame 93.

[2]"Marriage," *YIVO Encyclopedia of Jews in Eastern Europe* (http://www.yivoencyclopedia.org/article.aspx/Marriage : accessed 10 Nov 2017).

[3]Irving Howe, *World of Our Fathers: The Journey of the East European Jews to America and the Life They Found and Made* (New York: NYU Press, reprinted 2005), 13.

[4]ChaeRan Y. Freeze, *Jewish Marriage and Divorce in Imperial Russia* (London: Brandeis University Press, 2001), p. 30–31.

[5]Sylwia Kulczyk, "Mini Guidebook: The north-western Mazovia" (Warsaw: Mazowieckie Voivodeship, 2009), web copy of print pamphlet (https://www.mazovia.pl/gfx/mazovia/userfiles/m.guzowska/linki_nie_usuwac/mazowsze_polnocno-zachodnie_en_2.pdf : accessed 10 Nov 2017).

[6]"19th Century Russian Maps," database with images, *WWII Aerial Photos and Maps*, entry for " 1820" (http://www.wwii-photos-maps.com/19thcenturyrussianmaps/ : accessed 10 Nov 2017).

[7]Bella Zawierucha-Gutman, "I Remember," see chapter "Wyszogród Memories."

[8]Sarah Silberstein Swartz, "Return to Poland: In Search of My Parents' Memories," *From Memory to Transformation: Jewish Women's Voices* (Toronto: Second Story Press, 1998). Republished at sztetl.org.pl

[9]Marni Davis, *Jews and Booze: Becoming American in the Age of Prohibition* (New York: NYU Press, 2014), 73.

[10]Ibid, 74.

[11]Nahum Sokolov, "Vishogrod, Town of 'Schools,'" anthologized in online transcription of Vishogrod yizkor book (`http://www.jewishgen.org/yizkor/Wyszogrod/wyse003.html` : accessed 10 Nov 2017).

[12]Zawierucha-Gutman, "I Remember."

[13]Stephen Birmingham, *The Rest of Us: The Rise of America's Eastern European Jews*, first Syracuse University Press edition (Syracuse University Press, 1999), 80–81.

[14]Swartz, "Return to Poland: In Search of My Parents' Memories."

[15]*Ibid.*

[16]Zawierucha-Gutman, "I Remember."

[17]David Dawidowicz, "The Vishogrod Synagogue," anthologized in online transcription of Vishogrod yizkor book (`http://www.zchor.org/wyszogrod/wyszogrod_book` : accessed 10 Nov 2017).

[18]Zawierucha-Gutman, "I Remember."

[19]Abraham Millgram, "Pre-Modern Synagogue Architecture and Interior Design," *My Jewish Learning* (`http://www.myjewishlearning.com/article/synagogue-architecture-and-interior-design/` : accessed 10 Nov 2017).

[20]Zawierucha-Gutman, "I Remember."

[21]Millgram, "Pre-Modern Synagogue Architecture and Interior Design,"

[22]Dawidowicz, "The Vishogrod Synagogue."

[23]Gershon David Hundert, *Jews in Poland-Lithuania in the Eighteenth Century: A Genealogy of Modernity* (Berkeley: University of California Press, 2004), 140.

[24]Dawidowicz, "The Vishogrod Synagogue."

[25]Hayyim Schauss, "History of Bar Mitzvah," *My Jewish Learning* (`http://www.myjewishlearning.com/article/history-of-bar-mitzvah/` : accessed 11 Nov 2017).

[26]"Wyszogród Synagoga żydzi 1918r," product information page, *Sklep Kolekcjonerski Marczak* (`http://www.kolekcjonerski.com.pl/p,wyszogrod_synagoga_zydzi_1918r,2217,27.html` : accessed 11 Nov 2017).

[27]Selma Berrol, *East Side/East End: Eastern European Jews in*

London and New York, 1870–1920 (Westport, Conn.: Praeger, 1994), 4.

[28] *Ibid.*, 5.

[29] Samuel Joseph, "Jewish Immigration to the United States from 1881 to 1910," *Studies in History, Economics and Public Law*, volume 59 (New York: Columbia University, 1914), 474.

[30] John Klier, *Russians, Jews, and the Pogroms of 1881–1882* (New York: Cambridge University Press, 2011), 31.

[31] *Ibid.*

[32] Davis, 76.

[33] "The Photo Archive," database with images, *Yad Vashem* (`http://collections1.yadvashem.org/search.asp?lang=ENG&rsvr=7` : accessed 11 Nov 2017), entry "Wyszogrod, Poland, The market square," Item ID 97476.

[34] Joseph, 476–477.

[35] Birmingham, 137.

[36] Joseph, 479.

[37] "A People At Risk," article, *Immigration: Polish/Russian*, Library of Congress (`https://www.loc.gov/teachers/classroommaterials/presentationsandactivities/presentations/immigration/polish5.html` : accessed 10 Oct 2017).

[38] Joseph, 484.

[39] Ira A. Glazier, ed., *Migration from the Russian Empire: June 1889–July 1890*, vol. 5 (Baltimore: Genealogical Publishing, 1998), ix

[40] *Ibid.*, x.

[41] Howe, 119.

[42] Glazier, ix.

[43] Howe, 21.

[44] Davis, 76.

[45] *Ibid.*, 73.

[46] Translation of birth certificate for Abraham Arbeiter; see "Translations" appendix.

[47] Howe, 24.

[48] General Register Office of England, marriage entry no. 57 (1899

Mile End), Abraham Arbeiter and Sarah Jacobowitz; Her Majesty's Passport Office.

[49] Berrol, 13–14.

[50] Peter Stone, *The History of the Port of London: A Vast Emporium of All Nations* (South Yorkshire, England: Pen & Sword, 2017), 163.

[51] General Register Office of England, marriage entry no. 57 (1899 Mile End), Abraham Arbeiter and Sarah Jacobowitz.

[52] Berrol, 17.

[53] Philip MacDougall, *London and the Georgian Navy* (Stroud, United Kingdom: The History Press, 2013), online edition (`https://books.google.com/books?id=UvcSDQAAQBAJ` : accessed 15 Oct 2017).

[54] Michaels, 42. Though Michaels includes this photograph in his image-heavy book, he notes that the original source is unknown.

[55] Berrol, 43.

[56] *Ibid.*, 95.

[57] General Register Office of England, marriage entry no. 57 (1899 Mile End), Abraham Arbeiter and Sarah Jacobowitz.

[58] Marc Michaels, *The East London Synagogue: Outpost Of Another World*, fourth edition (London: Kulmus Publishing, 2013), 23.

[59] *Ibid.*, 22.

[60] *Ibid.*, 35.

[61] "East London Synagogue," *Jewish Communities & Records* (`https://www.jewishgen.org/jcr-uk/London/EE_eastlondon_utd/index.htm` : accessed 12 Oct 2017).

[62] Michaels, 52.

[63] "Search Our Database," *Jewish Records Indexing - Poland* (`http://jri-poland.org/jriplweb.htm`), Wyszogrod PSA Books of Residence, entry for Abram Arbajter, house 166.

[64] Louise Jordan Miln, *Wooings and Weddings in Many Climes* (Chicago: Herbert S. Stone & Company, 1900), 282.

[65] Manifest, S.S. *Celtic*, 27 May 1907, stamped p. 94, index number 17, Abraham Arbeiter.

[66] Manifest, S.S. *St. Paul*, 17 Nov 1907, stamped p. 19, index numbers 5–8, Sarah, Rebecca, Salomon [*sic*] and Benny Arbeiter; *Passenger and Crew Lists of Vessels Arriving at New York , NY, 1897-1957*, microfilm publication T715, (Washington: National Archives

and Records Service), roll 1042, frame 338–339.

[67] "82-86 Old Montague Street with 12-18 Greatorex Street," *Survey of London* (`https://surveyoflondon.org/map/feature/443/detail/` : accessed 11 Nov 2017).

[68] 1901 English census, Mile End Old Town civil parish, London, Stepney division, household 67, Davis, Hannah, Nelly, Jacob, Rosie and Miriam Arbeiter; image, *Ancestry.com* (`https://www.ancestry.com/interactive/7814/LNDRG13_330_331-0212/19573898` : accessed 11 Nov 2017).

[69] "Find a Grave," *US [United Synagogue] Burial*, database with images (`https://www.theus.org.uk/category/find-grave` : accessed 11 Oct 2017); entry for Hannah Yetta Arbiter; East Ham Cemetery.

[70] 1901 English census, Mile End Old Town civil parish, London, hhold 67, Davis, Hannah, Nelly, Jacob, Rosie and Miriam Arbeiter.

[71] 1901 English census, Mile End Old Town civil parish, London, Stepney division, household 304, Isaac, Betsy and Evelyn Arbiter; image, *Ancestry.com* (`https://www.ancestry.com/interactive/7814/LNDRG13_330_331-0212/19573898` : accessed 11 Nov 2017).

[72] Charles E. Goad Ltd., "Insurance Plan of London Vol. XI: sheet 322," *British Library Online Gallery*, online image of map (`http://www.bl.uk/onlinegallery/onlineex/firemaps/england/london/xi/mapsu145ubu22u11u2uf322r.html` : accessed 11 Nov 2017).

[73] "Chicksand Street to Old Montague Street - early history," *Survey of London* (`https://surveyoflondon.org/map/feature/179/detail/#chicksand-street-to-old-montague-street-early-history` : accessed 11 Nov 2017).

[74] London School of Economics & Political Science, "Charles Booth's London," online images of maps (`https://booth.lse.ac.uk/map/18/-0.0703/51.5174/100/0?marker=534132.0,181694.0` : accessed 11 Nov 2017).

[75] *Ibid.*

[76] General Register Office of England, birth registration no. 175 (1900 Mile End New Town, London), Rebecca Arbiter; Her Majesty's Passport Office.

[77] *Ibid.*, birth registration no. 402 (1903 Mile End, London), Solomon Arbeiter; Her Majesty's Passport Office.

[78] *Ibid.*, birth registration no. 309 (1905 Mile End Old Town South Western), Benjamin Arbeter; Her Majesty's Passport Office.

[79] Berrol, 5.

[80] General Register Office of England, death registration no. 91 (1919 Mile End Old Town South Western), Hannah Arbeiter; Her Majesty's Passport Office.

[81] "Find a Grave," *US Burial*, database with images (https://www. theus.org.uk/category/find-grave : accessed 11 Oct 2017); entry for Hannah Yetta Arbiter; East Ham Cemetery.

[82] General Register Office of England, death registration no. 118 (1929 Mile End Old Town), Davis Arbeiter; Her Majesty's Passport Office.

[83] Her Majesty's Courts & Tribunals Service, Grant of Letters of Administration for Davis Arbeiter, 22 Jan 1930.

[84] 1901 English census, Mile End Old Town civil parish, London, hhold 304, Isaac, Betsy and Evelyn Arbiter.

[85] "Find a Grave," *US Burial*, database with images (https://www. theus.org.uk/category/find-grave : accessed 19 Nov 2017); entry for Isaac Arbeiter, died 22 Nov 1923; East Ham Cemetery.

[86] "England & Wales, National Probate Calendar," image, *Ancestry.com* (https://www.ancestry.com/interactive/1904/32858_635001_2113-00073 : accessed 11 Nov 2017), entry for Joseph Hyman Arbiter, died 9 Mar 1962.

[87] Paul Alcantara and Sally J. Hall, "Ivor Arbiter, captain of the music industry and designer of the Beatles' 'drop-T' logo," obituary, *The Independent*, London, England, 23 Sep 2005, online version (http://www.independent.co.uk/news/obituaries/ivor-arbiter-314771.html : accessed 19 Nov 2017).

[88] "UK, Outward Passenger Lists, 1890–1960," image, *Ancestry.com* (https://www.ancestry.com/interactive/2997/41039_b001555-00373 : accessed 11 Nov 2017), ship *Duchess of Bedford*, departure 18 Jul 1940, entry for Ivor Arbiter, ticket no. 173094.

[89] 1911 English census, page 67 (written), Jacob, Sadie, Sidney and Emanuel Arbeiter, Jessie Lambert; image, *Ancestry.com* (https:// www.ancestry.com/interactive/2352/rg14_01287_0141_03/2482422 : accessed 11 Nov 2017).

[90] General Register Office of England, death registration no. 91 (1919 Mile End Old Town South Western), Hannah Arbeiter.

[91] *Ibid.*, death registration no. 221 (1923 Hackney, London), Isaac Arbiter; Her Majesty's Passport Office.

[92] Berrol, 13.

[93] Manifest, S.S. *St. Paul*, 17 Nov 1907, line 8, Sarah Arbeiter and

3 children; *Passenger and Crew Lists of Vessels Arriving at New York , NY, 1897-1957*, microfilm publication T715, (Washington: National Archives and Records Service), roll 1042, frame 294.

[94] Marian L. Smith, "Reading the Record of Detained Aliens." *Manifest Markings* (`https://www.jewishgen.org/InfoFiles/ Manifests/detained/` : accessed 12 Oct 2017).

[95] *Bomb Sight: Mapping the WW2 Bomb Census*, coordinates 51.51854:-0.06625, digital map (`http://bombsight.org` : accessed 11 Nov 2017).

[96] "Victory For East End Preservation Society!," *Spitalfields Life*, blog entry, 17 Apr 2014 (`http://spitalfieldslife.com/2014/04/ 17/victory-for-east-end-preservation-society/` : accessed 11 Nov 2017).

[97] London Borough of Tower Hamlets, "Stepney Green Conservation Area," *Conservation Area Character Appraisals and Management Guidelines*, digital image of report (`http://democracy. towerhamlets.gov.uk/mgConvert2PDF.aspx?ID=7773` : accessed 11 Nov 2017).

[98] Sherwin, 18.

[99] *Ibid.*, 22. This appears to be a mild misquotation: The quote appears to be from Itzhak Zuckerman, a Jewish resistance leader in Poland, who said in a documentary, "If you could lick my heart, it would poison you." He was also trapped *outside* of the Warsaw ghetto during the uprising.

[100] Agence France-Presse, "Used to rebuild Warsaw, Jewish tombstones return to cemeteries," reprinted in *Times of Israel*, online story 24 Oct 2014 (`https://www.timesofisrael.com/used-to- rebuild-warsaw-jewish-tombstones-return-to-cemeteries/` : accessed 16 Nov 2017).

[101] Michal Broniatowski and David M. Herszenhorn, "White nationalists call for ethnic purity at Polish demonstration," *Politico*, 15 Nov 2017 (`https://www.politico.eu/article/white-nationalists- call-for-ethnic-purity-at-polish-independence-day-march/` : accessed 16 Nov 2017).

[102] Anne Applebaum, "Why neo-fascists are making a shocking surge in Poland," *Washington Post*, 13 Nov 2017 (`https://www.washingtonpost. com/news/global-opinions/wp/2017/11/13/why-neo-fascists- are-making-a-shocking-surge-in-poland/` : accessed 16 Nov 2017).

[103] Avi Selk, "Poland defends massive far-right protest that called for a 'White Europe,'" *Washington Post*, 13 Nov 2017 (`https://www. washingtonpost.com/news/worldviews/wp/2017/11/12/pray-for-`

`an-islamic-holocaust-tens-of-thousands-from-europes-far-right-march-in-poland/` : accessed 16 Nov 2017).

[104] Adam Easton, "Polish museum celebrates 1,000 years of Jewish life," *BBC News*, 27 Oct 2014, online article (`http://www.bbc.com/news/world-europe-29741865` : accessed 11 Nov 2017). Also, entry for "Poland" community, *World Jewish Congress: Communities* (`http://www.worldjewishcongress.org/en/about/communities/PL` : accessed 11 Nov 2017).

[105] "Jewish Population of Europe in 1933: Population Data by Country," *United States Holocaust Museum* (`https://www.ushmm.org/wlc/en/article.php?ModuleId=10005161` : accessed 16 Nov 2017).

[106] Nathan Daicz, "From the diary," see chapter "Wyszogród memories."

[107] Swartz, "Return to Poland: In Search of My Parents' Memories."

[108] "European Jewish Cemeteries Initiative," database, *Lo Tishkach Foundation*, entry for "Wyszogrod New Jewish Cemetery (II)" (`http://admin.lo-tishkach.org/Search/Search/ShowCemeterySimple.aspx?QryCemeterySimple=6156` : accessed 11 Nov 2017).

[109] "Jewish gravestones found in Polish house's ceiling," *Times of Israel*, 2 Apr 2014, online version (`http://www.timesofisrael.com/jewish-gravestones-found-in-polish-homes-ceiling/` : accessed 19 Nov 2017). Also: "Jewish Tombstones Used to Pave Roads Return to Cemeteries," *Arutz Sheva*, 24 Oct 2014, online version (`http://www.israelnationalnews.com/News/News.aspx/186540` : accessed 19 Nov 2017).

[110] S. Lawrence, "Poland's Undead Gravestones," *Tablet* (`http://www.tabletmag.com/jewish-arts-and-culture/128998/poland-undead-gravestones` : accessed 19 Nov 2017).

[111] "Multiculture," *Muzeum of Vistula in Wyszogrod* (`http://muzeumwyszogrod.pl/en/ekspozycje/wielokulturowosc/` : accessed 19 Nov 2017).

[112] "European Jewish Cemeteries Initiative," database, *Lo Tishkach Foundation*, entry for "Wyszogrod Old Jewish Cemetery (I)" (`http://www.lo-tishkach.org/database/` : accessed 11 Nov 2017).

[113] Wyszogrod PSA Books of Residence, entry for Haim Aron Bilgoraj, house 124.

[114] Martin Gilbert, *The Routledge Atlas of the Holocaust*, third edition (London: Routledge, 2002), 136. It should be noted that there are many possibilities for how the family met their end, for reasons including a lack of clarity regarding where many Wyszogród resi-

dents were actually sent. It's possible they were sent to the Jewish ghetto at Nowy Dwor in late 1942 and later sent to Auschwitz.

[115] "Wyszogród," online article, *kirkuty.xip.pl* (http://www.kirkuty. xip.pl/wyszogrod.html : accessed 11 Nov 2017).

[116] Wyszogród synagogue aron ha-kodesh, ca. 1928; digitized by *Fotopolska* user Cristoforo (http://wyszogrod.fotopolska.eu/411892, foto.html?o=b100454 : accessed 11 Nov 2017).

[117] General Register Office of England, birth registration no. 402 (1903 Whitechapel), Solomon Arbeiter; Her Majesty's Passport Office.

[118] Jay Arbeiter (Delray Beach, Fla.), phone interview by Richard Abdill, 10 Jun 2017; transcript held privately by interviewer, Minneapolis, Minn.

[119] 1910 U.S. census, New York, NY, population schedule, Borough Manhattan, family 28, Abraham, Sarah, Rebecca, Soloman [*sic*] and Benjamin Arbeiter, Sam Finkle; image, *Ancestry.com* (https://www. ancestry.com/interactive/7884/4450086_01185/ : accessed 1 Oct 2017); citing NARA microfilm publication T624, roll 1024.

[120] Claire and Solomon Arbeiter, c. 1927; digitized and privately held by the author, Minneapolis, Minn., 2017. From the collection of Ann (Siegel) Dondero, courtesy of Mark Siegel.

[121] City of New York, birth certificate no. 12299 (1908 Brooklyn), Clara Reinstein; New York City Department of Records.

[122] C*Ibid.*, marriage certificate no. 1995 (1927 Brooklyn), Solomon Arbeiter and Clara Reinstein; New York City Department of Records.

[123] *Ibid.*, death certificate no. 8549 (1929, Bronx), Sylvia Arbeiter; New York City Department of Records.

[124] Jay Arbeiter, phone interview, 10 Jun 2017.

[125] Ann, Solomon and Jay Arbeiter, c. 1936; digitized and privately held by the author, Minneapolis, Minn., 2017. From the collection of Ann (Siegel) Dondero.

[126] City of New York, death certificate no. 8549 (1929, Bronx), Sylvia Arbeiter.

[127] "U.S. Public Records Index, 1950–1993, Volume 1," database, *Ancestry.com*, entry for Joan D Arbeiter, born 8 May 1937 (https: //search.ancestry.com/cgi-bin/sse.dll?indiv=1&dbid=1788 &h=63803232 : accessed 11 Nov 2017).

[128] 1920 U.S. census, New York NY, population schedule, Borough Manhattan, family 101, Abraham, Sarah, Rebecca, Solomon and

Benjamin Arbeiter; image, *Ancestry.com* (`https://www.ancestry.com/interactive/6061/4313940-01208/` : accessed 1 Oct 2017); citing NARA microfilm publication T625, roll 1217.

[129] 1930 U.S. census, Queens County, New York, population schedule, 2nd Assembly District, family 609, Soloman [*sic*] and Clara Arbeiter; image, *Ancestry.com* (`https://www.ancestry.com/interactive/6224/4639134_00729/` : accessed 1 Oct 2017).

[130] Jay Arbeiter, phone interview, 10 Jun 2017.

[131] 1930 U.S. census, Kings County, New York, population schedule, Brooklyn, family 396, Simon, Sarah and Eva Sovelove, Ester, Dora, Tillie and Lena Schwartz, David, Tillie and Jerome Reinstein; image, *Ancestry.com* (`https://www.ancestry.com/interactive/6224/4638827_00107/` : accessed 1 Oct 2017).

[132] 1940 U.S. census, Nassau County, New York, population schedule, Hempstead Town, household 66, Joseph, Goldie, Dorothy, Ethel and Martin Task, Rose Newman; image, *Ancestry.com* (`https://www.ancestry.com/interactive/2442/m-t0627-02690-00462/` : accessed 1 Oct 2017); citing NARA microfilm publication T627, roll 2690.

[133] Jay Arbeiter, phone interview, 10 Jun 2017.

[134] Florida Department of Health, "Florida Divorce Index, 1927–2001," database, *Ancestry.com* (`https://www.ancestry.com/interactive/8837/FLDIV_0116-0014/` : accessed 1 Oct 2017), entry for Solomon and Clarie [*sic*] Arbeiter, certificate 4850 (1955).

[135] Sol and Ina appear in photographs together at Mark Siegel's bar mitzvah in that year, though it's possible they were not married at the time.

[136] "Sweden, Emigrants Registered in Church Books, 1783-1991," database, *Ancestry.com* (`http://search.ancestry.com/cgi-bin/sse.dll?indiv=1&dbid=61085&h=880540&tid=84096417` : accessed 1 Oct 2017), entry for Aina Kristina Eriksson, departure 31 Jan 1925 from Maria Magdalena, Stockholm.

[137] *Ibid.*

[138] Manifest, S.S. *Drottningholm*, 24 Feb 1925, stamped list 5, index numbers 6–8, Helmer, Anna Viktoria and Aina Kristina Eriksson; *Passenger and Crew Lists of Vessels Arriving at New York , NY, 1897-1957*, microfilm publication T715, (Washington: National Archives and Records Service), roll 3611, frame 1158.

[139] *Ibid.*

[140] Social Security Administration, "Social Security Death Index,"

database, *Ancestry.com* (http://search.ancestry.com/cgi-bin/sse.dll?indiv=1&dbid=3693&h=1554288 : accessed 1 Oct 2017), entry for Ina Arbeiter, died 1 Dec 2002, SS no. 104-01-2842.

[141] Florida Department of Health, "Florida Divorce Index, 1927–2001," database, *Ancestry.com* (https://www.ancestry.com/interactive/8837/FLDIV_0036-0035/ : accessed 1 Oct 2017), entry for Rolf E. and Ina K. Myhrman, certificate 668 (1938).

[142] "New York City, Marriage Indexes, 1907–1995," database, *Ancestry.com* (http://search.ancestry.com/cgi-bin/sse.dll?indiv=1&dbid=61406&h=7582571&tid=84096417 : accessed 1 Oct 2017), entries for Aina Erikson and Rolph E Myhrman, license 6774, 27 Apr 1929.

[143] 1940 U.S. census, Kings County, New York, population schedule, Brooklyn, household 144, Helmer and Anna Erikson, Aina, Barbara and Ingegerd Myhrman; image, *Ancestry.com* (https://www.ancestry.com/interactive/2442/m-t0627-02589-00378/ : accessed 1 Oct 2017); citing NARA microfilm publication T627, roll 2589.

[144] "Florida Divorce Index, 1927–2001," database, *Ancestry.com*, entry for Rolf E. and Ina K. Myhrman.

[145] 1940 U.S. census, Kings County, NY, pop. sch., hhold 144, Helmer and Anna Erikson, Aina, Barbara and Ingegerd Myhrman.

[146] Nancy (Siegel) Abdill (Delran, NJ), phone interview by Richard Abdill, 20 Jun 2017; transcript held privately by interviewer, Minneapolis, Minn.

[147] Nancy (Siegel) Abdill and Richard Abdill Jr. (Delran, NJ), phone interview by the author, 28 Jun 2017; transcript held privately by interviewer, Minneapolis, Minn.

[148] David Shyovitz, "Yiddish: History & Development of Yiddish," *Jewish Virtual Library* (http://www.jewishvirtuallibrary.org/history-and-development-of-yiddish : accessed 1 Oct 2017).

[149] State of Florida, death certificate no. 73-002849, Solomon Arbeiter; Florida Department of Health.

[150] Social Security Administration, "Social Security Death Index," database, *Ancestry.com* (http://search.ancestry.com/cgi-bin/sse.dll?indiv=1&dbid=3693&h=1554288 : accessed 1 Oct 2017), entry for Ina Arbeiter, died 1 Dec 2002, SS no. 104-01-2842. Note: This record gives Ina's date of death as 1 Dec, which contradicts an obituary published 9 Dec 2002 giving the date as 8 Dec: "Ina Arbeiter," obituary, *Legacy.com* (http://www.legacy.com/obituaries/sunsentinel/obituary.aspx?n=ina-arbeiter&pid=643623 : accessed 1 Oct 2017). Given the inconsistency of precise dates found in the Social Security

databases, preference has been given to the obit.

[151] Borough of Metuchen, death certificate, Claire Arbeiter, died 5 Oct 1992; New Jersey State Department of Health.

[152] Ann (Arbeiter) Dondero, Nancy (Siegel) Abdill and and Claire (Reinstein) Arbeiter; digitized and privately held by the author, Minneapolis, Minn., 2017. From the collection of Ann (Siegel) Dondero.

[153] Claire, Ann and Jay Arbeiter, Arthur Gladstone, Sol Arbeiter; digitized and privately held by the author, Minneapolis, Minn., 2017. From the collection of Ann (Siegel) Dondero.

[154] Ann (Arbeiter) Dondero and Jay Arbeiter, 1968; digitized by the author; privately held by Nancy Abdill, Delran, NJ, 2017.

[155] Ann and Claire Arbeiter; digitized and privately held by the author, Minneapolis, Minn., 2017. From the collection of Ann (Siegel) Dondero.

[156] Abraham and Pearl Arbeiter; digitized and privately held by the author, Minneapolis, Minn., 2017. From the collection of Ann (Siegel) Dondero.

[157] Translation of birth certificate for Abraham Arbeiter; see "Translations" appendix.

[158] General Register Office of England, marriage entry no. 57 (1899 Mile End), Abraham Arbeiter and Sarah Jacobowitz.

[159] "JewishGen Online Worldwide Burial Registry," database, *JewishGen* (https://www.jewishgen.org/databases/jowbr.php?rec=J_NY_0081819 : accessed 2 Oct 2017), entry for Sarah (Arbeiter) Finkel, died 14 Jan 1963.

[160] 1901 English census, Whitechapel civil Parish, London, hhold 64, Abraham, Sharha and Rebecca Arbiter.

[161] "UK, Outward Passenger Lists, 1890–1960," database with images, *Ancestry.com* (https://www.ancestry.com/interactive/2997/40610_B000554-00092/41313930 : accessed 11 Nov 2017), entry for Abraha [*sic*] Arbeiter, ticket 366398.

[162] 1901 English census, Whitechapel civil Parish, London, Tower Hamlets division, household 64, Abraham, Sharha [*sic*] and Rebecca Arbiter; image, *Ancestry.com* (https://www.ancestry.com/interactive/7814/LNDRG13_301_303-0360/ : accessed 2 Oct 2017).

[163] 1940 U.S. census, New York, NY, population schedule, Manhattan Borough, household 135, Betty, Louis and Harold Buchalter; image, *Ancestry.com* (https://www.ancestry.com/interactive/2442/m-t0627-02636-00977/ : accessed 2 Oct 2017); citing NARA micro-

film publication T627, roll 2636. It's worth noting that even though Betty's husband Louis is listed in the census entry, Betty is listed as the head of household, the only example of the wife being given precedence over her husband in any census record cited in this book. The census was recorded 11 Apr 1940—six days after Louis Buchalter was sentenced to 30 years to life in prison on extortion charges.

[164] General Register Office of England, birth registration no. 175 (1900 Whitechapel), Rebecca Arbiter [*sic*]; Her Majesty's Passport Office. Betty's gravestone and an index of Florida death records gives her birth date as 12 Oct 1901, but her birth certificate shows that her birth was recorded at the end of 1900. In addition, she is recorded as being 6 months old in the 1901 English census, which, were she born in October 1901, would have been impossible.

[165] "Florida Death Index, 1877–1998," database, *Ancestry.com* (`http://search.ancestry.com/cgi-bin/sse.dll?indiv=1&dbid=7338&h=2788304` : accessed 2 Oct 2017), entry for Betty Jarwood, died 6 Mar 1983.

[166] *Find A Grave*, database with images (`https://www.findagrave.com/cgi-bin/fg.cgi?page=gr&GRid=147972312` : accessed 2 Oct 2017), memorial 147972312; Betty Jarwood; Temple Beth El Memorial Gardens; gravestone added by T. Jason Brown.

[167] "New York, New York, Marriage Certificate Index 1866-1937," database, *Ancestry.com* (`http://search.ancestry.com/cgi-bin/sse.dll?indiv=1&dbid=9105&h=2713420` : accessed 2 Oct 2017), entries for Betty Arbeiter and Jack Wasserman, certificate no. 23825 (1920, Manhattan).

[168] Kavieff, 79.

[169] Federal Bureau of Investigation, "Louis (Lepke) Buchalter Part 3 of 4," digitized docket, *FBI Records: The Vault* (`https://vault.fbi.gov/` : accessed 24 Sep 2017), p. 10.

[170] Social Security Administration, "Social Security Death Index," database, *Ancestry.com* (`http://search.ancestry.com/cgi-bin/sse.dll?indiv=1&dbid=3693&h=7801858` : accessed 2 Oct 2017), entry for Harold Buchalter, SS no. 112-01-8108.

[171] "New York City, Marriage License Indexes, 1907-1995," database, *Ancestry.com* (`http://search.ancestry.com/cgi-bin/sse.dll?indiv=1&dbid=61406&h=8291647` : accessed 2 Oct 2017), entries for Betty Wasserman and Louis Buchhalter [*sic*], certificate no. 18824 (1931, Manhattan).

[172] Social Security Administration, "Social Security Death Index," database, *Ancestry.com* (`http://search.ancestry.com/cgi-bin/sse.`

dll?indiv=1&dbid=3693&h=30503080 : accessed 2 Oct 2017), entry for Arthur Jarwood, SS no. 072-18-1410.

[173]General Register Office of England, birth registration no. 402 (1903 Whitechapel), Solomon Arbeiter.

[174]State of Florida, death certificate no. 73-002849, Solomon Arbeiter.

[175]General Register Office of England, birth registration no. 309 (1905 Mile End Old Town), Benjamin Arbeter [sic]; Her Majesty's Passport Office.

[176]Social Security Administration, "Social Security Death Index," database, *Ancestry.com* (http://search.ancestry.com/cgi-bin/sse.dll?indiv=1&dbid=3693&h=1554244 : accessed 2 Oct 2017), entry for Ben Arbeiter, SS no. 123-07-5850.

[177]Social Security Administration, "Social Security Applications and Claims Index, 1936–2007," database, *Ancestry.com* (https://search.ancestry.com/cgi-bin/sse.dll?indiv=1&dbid=60901&h=21881520 : accessed 11 Nov 2017), entry for Sylvia Greenberg Arbeiter, died 31 Jan 2001, SS no. 261-15-7171.

[178]1930 U.S. census, Bronx, New York, population schedule, family 61, Benjiman [sic], Sylvia and Elaine Arbeiter; image, *Ancestry.com* (https://www.ancestry.com/interactive/6224/4661149_00155/30780466 : accessed 11 Nov 2017); citing FHL microfilm 2,341,214.

[179]1940 U.S. census, Bronx, New York, population schedule, Jacob and Frieda Bersky, Sylvia and Elaine Arbeiter; image, *Ancestry.com* (https://www.ancestry.com/interactive/2442/m-t0627-02481-00652/3961034 : accessed 11 Nov 2017); citing NARA microfilm publication T627, roll 2481.

[180]A "Robert Arbeiter" married in Newburgh in 1964; the wedding announcement describes him as "son of Mr. and Mrs. Ben Arbeiter, also of Newburgh," and circumstantial evidence suggests the couple later moved to Florida, where "our" Ben lived. "Miss Hoyt Is Married," (Binghamton) *Press and Sun-Bulletin*, 25 Apr 1964, page 4, column 5.

[181]Mark Siegel (St. Petersburg, Fla.), text message conversation with Richard Abdill, 17 Jun 2017; transcript held privately by interviewer, Minneapolis, Minn.

[182]Mary Arbeiter identified by Mark Siegel; we have no documentation of her marriage to Ben.

[183]Arbeiter siblings and their spouses; digitized by the author, privately held by Nancy Abdill, Delran, NJ, 2017.

[184] "United States World War II Draft Registration Cards, 1942," images, Ancestry.com (https://www.ancestry.com/interactive/1002/2wwii_2370859-5839/7421625 : accessed 11 Nov 2017), card for Abraham Arbeiter.

[185] Jeffrey S. Gurock, *When Harlem Was Jewish, 1870–1930* (New York: Columbia University Press, 1979), 36.

[186] *Ibid.*, 28.

[187] *Ibid.*, 1.

[188] 1910 U.S. census, New York, New York, population schedule, Borough Manhattan, family 28, Abraham, Sarah, Rebecca, Soloman [*sic*] and Benjamin Arbeiter, Samuel Finkle [*sic*]; image, *Ancestry.com* (https://www.ancestry.com/interactive/7884/4450086_01185/18877691 : accessed 11 Nov 2017); citing NARA microfilm publication T624, roll 1024.

[189] Jay Arbeiter, phone interview, 10 Jun 2017.

[190] 1925 New York state census, Sullivan County, Mamakating town, Abraham, Sadie, Solomon and Benjamin Arbeiter; image, *Ancestry.com* (https://www.ancestry.com/interactive/2704/32849_b094363-00289/25335500 : accessed 11 Nov 2017).

[191] 1925 New York state census, New York City, assembly district 17, Sarah, Rebecca, Sol and Ben Arbeiter, Sam Finkel; image, *Ancestry.com* (https://www.ancestry.com/interactive/2704/32849_b119414-00034/17198870 : accessed 11 Nov 2017).

[192] "United States World War II Draft Registration Cards, 1942," images, Ancestry.com (https://www.ancestry.com/interactive/1002/2wwii_2370859-5839/7421625 : accessed 11 Nov 2017), card for Samuel Finkel.

[193] 1910 U.S. census, New York, NY, pop. sch., fam. 28, Abraham, Sarah, Rebecca, Soloman and Benjamin Arbeiter, Sam Finkle.

[194] *Ibid.*

[195] Annie Polland and Daniel Soyer, *Emerging Metropolis: New York Jews in the Age of Immigration, 1840–1920* (New York: New York University Press, 2015), 123.

[196] Howe, 179.

[197] Abraham and Blanche Arbeiter; digitized and privately held by the author, Minneapolis, Minn., 2017. From the collection of Ann (Siegel) Dondero.

[198] "New York, New York, Marriage Certificate Index 1866–1937," database, *Ancestry.com* (https://search.ancestry.com/cgi-bin/sse.

dll?indiv=1&dbid=9105&h=4636155 : accessed 11 Nov 2017), entry
for Sarah A Jakus marriage to Samuel Finkel, certificate no. 2555,
30 Mar 1936.

[199] Federal Bureau of Investigation, "Louis (Lepke) Buchalter Part
1 of 4," p. 10.

[200] "U.S. City Directories, 1822–1995," database, *Ancestry.com* (https:
//search.ancestry.com/cgi-bin/sse.dll?indiv=1&dbid=2469&h=60661303
: accessed 11 Nov 2017), entry for Samuel Finkel, 1939, in Newburgh,
New York.

[201] Jay Arbeiter, phone interview, 10 Jun 2017.

[202] "JewishGen Online Worldwide Burial Registry," database, *Jew-
ishGen.org* (https://www.jewishgen.org/databases/jowbr.php?rec=
J_NY_0081819 : accessed 11 Nov 2017), entry for Sarah (Arbeiter)
Finkel and Samuel Finkel, Congregation Agudas Israel Cemetery,
New Windsor, NY.

[203] *Ibid.*

[204] "New York City, Marriage License Indexes, 1907–1995," database
with images, *Ancestry.com* (https://search.ancestry.com/cgi-bin/
sse.dll?indiv=1&dbid=61406&h=8178281 : accessed 11 Nov 2017),
entry for Blanche Friedman marriage to Barney Satter [*sic*], license
dated 27 Dec 1912.

[205] 1940 U.S. census, Queens County, New York, population schedule, household 99, Abraham and Blanch [*sic*] Arbeiter, Joseph Salter;
image, *Ancestry.com* (https://www.ancestry.com/interactive/2442/
m-t0627-02741-00811/6344885 : accessed 19 Nov 2017); citing NARA
microfilm publication T627, roll 2741.

[206] "New York, New York, Marriage Certificate Index 1866–1937,"
database, *Ancestry.com* (https://search.ancestry.com/cgi-bin/sse.
dll?indiv=1&dbid=9105&h=2671237 : accessed 11 Nov 2017), entry
for Blanche Friedman marriage to Barney Salter, 4 Jan 1913, certificate 1236.

[207] "New York, New York, Death Index, 1862–1948," database, *An-
cestry.com* (https://search.ancestry.com/cgi-bin/sse.dll?indiv=
1&dbid=9131&h=2358401 : accessed 11 Nov 2017), entry for Bernard
Salter, died 14 Dec 1918, Manhattan, certificate no. 42252.

[208] 1915 New York state census, Kings County, New York, Brooklyn, Barney, Blanche, Henry and Joseph Salter; image, *Ancestry.com*
(https://www.ancestry.com/interactive/2703/32848_B094153-00160/
7113398 : accessed 11 Nov 2017).

[209] "U.S., Department of Veterans Affairs BIRLS Death File, 1850-

2010," database, *Ancestry.com* (https://search.ancestry.com/cgi-bin/sse.dll?indiv=1&dbid=2441&h=7760657 : accessed 11 Nov 2017), entry for Joseph Salter, died 23 Aug 1983.

[210] 1940 U.S. census, Queens County, New York, pop. sch., hhold 99, Abraham and Blanch Arbeiter, Joseph Salter.

[211] "U.S., Department of Veterans Affairs BIRLS Death File, 1850-2010," entry for Joseph Salter, died 23 Aug 1983.

[212] FBI investigatory files show that they picked up on a "Blanche Arbeiter" in November 1937 whom they believed to be linked to Abraham's family. Federal Bureau of Investigation, "Louis (Lepke) Buchalter Part 2 of 4," 11.

[213] Mount Hebron Cemetery (Flushing, NY), online interment search (http://www.mounthebroncemetery.com/location.asp?id=5669454 : accessed 11 Nov 2017), entry for Blanche Arbeiter, died 26 Oct 1959.

[214] *Ibid.* (http://www.mounthebroncemetery.com/location.asp?id=5693916 : accessed 11 Nov 2017), entry for Abraham Arbeiter, died 8 Sep 1966.

[215] Social Security Administration, "Social Security Applications and Claims Index, 1936–2007," database, *Ancestry.com* (https://search.ancestry.com/cgi-bin/sse.dll?indiv=1&dbid=60901&h=13158633 : accessed 11 Nov 2017), entry for Louis Buchalter, born 6 Feb 1897, SS no. 150-01-4877.

[216] Paul R. Kavieff, *The Life and Times of Lepke Buchalter: America's Most Ruthless Labor Racketeer* (Fort Lee, NJ: Barricade Books, 2006).

[217] Jay, Betty and Ann Arbeiter at Camp Allegro, New York, ca. 1946; digitized and privately held by the author, Minneapolis, Minn., 2017. From the collection of Ann (Siegel) Dondero.

[218] Kavieff, 80.

[219] Scott Alexander, "Duke Ellington and his Kentucky Club Orchestra," *The Red Hot Jazz Archive* (http://www.redhotjazz.com/kentucky.html : accessed 19 Nov 2017).

[220] Mark Tucker, *Ellington: The Early Years* (Champaign, Ill.: University of Illinois Press, 1995), 110.

[221] Kavieff, 80.

[222] "Ben Marden, 77, Who Owned The Riviera Nightclub, Is Dead," *New York Times*, 8 Apr 1973, online edition (http://www.nytimes.com/1973/04/08/archives/ben-marden-77-who-owned-the-riviera-nightclub-is-dead-ran-havana.html : accessed 19 Oct

2017).

[223] Rusty E. Frank, *TAP! The Greatest Tap Dance Stars and Their Stories, 1900–1955* (Cambridge: Da Capo Press, 1995), 31.

[224] Ellen NicKenzie Lawson, "Geographical List of Manhattan Prohibition Sites," *Smugglers, Bootleggers, And Scofflaws: Prohibition And New York City,* online addenda
(`http://smugglersbootleggersandscofflaws.com/geography-significant-sites-prohibition-new-york-city/` : accessed 19 Oct 2017).

[225] "Ben Marden, 77, Who Owned The Riviera Nightclub, Is Dead," *New York Times*, 8 Apr 1973.

[226] Turkus and Feder, 4.

[227] Kavieff, 1.

[228] *Ibid.*, 80.

[229] *Ibid.*

[230] Nancy (Siegel) Abdill (Delran, NJ), phone interview by Richard Abdill, 21 Oct 2017; transcript held privately by interviewer, Minneapolis, Minn.

[231] Federal Bureau of Investigation, "Louis (Lepke) Buchalter Part 2 of 4," 14.

[232] Nancy Abdill, phone interview, 21 Oct 2017.

[233] Federal Bureau of Investigation, "Louis (Lepke) Buchalter Part 3 of 4," 10.

[234] "Defense Rests in Lepke Trial; Closing Arguments to Jury Begin on Monday," *New York Sun*, 23 Feb 1940.

[235] Al Aumuller, "Louis "Lepke" Buchalter, center, handcuffed to J. Edgar Hoover, on the left, with another man on the right, at entrance to courthouse," *New York World-Telegram & Sun Newspaper Photograph Collection*, Library of Congress Prints and Photographs Division, reproduction LC-USZ62-134663.

[236] Federal Bureau of Investigation, "Louis (Lepke) Buchalter Part 2 of 4," 11.

[237] *Ibid.*, pgs. 11 and 13.

[238] Kavieff, 80.

[239] *Ibid.*, 83.

[240] Zwillman implicated by Carl Sifakis, *The Mafia Encyclopedia*, third edition (New York: Facts On File, 1999), 261. The others

included in Albert Fried, *The Rise and Fall of the Jewish Gangster in America* (New York: Columbia University Press, 1980), 212–213.

[241] Kavieff, 127.

[242] Walter Winchell, "Winchell Relates Dramatic Story Of Delivering Lepke To Hoover," *Rochester Democrat and Chronicle*, 26 Aug 1939, page 5, columns 2–3.

[243] The chair used in Buchalter's execution was first used in 1890, in the first execution by electric chair in the world. "1890: First execution by electric chair," *This Day In History* (http://www.history.com/this-day-in-history/first-execution-by-electric-chair : accessed 6 Oct 2017).

[244] Turkus and Feder, 409–412, 416.

[245] Nancy Abdill, phone interview, 21 Oct 2017.

[246] The Reinstein siblings at the Riobamba, early 1940s; digitized and privately held by the author, Minneapolis, Minn., 2017. From the collection of Ann (Siegel) Dondero.

[247] "Visit Lepke In Death House," *Daily Mail*, Hagerstown, Md., 3 Mar 1944, pg. 2; online image of print edition (https://www.newspapers.com/image/22163551/ : accessed 11 Nov 2017).

[248] 1901 English census, Mile End Old Town civil parish, London, hhold 67, Davis, Hannah, Nelly, Jacob, Rosie and Miriam Arbeiter.

[249] Wyszogrod PSA Books of Residence, entry for Dawid Arbajter, born 1845, house 166.

[250] Translated birth certificate for Hana Itta Biłgoraj, see "Translations" appendix.

[251] 1911 England census, Davis and Annie Arbieter [*sic*]; image, *Ancestry.com* (https://www.ancestry.com/interactive/2352/rg14_01601_0475_03/323331 : accessed 11 Nov 2017).

[252] Wyszogrod PSA Books of Residence, entry for Isak Arbajter, house 166.

[253] 1911 England census, Isaac, Betsy, Evline [*sic*], Ester and Joseph Arbiter; image, *Ancestry.com* (https://www.ancestry.com/interactive/2352/rg14_01590_0397_03/307352 : accessed 11 Nov 2017).

[254] Wyszogrod PSA Books of Residence, entry for Isak Arbajter, house 166.

[255] General Register Office of England, death registration no. 221 (1923 Hackney), Isaac Arbiter; Her Majesty's Passport Office.

256 Wyszogrod PSA Books of Residence, entry for Isak Arbajter, house 166.

257 "England & Wales, Civil Registration Birth Index, 1837–1915," database with images, *Ancestry.com* (https://search.ancestry.com/cgi-bin/sse.dll?indiv=1&dbid=8912&h=43777960 : accessed 11 Nov 2017), entry for Esther Arbiter, birth registered first quarter 1902, Mile End Old Town, pg. 476.

258 1911 England census, Isaac, Betsy, Evline, Ester and Joseph Arbiter.

259 Geoff Nicholls, *The Drum Book: A History of the Rock Drum Kit* (London: Backbeat Books, 2008).

260 "UK, Outward Passenger Lists, 1890–1960," entry for Ivor Arbiter, ticket no. 173094.

261 Wyszogrod PSA Books of Residence, entry for Laja Arbajter, house 166.

262 *FreeBMD* vital records index (https://www.freebmd.org.uk/ : accessed 11 Nov 2017), entry for Leah Arbiter, age 36, died third quarter 1906, Whitechapel district, volume 1c, page 192.

263 Wyszogrod PSA Books of Residence, entry for Laja Arbajter, house 166.

264 *Ibid.*, entry for Abram Arbajter, house 166.

265 "United States World War II Draft Registration Cards, 1942," card for Abraham Arbeiter.

266 Wyszogrod PSA Books of Residence, entry for Nauma Arbajter, house 166.

267 1901 English census, Mile End Old Town civil parish, London, Davis, Hannah, Nelly, Jacob, Rosie and Miriam Arbeiter.

268 *FreeBMD* vital records index, entry for Nancy Arbiter, age 40, died third quarter 1918, Whitechapel district, volume 1c, page 190.

269 Wyszogrod PSA Books of Residence, entry for Jakow Arbajter, house 166.

270 "England & Wales, National Probate Calendar," image, *Ancestry.com* (https://www.ancestry.com/interactive/1904/32858_635001_2113-00073 : accessed 11 Nov 2017), entry for Jacob Arbeiter, died 21 May 1946.

271 1901 English census, Mile End Old Town civil parish, London, Davis, Hannah, Nelly, Jacob, Rosie and Miriam Arbeiter.

272 1911 English census, Jacob, Sadie, Sidney and Emanuel Arbeiter,

Jessie Lambert.

[273]Third child referenced in "England & Wales, National Probate Calendar," entry for Jacob Arbeiter, died 21 May 1946.

[274]Wyszogrod PSA Books of Residence, entry for Rasza Arbajter, house 166.

[275]1901 English census, Mile End Old Town civil parish, London, Davis, Hannah, Nelly, Jacob, Rosie and Miriam Arbeiter.

[276]*FreeBMD* vital records index, entry for Rose Arbiter, married third quarter 1906, Whitechapel district, volume 1c, page 503.

[277]1911 England census, Hyman, Rose and Davie Appleby; image, *Ancestry.com* (https://www.ancestry.com/interactive/2352/rg14_01600_0015_03/320953 : accessed 11 Nov 2017).

[278]"Search Our Database," *Jewish Records Indexing - Poland* (http://jri-poland.org/jriplweb.htm), Wyszogrod PSA Births, Marriages, Deaths 1886-1906, entry for birth of Ryfka Arbajter, document 43.

[279]Wyszogrod PSA Books of Residence, entry for Rasza Arbajter, house 166.

[280]Wyszogrod PSA Births, Marriages, Deaths 1886-1906, entry for death of Ryfka Arbajter, document 24.

[281]Wyszogrod PSA Books of Residence, entry for Mariem Arbajter, house 166.

[282]*FreeBMD* vital records index, entry for Mariam Arbiter, married first quarter 1910, Whitechapel district, volume 1c, page 689.

[283]1911 England census, Maurice, Miriam and Hyman Peters; image, *Ancestry.com* (https://www.ancestry.com/interactive/2352/rg14_01601_0115_03/322529 : accessed 11 Nov 2017).

[284]1911 England census, Isaac, Betsy, Evline [*sic*], Ester and Joseph Arbiter.

[285]General Register Office of England, death registration no. 91 (1919 Mile End Old Town), Hannah Arbeiter; Her Majesty's Passport Office.

[286]General Register Office of England, marriage entry no. 57 (1899 Mile End), Abraham Arbeiter and Sarah Jacobowitz.

[287]General Register Office of England, death registration no. 118 (1929 Stepney), Davis Arbeiter; Her Majesty's Passport Office.

[288]Her Majesty's Courts & Tribunals Service, Grant of Letters of Administration for "Davis Arbeiter otherwise Davis Albeiter," died 27 Dec 1929, probate adjudicated 22 Jan 1930.

[289] "Find a Grave," *US Burial*, database with images (`https://www.theus.org.uk/category/find-grave` : accessed 11 Oct 2017); entry for Davis Arbiter; East Ham Cemetery.

[290] George Pope Morris, *Poems*, Project Gutenberg edition (`http://www.gutenberg.org/ebooks/2558` : accessed 12 Oct 2017).

[291] Richard Abdill, discussion thread on gravestone of "Annie" Arbiter, 11 Oct 2017, "Tracing the Tribe - Jewish Genealogy on Facebook," *Facebook.com* (`https://www.facebook.com/groups/tracingthetribe/permalink/10155770658410747/` : accessed 12 Oct 2017). Translation by Leah Cohen and Sara Sarit Nakash.

[292] "Find a Grave," *US Burial*, entry for Hannah Yetta Arbiter; East Ham Cemetery.

[293] Josiah Lafayette Seward, *A History of the town of Sullivan, New Hampshire*, vol. 1 (Keene, NH: published by the author, 1921), 347.

[294] Terence Jenkins, *The Most Dangerous Woman in Europe (And Other Londoners)* (Leicester, UK: Matador Publishing, 2016), 138.

[295] Translated marriage record of Zelman Arbajter and Ryfka Chrzanowska; see "Translations" appendix.

[296] *Ibid.*

[297] Wyszogrod PSA Books of Residence, entry for Jakow Arbajter, house 218.

[298] *Ibid.*

[299] "Search Our Database," *Jewish Records Indexing - Poland* (`http://jri-poland.org/jriplweb.htm`), Wyszogrod Births, Marriages, Deaths 1886-1906, entries for Estera Sura Grynbaum and Mendel Arbajter, married 1888, document 4.

[300] Wyszogrod PSA Books of Residence, entry for Moszek Aron Arbajter, house 218.

[301] *Ibid.*, entry for Lipa Arbajter, house 218.

[302] *Ibid.*, entry for Hena Ryfka Arbajter, house 218.

[303] *Ibid.*, entry for Bela Arbajter, house 218.

[304] JRI-Poland search. Licpo ARBAJTER, grenadier from Wyszogrod, collection "Russian Jewish Fallen Soldiers."

[305] "Background [Russian Jewish Fallen Soldiers, WW1]," *JRI-Poland* (`http://jri-poland.org/russian-jewish-fallen-soldiers-ww1.htm` : accessed 11 Nov 2017).

[306] "For Independence. Year 1914," *The Royal Castle In War-*

saw - Museum (`https://www.zamek-krolewski.pl/en/your-visit/`
`temporary-exhibitions/for-independence.-year-1914-`
`institute-of-national-remembrances-exhibition` : accessed 6 Oct
2017).

[307]Translated death record of Berek Arbajter; see "Translations"
appendix.

[308] "Search Our Database," *Jewish Records Indexing - Poland* (`http:`
`//jri-poland.org/jriplweb.htm`), Biezun Births, Marriages, Deaths,
entry for Ryfka Chrzanoska, married 1843.

[309]Wyszogrod PSA Books of Residence, entry for Mosek Arbajter,
house 218.

[310]Translated death record of Berek Arbajter; see "Translations"
appendix.

[311] *Ibid.*

[312]Wyszogrod PSA Books of Residence, entry for Tauba Arbajter,
house 218.

[313]Wyszogrod PSA Books of Residence, entry for Josek Arbajter,
house 218.

[314]Mikołaj Glinski, "A Foreigner's Guide to Polish Names," *Cul-
ture.pl* (`http://culture.pl/en/article/a-foreigners-guide-`
`to-polish-names` : accessed 12 Oct 2017).

[315]Wyszogrod PSA Books of Residence, entry for Tauba Arbajter,
house 218.

[316] *Ibid.*, entry for Raca Arbajter, house 218.

[317] *Ibid.*, entry for Tauba Arbajter, house 218.

[318] *Ibid.*, entry for Sura Mindla Zauraj.

[319] *Ibid.*

[320] *Ibid.*, entry for Ruchla Akawiec, house 209.

[321] *Ibid.*, entry for Alta Haja Akawiec, house 209.

[322] *Ibid.*, entry for Hena Malka Akawiec, house 76.

[323] *Ibid.*

[324] *Ibid.*, entry for Moszek Akawiec, house 209.

[325] *Ibid.*, entry for Ruda Akawiec, house 209.

[326] *Ibid.*, entry for Hana Maria Akawiec, house 209.

[327] *Ibid.*, entry for Golda Akawiec, house 209.

Chapter 2 Biłgoraj

[1] James L. Fidelholtz, "Stress in Polish – With Some Comparisons to English Stress," *Papers and Studies in Contrastive Linguistics*, edition 9 (1979): 47–61, specifically 47.

[2] Wyszogrod PSA Books of Residence, entry for Szmul Haim Bilgoraj, house 124.

[3] Wyszogrod PSA Books of Residence, entry for Sura Estera (Wejs) Bilgoraj, house 124.

[4] "Wyszogrod PSA Births, Marriages, Deaths 1886–1906," *Jewish Records Indexing – Poland* (http://jri-poland.org/jriplweb.htm : accessed 30 Sep 2017) entry for Szulim Chaim Bilgoraj, year 1887 akta 29.

[5] *Ibid.*, entry for Sura Estera (Wejs) Bilgoraj, house 124.

[6] Wyszogrod PSA Books of Residence, entry for Zelmen Ber Bilgoraj, house 126.

[7] *Ibid.*, entry for Łaja Rasza Bilgoraj, house 126.

[8] *Ibid.*, entry for Ryfka Bilgoraj, house 126.

[9] *Ibid.*, entry for Hawa Bilgoraj, house 126.

[10] *Ibid.*, house 126.

[11] General Register Office of England, death registration no. 91 (1919 Mile End Old Town), Hannah Arbeiter.

[12] Wyszogrod PSA Books of Residence, entry for Szymon Boruch Bilgoraj, house 123.

[13] *Ibid.*, entry for Lewek Icek Bilgoraj, house 123.

[14] *Ibid.*, entry for Abram Haskel Bilgoraj, house 123.

[15] *Ibid.*, entry for Haja Gitel Bilgoraj, house 123.

[16] *Ibid.*, entry for Szulim Haim Bilgoraj, house 123.

[17] *Ibid.*, entry for Icek Bilgoraj, house 124.

[18] *Ibid.*, entry for Haim Aron Bilgoraj, house 124.

[19] *Ibid.*, entry for Ryfka Maria Bilgoraj, house 124.

[20] *Ibid.*, entry for Hana Bilgoraj, house 124.

[21] *Ibid.*, entry for Noech Bilgoraj, house 124.

[22] *Ibid.*, entry for Izrael Moszek Bilgoraj, house 124.

[23] *Ibid.*, entry for Matys Bilgoraj, house 124.

[24] *Ibid.*, entry for Szmul Bilgoraj, house 124.

[25] *Ibid.*, house 124.

[26] Translated death record of Szymon Biłgoraj; see "Translations" appendix.

[27] Wyszogrod PSA Books of Residence, entry for Icek Szulem Bilgoraj, house 191.

[28] Wyszogrod Births, Marriages, Deaths, Szymon Bilgoray, year 1846 akta 187.

[29] *Ibid.*

[30] *Ibid.*

[31] *Ibid.*

[32] Wyszogrod PSA Books of Residence, entry for Lajzer Bilgoraj, house 215.

[33] *Ibid.*, entry for Maria (Moszkow) Bilgoraj, house 215.

[34] *Ibid.*, entry for Ester Szajna Dzedzic [*sic*], house 215.

[35] *Ibid.*, entry for Estera Dziedzic [*sic*], house 122.

[36] Wyszogrod Births, Marriages, Deaths, Szymon Bilgoray, year 1846 akta 187.

[37] Wyszogrod Births, Marriages, Deaths, entry for Rasza Bilgoraj, death, 1864 akta 13.

Chapter 3   Chrzanowski

[1] Susana Leistner Block, "Polish Patronymics and Surname Suffixes," *KehilaLinks* (https://kehilalinks.jewishgen.org/Suchostaw/polish_patronymics_and_surname_suffixes.htm : accessed 21 Oct 2017).

[2] Biezun Births, Marriages, Deaths, entry for Jakob Szoel Chrzanowski, died 1857.

[3] "Frequently Asked Questions," *JewishGen.org* (https://www.jewishgen.org/InfoFiles/faq.html : accessed 11 Nov 2017).

[4] Biezun Births, Marriages, Deaths, entry for Ester Chrzanowski.

[5] Biezun Births, Marriages, Deaths, entry for Lewin Chrzanowski.

[6] Biezun Births, Marriages, Deaths, entry for Hana Laja Chrzan-owski.

[7] Biezun Births, Marriages, Deaths, entry for Ester Chrzanowski.

[8] Warren Blatt, "Polish-Jewish Genealogy: Questions and Answers," *JewishGen.com* (https://www.jewishgen.org/InfoFiles/Poland/Questions.htm : accessed 11 Nov 2017).

[9] Biezun Births, Marriages, Deaths, entries for Ruchla Chrzanoska and Jcick Bekier, year 1849, akta 2.

[10] Biezun Births, Marriages, Deaths, entry for birth of Abram Bekier, year 1857, akta 3.

[11] Biezun Births, Marriages, Deaths, entry for death of Chaim Chrzanowski, year 1837, akta 109.

[12] Biezun Births, Marriages, Deaths, entry for death of Hana Laja Chrzanowski, birth, year 1839, akta 236.

[13] Biezun Births, Marriages, Deaths, entry for death of Ester Chrzanowski, birth, year 1841, akta 308.

[14] Biezun Births, Marriages, Deaths, entry for death of Jakob Szoel Chrzanowski, year 1857, akta 7.

Chapter 4 Jacobowitz

[1] "Louis (Lepke) Buchalter Part 2 of 4," 30.

[2] "JewishGen Online Worldwide Burial Registry," entry for Sarah (Arbeiter) Finkel, died 14 Jan 1963.

[3] Richard Abdill, discussion thread on existance of "Kisminsk," 13 Jun 2017, "Tracing the Tribe - Jewish Genealogy on Facebook," *Facebook.com* (https://www.facebook.com/groups/tracingthetribe/permalink/10155407710350747/ : accessed 2 Oct 2017).

[4] "JewishGen Online Worldwide Burial Registry," entry for Sarah (Arbeiter) Finkel, died 14 Jan 1963.

[5] Manifest, S.S. *St. Paul*, 17 Nov 1907, list 3, line 5, Sarah Arbeiter; *Passenger and Crew Lists of Vessels Arriving at New York , NY, 1897-1957*, microfilm publication T715, (Washington: National Archives and Records Service), roll 1042, frame 537.

[6] "JewishGen Online Worldwide Burial Registry," entry for Sarah (Arbeiter) Finkel, died 14 Jan 1963.

[7] General Register Office of England, marriage entry no. 57 (1899 Mile End), Abraham Arbeiter and Sarah Jacobowitz.

[8]General Register Office of England, birth registration no. 175 (1900 Mile End New Town, London), Rebecca Arbiter; Her Majesty's Passport Office.

[9]General Register Office of England, birth registration no. 402 (1903 Mile End, London), Solomon Arbeiter; Her Majesty's Passport Office.

[10] "New York, New York, Marriage Certificate Index 1866-1937," database, *Ancestry.com* (`http://search.ancestry.com/cgi-bin/sse.dll?indiv=1&dbid=9105&h=4636155&pid=110011185921` : accessed 24 Sep 2017), entries for Sarah A Jakus and Samuel Finkel, certificate no. 2555.

Chapter 5 Reinstein

[1] "The Weather," *The New York Sun*, 6 Jul 1905, pg. 3; digital scan of original (`https://www.newspapers.com/image/163865131/` : accessed 20 Oct 2017).

[2]Berrol, 5.

[3]Grose, 62.

[4]*Ibid.*

[5]Ellis Island Immigration Museum, "The 'Stairs of Separation,' " *Flickr* (`https://www.flickr.com/photos/ellisislandnps/7093756569/` : accessed 20 Oct 2017)

[6] "Jewish Immigration to the United States," 516.

[7]Joseph, 516.

[8]Howe, 27.

[9]Manifest, S.S. *Corinthian*, 11 Mar 1904, index no. 14, Hersch Reinstein; *Passenger and Crew Lists of Vessels Arriving at New York , NY, 1897-1957*, microfilm publication T715, (Washington: National Archives and Records Service), roll 435, frame 740.

[10]Berrol, 17.

[11]Birmingham, 31.

[12]Howe, 5.

[13]Joseph, 543.

[14]Howe, 27.

[15]Pelo, *Genealogy Research.*

[16] OhRanger, "The Immigrant Journey," *Ellis Island National Monument* (http://www.ohranger.com/ellis-island/immigration-journey : accessed 21 Oct 2017).

[17] There is no documentation stating that Ellis Island was closed to the public on the 4th of July. This conclusion is based on the *Astoria* records of detained aliens—of the dozens on the roster, none were released on July 4; several were released July 3, and the remainder on July 5 and 6.

[18] "Detained at Ellis Island," *Ellis Island Videos*, online video clip (http://www.history.com/topics/ellis-island/videos/detained-at-ellis-island : accessed 12 Oct 2017).

[19] *Ibid.*

[20] From Pelo, *Genealogy Research*, though its provenance is unclear. It may be excerpted from *Liberty*, by Leslie Allen.

[21] Howe, 42.

[22] U.S. Citizenship and Immigration Services, "Immigrant Name Changes," *Genealogy Notebook* (https://www.uscis.gov/history-and-genealogy/genealogy/genealogy-notebook/immigrant-name-changes/ : accessed 16 Oct 2017.)

[23] *Ibid.*

[24] "History," *HIAS* (https://www.hias.org/history : accessed 17 Oct 2017).

[25] Howe, 48.

[26] "History," *HIAS.*

[27] Howe, 50.

[28] "Hilfsverein der Deutschen Juden," *SHOAH Resource Center* (http://www.yadvashem.org/odot_pdf/Microsoft%20Word%20-%206371.pdf : accessed 19 Oct 2017).

[29] Birmingham, 41.

[30] Howe, 30.

[31] Ada's age here is an estimation; her birthday is unknown, but is likely around 1876 or 1877.

[32] "Markings on the Manifest's Left Margin," *Manifest Markings* (https://www.jewishgen.org/InfoFiles/Manifests/left/ : accessed 11 Nov 2017).

[33] Howe, 37.

[34] Birmingham, 43.

[35] Record of Detained Aliens, S.S. *Astoria*, 3 Jul 1905, index no. 13, Edel Reinstein and three children; *Passenger and Crew Lists of Vessels Arriving at New York , NY, 1897-1957*, microfilm publication T715, (Washington: National Archives and Records Service), roll 596, frame 324.

[36] "House: 39 Essex Street," *StreetEasy* (https://streeteasy.com/building/39-essex-street-manhattan : accessed 21 Oct 2017).

[37] Howe, 43.

[38] Berol, 90.

[39] *Ibid.*

[40] Berrol, 25.

[41] Jason Barr and Teddy Ort, "Population Density across the City: The Case of 1900 Manhattan," Department of Economics, Rutgers University (http://andromeda.rutgers.edu/~jmbarr/skyscrapers/tenementsdraftv1_18aug2013.pdf : accessed 19 Nov 2017).

[42] Howe, 148.

[43] Arnold Bennett, "Your United States," *Hearst's International*, vol. 23 (New York: World Review Company, 1913), 498.

[44] Berrol, 24.

[45] *Ibid.*

[46] Birmingham, 45.

[47] Howe, 68.

[48] Pelo, *Genealogy Research.*

[49] Howe, 174–175.

[50] Birmingham, 45.

[51] Pelo, *Genealogy Research.*

[52] Birmingham, 47.

[53] *Ibid.*, 45.

[54] Howe, 74.

[55] *Ibid.*, 116.

[56] Birmingham, 14.

[57] *Ibid.*, 23.

[58] *Ibid.*, 16.

[59] Berrol, 39.

[60] *Ibid.*, 39–40.

[61] Berrol, 119.

[62] Polland and Soyer, 118.

[63] *Ibid.*

[64] Howe, 57.

[65] Ted Merwin, "Unbuttoned: Clothing as a Theme in American Jewish Comedy," *Fashioning Jews: Clothing, Culture, and Commerce*, Leonard J. Greenspoon, editor (West Lafayette, Ind: Purdue University Press, 2013), 137.

[66] Polland and Soyer, 120.

[67] Manifest, S.S. *Westernland*, 26 Mar 1906, stamped p. 18, index no. 16, Ruchel Reinstein, *Passenger and Crew Lists of Vessels Arriving at New York , NY, 1897-1957*, microfilm publication T715, (Washington: National Archives and Records Service), roll 681, frame 259.

[68] Manifest, S.S. *Livonia*, 23 Jun 1907, list 22, index no. 20, Schmiel Reinstein, *Passenger and Crew Lists of Vessels Arriving at New York , NY, 1897-1957*, microfilm publication T715, (Washington: National Archives and Records Service), roll 929, frame 7.

[69] Alex Dean, "'Moving Day': How 1 million New Yorkers used to move house on the same day every year," *New Statesman*, 14 Aug 2015 (http://www.citymetric.com/horizons/moving-day-how-1-million-new-yorkers-used-move-house-same-day-every-year-1320 : accessed 21 Oct 2017).

[70] Davy Crockett, *An Account of Col. Crockett's Tour to the North and Down East* (Baltimore: Carey, Hart, and Co., 1835), 47–48.

[71] John B. Manbeck, *The Neighborhoods of Brooklyn* (New Haven: Yale University Press, 1998), 226.

[72] Berrol, 136.

[73] 1910 U.S. census, Kings County, New York, population schedule, family 121, Harry, Ada, Pearl, David, Anna, Nathan and Clara Reinstein; image, *Ancestry.com* (https://www.ancestry.com/interactive/7884/4449796_00304/17849398 : accessed 11 Nov 2017); citing NARA microfilm publication T624, roll 968.

[74] Berrol, "Education and Economic Mobility: the Jewish Experience in New York City, 1880-1920," 263.

[75] Manifest, S.S. *Livonia*, 23 Jun 1907, list 22, index no. 20,

Schmiel Reinstein.

[76] Record of detained aliens, S.S. *Westernland*, 26 Mar 1906, stamped p. 51, index no. 43, Ruchel Reinstein, *Passenger and Crew Lists of Vessels Arriving at New York , NY, 1897-1957*, microfilm publication T715, (Washington: National Archives and Records Service), roll 681, frame 320.

[77] Polland and Soyer, 6.

[78] *Ibid.*, 117.

[79] Polland and Soyer, 121.

[80] *Ibid.*, 112.

[81] "From Pickle Day Exhibits: What is a Pickle?" *New York Food Museum* (http://www.nyfoodmuseum.org/_pkwhat.htm : accessed 18 Oct 2017).

[82] Polland and Soyer, 123.

[83] "U.S., World War I Draft Registration Cards, 1917–1918," images, Ancestry.com (https://www.ancestry.com/interactive/6482/005262931_00399/1411833 : accessed 12 Nov 2017), card for Harry Reinstein.

[84] "Selected U.S. Naturalization Records, Original Documents, 1790–1974," images, Ancestry.com (https://www.ancestry.com/interactive/1554/32126_22319183132018-00378/3311426 : accessed 12 Nov 2017), Declaration of Intention no. 9618 (19 Mar 1904) and Petition for Naturalization no. 8128 (7 Feb 1912), Harry Reinstein, Kings County, NY, New York State Supreme Court.

[85] City of New York, death certificate no. 21640 (1944 Brooklyn), Harry Reinstein; New York City Department of Records.

[86] Manifest, S.S. *Astoria*, 3 Jul 1905, index nos. 19–22, Edel, Perl, David and Chane Reinstein; *Passenger and Crew Lists of Vessels Arriving at New York , NY, 1897-1957*, microfilm publication T715, (Washington: National Archives and Records Service), roll 596, frame 308.

[87] City of New York, death certificate no. 17894 (1931 Brooklyn), Ada Reinstein, died 18 Aug 1931; New York City Department of Records.

[88] 1910 U.S. census, Kings County, New York, pop. sch., fam. 121, Harry, Ada, Pearl, David, Anna, Nathan and Clara Reinstein.

[89] Manifest, S.S. *Corinthian*, 11 Mar 1904, index no. 14, Hersch Reinstein.

[90] "UK, Outward Passenger Lists, 1890–1960," image, *Ancestry.com* (https://www.ancestry.com/interactive/2997/40610_B000424-00043/48225395 : accessed 12 Nov 2017), ship *Corinthian*, departure 27 Feb 1904, entry for Hersch Reinstein, ticket no. 103.

[91] Manifest, S.S. *Corinthian*, 11 Mar 1904, index no. 14, Hersch Reinstein.

[92] *Ibid.*

[93] Jacob A. Riis, *How The Other Half Lives: Studies Among the Tenements of New York* (New York: Charles Scribner's Sons, 1897), 104–105.

[94] Riis, 108.

[95] Photo ca. 1890, by Jacob Riis.

[96] Riis, 123–124.

[97] Jay Arbeiter, phone interview, 10 Jun 2017.

[98] 1910 U.S. census, Kings County, New York, pop. sch., fam. 121, Harry, Ada, Pearl, David, Anna, Nathan and Clara Reinstein.

[99] Manifest, S.S. *Livonia*, 23 Jun 1907, list 22, index no. 20, Schmiel Reinstein.

[100] Social Security Administration, "Social Security Applications and Claims Index," database, *Ancestry.com* (https://search.ancestry.com/cgi-bin/sse.dll?indiv=1&dbid=60901&h=24857266 : accessed 12 Nov 2017), entry for Selma Reinstein, died 9 Oct 2007, SS no. 054-07-5748.

[101] 1915 New York state census, Kings County, Brooklyn, Harry, Ida, Pearl, Anna, Clara, David, Nathan, Hyman, Samuel and Dora Reinstein; image, *Ancestry.com* (https://www.ancestry.com/interactive/7884/31111_4330909-00880/ : accessed 11 Nov 2017).

[102] Jay Arbeiter, phone interview, 10 Jun 2017.

[103] *Ibid.*

[104] Manifest, S.S. *Astoria*, 3 Jul 1905, index nos. 19–22, Edel, Perl, David and Chane Reinstein.

[105] "Selected U.S. Naturalization Records, Original Documents, 1790–1974," Declaration of Intention no. 9618 (19 Mar 1904) and Petition for Naturalization no. 8128 (7 Feb 1912), Harry Reinstein.

[106] *Find A Grave*, database with images (https://www.findagrave.com/memorial/161272866 : accessed 12 Nov 2017), memorial 161272866; Pearl Reinstein Gitlin; Washington Cemetery.

107 "New York, Abstracts of World War I Military Service, 1917–1919," image, *Ancestry.com* (https://www.ancestry.com/interactive/3030/40808_1120704930_0237-00412/405046 : accessed 12 Nov 2017), entry for Harry J Gitlin, serial number 4,883,881.

108 *Find A Grave*, database with images (https://www.findagrave.com/memorial/161273035 : accessed 12 Nov 2017), memorial 161273035; Harry Joseph Gitlin; Washington Cemetery.

109 Social Security Administration, "Social Security Death Index," database, *Ancestry.com* (https://search.ancestry.com/cgi-bin/sse.dll?indiv=1&dbid=3693&h=22399552 : accessed 12 Nov 2017), entry for Harry Gitlin, died Feb 1979, SS no. 117-09-3413.

110 1905 New York state census, Kings County, Nathan, Becky, Ettie and Harry Gitlin; image, *Ancestry.com* (https://www.ancestry.com/interactive/7364/004296330_00439/692526 : accessed 12 Nov 2017).

111 1910 U.S. census, Kings County, New York, population schedule, Brooklyn Borough, dwelling 23, family 115, Nathan, Rebecca, Harry and Yetta Gitlin; image, *Ancestry.com* (https://www.ancestry.com/interactive/7884/4449796_00362/102653370 : accessed 12 Nov 2017); citing NARA microfilm publication T624, roll 968.

112 "New York, New York, Marriage Certificate Index 1866–1937," database, *Ancestry.com* (https://search.ancestry.com/cgi-bin/sse.dll?indiv=1&dbid=9105&h=2502646 : accessed 12 Nov 2017), entry for Harry J Gitlin and Pearl Reinstein, certificate 1527, 4 Jan 1920.

113 1930 U.S. census, Kings County, New York, population schedule, Brooklyn Borough, dwelling 114, family 446, Harry, Pearl, Shirley and Saul Gitlin; image, *Ancestry.com* (https://www.ancestry.com/interactive/6224/4638827_00329/1105557527 : accessed 12 Nov 2017).

114 "WWII Draft Registration Cards," image, *Fold3* (https://www.fold3.com/image/598690771 : accessed 12 Nov 2017), card for David Reinstein, serial number 1591, Richmond, Va.

115 "New York City, Marriage License Indexes, 1907–1995," database, *Ancestry.com* (https://search.ancestry.com/cgi-bin/sse.dll?indiv=1&dbid=61406&h=6395799 : accessed 18 Nov 2017), entries for David Reinstein and Lillie [*sic*] Sovelove, license 7798 (Brooklyn).

116 1930 U.S. census, Kings County, New York, population schedule, Brooklyn Borough, dwelling 145, family 396, Simon, Sarah and Eva Sovelove, Ester, Dora, Tillie and Lena Schwartz, David, Tillie and Jerome Reinstein; image, *Ancestry.com* (https://www.ancestry.com/interactive/6224/4638827_00107/1105549949 : accessed 18 Nov 2017).

[117] Jay Arbeiter, phone interview, 10 Jun 2017.

[118] Commonwealth of Virginia, death certificate no. 71-028225, David Reinstein; Virginia Department of Health, Richmond.

[119] "WWII Draft Registration Cards," card for David Reinstein, serial number 1591, Richmond, Va.

[120] Commonwealth of Virginia, divorce report no. 66-001955, David Reinstein and Tillie Sovelove Reinstein, digital scan of document, *Ancestry.com* (`https://www.ancestry.com/interactive/9280/43072_162028006074_0760-00456/2112688` : accessed 18 Nov 2017).

[121] Jay Arbeiter, phone interview, 10 Jun 2017.

[122] Commonwealth of Virginia, divorce report no. 66-001955, David Reinstein and Tillie Sovelove Reinstein.

[123] Commonwealth of Virginia, death certificate no. 71-028225, David Reinstein.

[124] Nancy Abdill, phone interview, 20 Jun 2017.

[125] Manifest, S.S. *Astoria*, 3 Jul 1905, index nos. 19–22, Edel, Perl, David and Chane Reinstein.

[126] We have multiple dates given for Anna's date of birth: Social Security records say 15 May 1901, but that date is impossible if David's is correct. Her father gave the date as 5 Dec 1903 in his application for citizenship, but at least one of the dates on the application looks to be a guess. An index of Florida death records gives the date as 18 Jan 1903—the source of this information was likely Anna's son Daniel; we're going to take his word for it.

[127] "Selected U.S. Naturalization Records, Original Documents, 1790–1974," Declaration of Intention no. 9618 (19 Mar 1904) and Petition for Naturalization no. 8128 (7 Feb 1912), Harry Reinstein.

[128] "Florida Death Index, 1877–1998," database, *Ancestry.com* (`https://search.ancestry.com/cgi-bin/sse.dll?indiv=1&dbid=7338&h=2648643` : accessed 18 Nov 2017), entry for Anna Gladstone, died 6 May 1984.

[129] Social Security Administration, "Social Security Death Index," database, *Ancestry.com* (`https://search.ancestry.com/cgi-bin/sse.dll?indiv=1&dbid=3693&h=22430318` : accessed 18 Nov 2017), entry for Arthur Gladstone, died Oct 1981, SS no. 061-01-7982.

[130] "United States World War II Draft Registration Cards, 1942," images, Ancestry.com (`https://www.ancestry.com/interactive/1002/NY-2369699-4509/2894686` : accessed 19 Nov 2017), card for Arthur Gladstone.

[131] "Social Security Death Index," entry for Arthur Gladstone, SS

no. 061-01-7982.

[132] 1940 U.S. census, Kings County, New York, population schedule, household 108, Arthur, Anna and Daniel Gladstone, Lula Smith; image, *Ancestry.com* (https://www.ancestry.com/interactive/2442/m-t0627-02558-00496/3235592 : accessed 20 Nov 2017); citing NARA microfilm publication T627, roll 2558.

[133] "New York, New York, Birth Index, 1878–1909," database, *Ancestry.com* (https://search.ancestry.com/cgi-bin/sse.dll?indiv=1&dbid=9089&h=701041 : accessed 19 Nov 2017), entry for Nathan Reinstein, born 23 Aug 1906, certificate no. 22667 (Kings County). It appears Nathan's father gave his date of birth as 14 Jul 1906 when Nathan died, but his birth certificate gives the August date.

[134] City of New York, death certificate no. 2236 (1938 Brooklyn), Nathan Reinstein; New York City Department of Records.

[135] *Ibid.*, birth certificate no. 12299 (1908 Brooklyn), Clara Reinstein; New York City Department of Records.

[136] Borough of Metuchen, death certificate, Claire Arbeiter, died 5 Oct 1992.

[137] Social Security Administration, "Social Security Death Index," database, *Ancestry.com* (https://search.ancestry.com/cgi-bin/sse.dll?indiv=1&dbid=3693&h=51442797 : accessed 19 Nov 2017), entry for Herman Reinstein, died Feb 1972, SS no. 111-36-3439.

[138] *Ibid.* (https://search.ancestry.com/cgi-bin/sse.dll?indiv=1&dbid=3693&h=51442851 : accessed 19 Nov 2017), entry for Lillian Reinstein, SS no. 102-07-0463.

[139] "Florida Death Index, 1877–1998," database, *Ancestry.com* (https://search.ancestry.com/cgi-bin/sse.dll?indiv=1&dbid=7338&h=3141779 : accessed 19 Nov 2017), entry for Lillian Reinstein, died 6 Nov 1982.

[140] Social Security Administration, "Social Security Death Index," database, *Ancestry.com* (https://search.ancestry.com/cgi-bin/sse.dll?indiv=1&dbid=3693&h=32393323 : accessed 19 Nov 2017), entry for Ruth Kaufman, died 9 Jun 1998, SS no. 053-14-2038.

[141] S*Ibid.* (https://search.ancestry.com/cgi-bin/sse.dll?indiv=1&dbid=3693&h=32391431 : accessed 19 Nov 2017), entry for Milton A. Kaufman, died 7 Aug 1998, SS no. 057-05-7242.

[142] Reinstein family, c. 1909; digitized and privately held by the author, Minneapolis, Minn., 2017. From the collection of Ann (Siegel) Dondero.

[143] City of New York, death certificate no. 17894 (1931 Brooklyn),

Ada Reinstein, died 18 Aug 1931.

[144] 1940 U.S. census, Kings County, New York, population schedule, Solomon, Pearl, Anne [*sic*], and Jay D Arbeiter, Ruth Reinstein; image, *Ancestry.com* (https://www.ancestry.com/interactive/2442/m-t0627-02615-00388/5008082 : accessed 19 Nov 2017).

[145] City of New York, death certificate no. 21640 (1944 Brooklyn), Harry Reinstein

[146] "New York, New York, Marriage Certificate Index 1866–1937," database, *Ancestry.com* (https://search.ancestry.com/cgi-bin/sse.dll?indiv=1&dbid=9105&h=4770879 : accessed 19 Nov 2017), entries for Esther Siegel and Harry Reinstein, certificate no. 16519.

[147] City of New York, death certificate no. 21640 (1944 Brooklyn), Harry Reinstein

[148] Montefiore Cemetery (Springfield, NY), online interment search (http://montefiorecemetery.org/interment/?id=5451093 : accessed 19 Nov 2017), entry for Esther Reinstein, died 17 Apr 1950.

[149] Google Street View, online images (https://maps.google.com), 441 Pine St., Brooklyn, NY. City real estate records indicate the house was build in 1930; Ada died in 1931.

[150] Arbeiter siblings, c. 1946; digitized and privately held by the author, Minneapolis, Minn., 2017. From the collection of Ann (Siegel) Dondero.

[151] Herman Reinstein receiving military commendation; digitized and privately held by the author, Minneapolis, Minn., 2017. From the collection of Ann (Siegel) Dondero.

[152] Ruth and Milton Kaufman; digitized and privately held by the author, Minneapolis, Minn., 2017. From the collection of Ann (Siegel) Dondero.

[153] Rachel, the couple's eldest known child, was born abt 1868.

[154] 1910 U.S. census, Kings County, New York, pop. sch., fam. 121, Harry, Ada, Pearl, David, Anna, Nathan and Clara Reinstein.

[155] Harry Reinstein gravestone, 2017; photograph by Kevin LaCherra, used by permission.

[156] Manifest, S.S. *Astoria*, 3 Jul 1905, index no. 18, Zipre Reinstein; *Passenger and Crew Lists of Vessels Arriving at New York , NY, 1897-1957*, microfilm publication T715, (Washington: National Archives and Records Service), roll 596, frame 308.

[157] "Reading Hebrew Tombstones," *JewishGen InfoFiles* (http://www.jewishgen.org/InfoFiles/tombstones.html : accessed 19 Nov

2017).

158 Doron M. Behar et. al, "Multiple Origins of Ashkenazi Levites: Y Chromosome Evidence for Both Near Eastern and European Ancestries," *American Journal of Human Genetics* (`https://www.ncbi.nlm.nih.gov/pmc/articles/PMC1180600/`).

159 1910 U.S. census, Kings County, New York, pop. sch., fam. 121, Harry, Ada, Pearl, David, Anna, Nathan and Clara Reinstein.

160 Manifest, S.S. *Astoria*, 3 Jul 1905, index no. 18, Zipre Reinstein.

161 Manifest, S.S. *Corinthian*, 11 Mar 1904, index no. 14, Hersch Reinstein; *Passenger and Crew Lists of Vessels Arriving at New York , NY, 1897-1957*, microfilm publication T715, (Washington: National Archives and Records Service), roll 435, frame 740.

162 Charles Burns, "Medzhybizh," *Galician Traces* (`http://galiciantraces.com/medzhybizh/` : accessed 19 Nov 2017).

163 Samuel D. Gruber, "Jewish Cemeteries, Synagogues, and Mass Grave Sites in Ukraine" (2005), *Surface*, Syracuse University, p. 70.

164 1910 U.S. census, Kings County, New York, pop. sch., fam. 121, Harry, Ada, Pearl, David, Anna, Nathan and Clara Reinstein.

165 "JewishGen Online Worldwide Burial Registry," database, *JewishGen* (`https://www.jewishgen.org/databases/jowbr.php?rec=J_NY_0014982` : accessed 19 Nov 2017), entry for Sam Reinstein, died 1975.

166 "U.S., World War I Draft Registration Cards, 1917–1918," images, Ancestry.com (`https://www.ancestry.com/interactive/6482/005262792_02750/71790288` : accessed 19 Nov 2017), card for Hyman Dreizen.

167 *Ibid.*

168 Email communication between the author and James Manchester, June 7–30, 2017.

169 "United States World War II Draft Registration Cards, 1942," images, Ancestry.com (`https://www.ancestry.com/interactive/1002/NY-2370486-2237/2933119` : accessed 19 Nov 2017), card for Sam Reinstein. When Sam registered for the World War I draft, he said he was born in July 1891, but did not know the date. When the World War II draft came around, he gave his birth date as 25 Jul.

170 "JewishGen Online Worldwide Burial Registry," entry for Sam Reinstein, died 1975.

171 Manifest, S.S. *Livonia*, 23 Jun 1907, list 22, index no. 20, Schmiel Reinstein.

[172] Jay Arbeiter, phone interview, 10 Jun 2017.

[173] Joel Weintraug, "The Ellis Island Name Change Myth," *Jewish-Gen InfoFiles* (`http://www.jewishgen.org/InfoFiles/ellismythnames.html` : accessed 19 Nov 2017).

[174] Manchester to Abdill, 19 Jun 2017.

[175] Social Security Administration, "Social Security Applications and Claims Index," database, *Ancestry.com* (`https://search.ancestry.com/cgi-bin/sse.dll?indiv=1&dbid=60901&h=24857266` : accessed 19 Nov 2017), entry for Selma Reinstein, died 8 Oct 2007, SS no. 054-07-5748.

[176] 1915 New York state census, Kings County, Harry, Ida, Pearl, Anna, Clara, David, Nathan, Hyman, Samuel and Dora Reinstein.

[177] 1940 U.S. census, Kings County, New York, population schedule, Brooklyn Borough, household 121, Sam, Dora, Selma, Sol, Shirley and Marilyn Reinstein; image, *Ancestry.com* (`https://www.ancestry.com/interactive/2442/m-t0627-02618-00320/4017136` : accessed 19 Nov 2017); citing NARA microfilm publication T627, roll 2618.

[178] Manifest, S.S. *Gothland*, 29 Jul 1913, written p. 27, index no. 21, Chaim Renistein, *Passenger and Crew Lists of Vessels Arriving at New York , NY, 1897-1957*, microfilm publication T715, (Washington: National Archives and Records Service), roll 2140, frame 654.

[179] Jay Arbeiter, phone interview, 10 Jun 2017.

[180] "U.S., World War I Draft Registration Cards, 1917–1918," card for Hyman Dreizen.

[181] Montefiore Cemetery (Springfield, NY), online interment search (`http://montefiorecemetery.org/interment/?id=5482014` : accessed 19 Nov 2017), entry for Hyman Dreizen, died 20 Oct 1964.

[182] 1930 U.S. census, Kings County, New York, population schedule, Brooklyn Borough, dwelling 80, family 459, Hyman, Mary, Florence, Slyvia [*sic*], Ray and Edith Dreizen, *Ancestry.com* (`https://www.ancestry.com/interactive/6224/4661163_00425/38735337` : accessed 19 Nov 2017).

[183] Montefiore Cemetery (Springfield, NY), online interment search (`http://montefiorecemetery.org/interment/?id=5456213` : accessed 19 Nov 2017), entry for Mary Dreizen, died 9 Sep 1952.

[184] 1940 U.S. census, Kings County, New York, population schedule, Brooklyn Borough, household 298, Hyman, Mary, Florence, Sylvia, Ray and Edith Dreizen, *Ancestry.com* (`https://www.ancestry.com/interactive/2442/m-t0627-02549-00610/6266608` : accessed 19 Nov

2017).

[185] Manchester to Abdill, 19 Jun 2017.

[186] *Ibid.*

Chapter 6   Newman

[1] City of New York, death certificate no. 17894 (1931), Ada Reinstein; New York City Department of Records.

[2] 1910 U.S. census, Kings County, New York, population schedule, Borough of Brooklyn, family 121, Harry, Ada, Pearl, David, Anna, Nathan and Clara Reinstein; image, *Ancestry.com* (https://www.ancestry.com/interactive/7884/4449796_00304/ : accessed 54 Sep 2017); citing NARA microfilm publication T624, roll 968.

[3] "Basic Explanation of Surname Endings," *PolishRoots* (http://www.polishroots.org/Resources/SurnameSearch/Surnamesendings/tabid/118/Default.aspx : accessed 21 Oct 2017). Also: Block, "Polish Patronymics and Surname Suffixes."

[4] Ray appears in a photo dated February 1955.

[5] Italian Genealogical Group, "Bronx, Kings, Manhattan, Richmond, and Queens County Brides," database (http://www.italiangen.org/records-search/brides.php : accessed 25 Sep 2017), entries for Golda Newman and Joseph Task, certificate no. 3940 (1920). Note: A request was submitted to the New York City Department of Records for a copy of this certificate; they responded later with a letter saying the record could not be found.

[6] *Find A Grave*, database with images (https://www.findagrave.com/cgi-bin/fg.cgi?page=gr&GRid=31892198 : accessed 25 Sep 2017), memorial 31892198; Rose Newman; Mount Ararat Cemetery; gravestone added by GLENN.

[7] 1930 U.S. census, Nassau County, New York, population schedule, Town of Hempstead, dwelling 301, family 456, Joseph, Goldie, Dorothy, Ethel and Martin Task; image, *Ancestry.com* (https://www.ancestry.com/interactive/6224/4661130_00478/ : accessed 25 Sep 2017).

[8] Mount Ararat Cemetery (Lindenhurst, NY), online interment search (http://www.mountararatcemetery.com/location.asp?id=1126806 : accessed 24 Sep 2017), entry for Goldie Task, died 24 Sep 1970.

[9] "U.S. World War I Registration Cards, 1917–1918," database, *Ancestry.com* (https://www.ancestry.com/interactive/6482/

005262931_02024/ : accessed 29 Sep 2017), card for Joseph Task, serial no. 254, Precinct 153, Kings County, NY.

[10]Mount Ararat Cemetery (Lindenhurst, NY), online interment search (http://www.mountararatcemetery.com/ location.asp?id=1132224 : accessed 29 Sep 2017), entry for Joseph Task, died 3 Jul 1970.

[11] "Bronx, Kings, Manhattan, Richmond, and Queens County Brides," database, entries for Golda Newman and Joseph Task.

[12]1940 U.S. census, Nassau County, New York, population schedule, Hempstead Town, household 66, Joseph, Goldie, Dorothy, Ethel and Martin Task, Rose Newman; image, *Ancestry.com* (https:// www.ancestry.com/interactive/2442/m-t0627-02690-00462/ : accessed 29 Sep 2017); citing NARA microfilm publication T627, roll 2690.

[13]1925 New York state census, Nassau County, Hempstead town, Assembly District 1, Joseph, Goldie, Dorothy and Ethel Task, Rose Newman; image, *Ancestry.com* (https://www.ancestry.com/ interactive/2704/32849_b094348-00416/ : accessed 29 Sep 2017).

[14]*Find A Grave*, database with images, memorial 31892198; Rose Newman; Mount Ararat Cemetery; gravestone added by GLENN.

[15]Rose Newman, in an undated photo; digitized and privately held by the author, Minneapolis, Minn., 2017. From the collection of Ann (Siegel) Dondero.

[16]Ray Newman, Harry Gitlin and Claire Arbeiter, 1955; digitized and privately held by the author, Minneapolis, Minn., 2017. From the collection of Ann (Siegel) Dondero.

Chapter 7 Siegel

[1] "Russians to the rescue—Icefield described," online clipping of article from 25 Apr 1912, in *The Daily Telegraph*, by Charles E. Walters; *Encyclopedia Titanica*, reproduced online by Senan Molony; accessed 23 Sep 2017, https://www.encyclopedia-titanica.org/ russians-rescue-icefield-described.html

[2] "Russians to the rescue," *Encyclopedia Titanica*.

[3]1,517 passengers died in total; one died after being rescued, and three people were found dead in lifeboats.

[4]Manifest, S.S. *Kaiserin Auguste Victoria*, 28 Nov 1910, list 18, Salman, Jakob, Aron and Dwoire Sigal; *Passenger and Crew Lists*

of Vessels Arriving at New York , NY, 1897-1957, microfilm publication T715, (Washington: National Archives and Records Service), roll 1601, frames 222–223.

5 Joseph, 444.

6 *Ibid.*, 458–459.

7 *Ibid.*, 460.

8 Polland and Soyer, 114.

9 "Primer on Emigration and Immigration," Polish Genealogical Society of America, *How to Begin Your Family Research*; accessed 23 Sep 2017, https://pgsa.org/how-to/primer-on-emigration-and-immigration/

10 Geoff Chester, "Final Point of the Russian Empire: Liepaja's Half a Million Emigrants," *Deep Baltic: Inside the Lands Between*; accessed 23 Sep 2017; https://deepbaltic.com/2015/12/02/final-point-of-the-russian-empire-the-story-of-liepajas-half-a-million-emigrants/

11 Howe, 28.

12 Senan Molony, "Birma's wireless bears witness!" *Encyclopedia Titanica*; accessed 23 Sep 2017, https://www.encyclopedia-titanica.org/birma-bears-witness.html

13 Chester, "Final Point of the Russian Empire."

14 The experiences of the *Birma* in spring 1912 were based on multiple documents, including: Associated Press, "Bury Four of the Dead At Sea; Impressive Services Over Victims Are Held Aboard the Carpathia," *Chicago Daily News*, 19 Apr 1912, transcription via *Encyclopedia Titanica* (https://www.encyclopedia-titanica.org/bury-four-of-the-titanic-dead-at-sea.html : accessed 19 Nov 2017). Paul Lee, *Titanic Pages*, "The SS Birma's PV resurfaces at last" (http://www.paullee.com/titanic/Birma.html : accessed 19 Nov 2017). Samuel Halpern, "The Enigmatic Excursion of the SS Birma," *Titanicology* (http://www.titanicology.com/Titanica/Inigmatic_Excursion_of_SS_Birma.pdf : accessed 19 Nov 2017). "Birma (ex-Arundel Castle)," *Titanic Inquiry Project* (http://www.titanicinquiry.org/ships/birma.php : accessed 19 Nov 2017).

15 Senan Molony, "Captain Ludwig Stulping of the s.s. Birma" *Encyclopedia Titanica*; accessed 23 Sep 2017, https://www.encyclopedia-titanica.org/captain-ludwig-stulping-ss-birma.html

16 "Baltic American Line Steamship Brochures and Historical Archives," *Gjenvick-Gjonvik Archives*; accessed 23 Sep 2017; http://www.gjenvick.com/SteamshipLines/BalticAmericaLine/index.html

[17]Keith Wilson, editor, *Decisions for War 1914* (London: Routledge, 2016), 52–53.

[18]Manifest, S.S. *Birma*, 19 May 1912, list 23, Sigalow family; *Passenger and Crew Lists of Vessels Arriving at New York , NY, 1897-1957*, microfilm publication T715, (Washington: National Archives and Records Service), roll 1864, frames 253–254.

[19]Record of Aliens Held for Special Inquiry, S.S. *Birma*, 19 May 1912, stamped p. 137, index numbers 2–3, Sigalow family; *Passenger and Crew Lists of Vessels Arriving at New York , NY, 1897-1957*, microfilm publication T715, (Washington: National Archives and Records Service), roll 1864, frame 264.

[20]"Trade treaty through vessels by name – Bor," United States Immigration and Naturalization Service, *Subject index to correspondence and case files of the Immigration and Naturalization Service, 1903-1952*; FHL roll 1527631, image 4112 (`https://www.familysearch.org/search/catalog/589325` : accessed 23 Sep 2017).

[21]Nancy Abdill, phone interview, 20 Jun 2017.

[22]Martin Stanley Siegel, SS no. 109-20-2365, 7 Jul 1943, Application for Social Security Account Number (Form SS-5), Social Security Administration, Baltimore, Md.

[23]Martin Stanley Siegel, SS no. 109-20-2365, 1943, Application for Social Security Account No. (Form SS-5), Social Security Administration.

[24]City of New York, death certificate no. 156-95-051851 (1995), Martin Siegel; New York City Department of Health.

[25]1940 U.S. census, Kings County, New York, population schedule, page 10B, households 277–278, Henry and Rose Steinman, Helen and Martin Seigal [*sic*], Frank and Adele Katz; image, *Ancestry.com* (`https://www.ancestry.com/interactive/2442/m-t0627-02606-00250` : accessed 24 Sep 2017); citing NARA microfilm publication T627, roll 2606.

[26]Mark Siegel, phone interview, 10 Apr 2017.

[27]Steven D. Ginsburg to Richard Abdill, online message, 1 Jul 2017, relationship of Morris Siegel to Berdie Siegel; miscellaneous manuscripts; volume III documents; privately held by Abdill, Minneapolis, Minn.

[28]Nancy Abdill, interview, 28 Jun 2017. Their marriage license is dated 17 May 1952: City of New York, "NYC Marriage Index—Brooklyn 1952," microfilm publication, digitized by Reclaim the Records, *Archive.org* (`https://archive.org/stream/NYC_Marriage_`

Index_Brooklyn_1952/Reclaim_The_Records_-_NYC_Marriage_Index_
-_Brooklyn_-_1952 : accessed 17 Nov 2017), frames 34 and 838; entries for Ann Arbeiter and Martin Siegel, index no. 648.

[29] Social Security Administration, "Social Security Applications and Claims Index," database, *Ancestry.com* (http://search.ancestry.com/cgi-bin/sse.dll?indiv=1&dbid=60901&h=21517553 : accessed 24 Sep 2017), entry for Denise Barbara Luftman, died 19 Aug 2006, SS no. 143-38-8572.

[30] Nancy Abdill, phone interview, 28 Jun 2017.

[31] "Florida, Divorce Index, 1927–2001," database, *Ancestry.com* (http://search.ancestry.com/cgi-bin/sse.dll?indiv=1&dbid=8837&h=8736963 : accessed 24 Sep 2017), entry for Mark R. and Denise Siegel, divorced 29 Apr 1999.

[32] Mark Siegel (St. Petersburg, Fla.), phone interview by Richard Abdill, 25 Jul 2017; transcript held privately by interviewer, Minneapolis, Minn.

[33] City of New York, birth certificate no. 156-59-348567 (1959), Nancy Elizabeth Siegel; New York City Department of Health.

[34] State of New Jersey, marriage certificate, Richard John Abdill, Jr. and Nancy Elizabeth Siegel, 6 Sep 1986; Office of Registrar of Vital Statistics of Wrightstown Borough, Burlington County.

[35] City of New York, birth certificate no. 156-89-109756 (1989), Richard John Abdill III; New York City Department of Health.

[36] Nancy Abdill, phone interview, 26 Aug 2017.

[37] Mark Siegel, phone interview, 27 May 2017.

[38] Mark Siegel (St. Petersburg, Fla.), phone interview by Richard Abdill, 19 Nov 2017; transcript held privately by interviewer, Minneapolis, Minn.

[39] Nancy Abdill, interview, 28 Jun 2017.

[40] *Ibid.*

[41] *Ibid.*

[42] "U.S. Public Records Index, 1950–1993, Volume 1," database, *Ancestry.com* (http://search.ancestry.com/cgi-bin/sse.dll?indiv=1&dbid=1788&h=348504160&pid=110011109701 : accessed 24 Sep 2017), entry for Ronald J Dondero, 23 McCoy Ave, Metuchen, NJ.

[43] They bought their house in the early 2000s, but moved permanently later.

[44] Hudson County, NJ, birth recording extract no. 5681 (1954),

Ronald Dondero, born 15 May 1935; Board of Health and Vital Statistics.

[45] 1940 U.S. census, Hudson County, New Jersey, population schedule, page 702 (stamped), household 290, John, Carmella, John and Ronald Dondero; image, *Ancestry.com* (https://www.ancestry.com/interactive/2442/m-t0627-02351-00046/ : accessed 24 Sep 2017).

[46] "Today's Log: Births," *The Lima News*, 28 Feb 1963, p. 2, col. 3; digital image, *Ancestry.com* (https://www.ancestry.com/interactive/7751/NEWS-OH-LI_NE.1963_02_28_0002/ : accessed 24 Sep 2017).

[47] Nancy Abdill, interview, 28 Jun 2017.

[48] "Ohio, Birth Index, 1908–1964," database, *Ancestry.com* (http://search.ancestry.com/cgi-bin/sse.dll?indiv=1&dbid=3146&h=7818912 : accessed 24 Sep 2017), entry for John E Dondero, born 22 Feb 1963, state file no. 1963013788.

[49] Barbara Snyder, "High School Report: Drama Club Learns at Festival," *Asbury Park Press*, 4 Mar 1966, p. 12, col. 5.

[50] Nancy (Siegel) Abdill (Delran, NJ), phone interview by Richard Abdill, 21 Oct 2017; transcript held privately by interviewer, Minneapolis, Minn.

[51] Social Security Administration, "Social Security Death Index," database, *Ancestry.com* (http://search.ancestry.com/cgi-bin/sse.dll?indiv=1&dbid=3693&h=16063236 : accessed 24 Sep 2017), entry for John Dondero, died May 1980, SS no. 142-05-7812.

[52] "John Dondero," obituary, *Fremont News-Messenger*, 3 May 1980, p. 2, col. 2.

[53] *Ibid.*

[54] 1910 U.S. census, Hudson County, New Jersey, population schedule, Hoboken City, family 13, John, Jennie, Joseph, Ernest, Tessie, Florence, Raymond, Madeline, Grace and John Dondero; image, *Ancestry.com* (https://www.ancestry.com/interactive/7884/31111_4330909-00880/ : accessed 24 Sep 2017); citing NARA microfilm publication T624, roll 887.

[55] 1910 U.S. census, Hudson County, New Jersey, pop. sch., family 13, John, Jennie, Joseph, Ernest, Tessie, Florence, Raymond, Madeline, Grace and John Dondero.

[56] "John Dondero," *Fremont News-Messenger*, 3 May 1980.

[57] 1910 U.S. census, Hudson County, New Jersey, pop. sch., family 13, John, Jennie, Joseph, Ernest, Tessie, Florence, Raymond, Made-

line, Grace and John Dondero.

[58]Social Security Administration, "Social Security Death Index," database, *Ancestry.com* (`http://search.ancestry.com/cgi-bin/sse.dll?indiv=1&dbid=3693&h=16063021&pid=110011199072` : accessed 24 Sep 2017), entry for Carmella Dondero, died Sep 1976, SS no. 137-34-6642.

[59]"Mrs. John Dondero Sr.," obituary, *Fremont News-Messenger*, 15 Sep 1976, p. 8, col. 1.

[60]"Ohio, Deaths, 1908–1932, 1938–2007," database, *Ancestry.com* (`http://search.ancestry.com/cgi-bin/sse.dll?indiv=1&dbid=5763&h=1166156&pid=110011127089` : accessed 24 Sep 2017), entry for John J Dondero, died 2 May 1980, certificate 058731.

[61]Mark and Nancy Siegel, 1985, digitized and privately held by the author, Minneapolis, Minn., 2017. From the collection of Ann (Siegel) Dondero.

[62]The Siegel family at Mark's bar mitzvah celebration, 1968; digitized by the author; privately held by Nancy (Siegel) Abdill, Delran, NJ, 2017. Date of bar mitzvah from phone interview by the author with Mark Siegel, 27 May 2017.

[63]Mark and Nancy Siegel, abt 1963; digitized and privately held by the author, Minneapolis, Minn., 2017. From the collection of Ann (Siegel) Dondero.

[64]Ann Arbeiter and Marty Siegel wedding photo, 1952; digitized and privately held by the author, Minneapolis, Minn., 2017. From the collection of Ann (Siegel) Dondero.

[65]City of New York, death certificate no. 2292 (1932), Morris Seigel [sic]; New York City Department of Records.

[66]Mount Hebron Cemetery (Queens, New York, NY), online interment search (`http://www.mounthebroncemetery.com/location.asp?id=5826883` : accessed 24 Sep 2017), entry for Morris Seigel [*sic*], burial society "MEDWIN BEN ASSN."

[67]"Kiev Gubernia Duma Voters Lists Database," *JewishGen* (`https://www.jewishgen.org/databases/Ukraine/KievDuma.htm` : accessed 30 Sep 2017).

[68]Given name via Google Translate (`https://translate.google.com` : accessed 24 Sep 2017) translation of English "Moses" to Russian. Surname via list of Medvin Holocaust victims: "Medvin," *History of Jewish Communities in Ukraine* (`http://jewua.org/medvin/` : accessed 24 Sep 2017).

[69]1920 U.S. census, Kings County, New York, population schedule,

Brooklyn, dwelling 65, family 298, Samuel, Hannah, Jack, Bessie, Bertha, Sophia, Sylvia and Maurice [*sic*] Siegel; image, *Ancestry.com* (https://www.ancestry.com/interactive/6061/4313513-00338/ : accessed 24 Sep 2017); citing NARA microfilm publication T625, roll 1165.

[70]Marty and Helen Siegel, 1968; digitized by the author; privately held by Nancy (Siegel) Abdill, Delran, NJ, 2017.

[71]1905 New York state census, Kings County, election district 23, block A, Max, Sarah, Henry, Rose, Emma, William, Amelia and Helen Steinman; image, *Ancestry.com* (https://www.ancestry.com/interactive/7364/004296311_00503 : accessed 24 Sep 2017).

[72]City of New York, marriage certificate no. 9315 (1928), Morris Siegel and Helen Steinman; New York City Department of Records.

[73]1920 U.S. census, Kings County, New York, population schedule, Brooklyn, dwelling 117, family 318, Sarah, Henry, Rose, William, Amelia and Helen Steinman; image, *Ancestry.com* (https://www.ancestry.com/interactive/6061/4313503-01022/ : accessed 24 Sep 2017); citing NARA microfilm publication T625, roll 1153.

[74]NYC, marriage certificate no. 9315 (1928), Morris Siegel and Helen Steinman.

[75]NYC, death certificate no. 156-95-051851 (1995), Martin Siegel.

[76]Ginsburg to Abdill, 1 Jul 2017.

[77]NYC, death certificate no. 2292 (1932), Morris Seigel.

[78]1940 U.S. census, Kings County, New York, pop. sch., p. 10B, hholds 277–278, Henry and Rose Steinman, Helen and Martin Seigal, Frank and Adele Katz.

[79]Martin Stanley Siegel, SS no. 109-20-2365, 1943, Application for Social Security Account No. (Form SS-5), Social Security Administration.

[80]Manifest, S.S. *Kaiserin Auguste Victoria*, 28 Nov 1910, list 18, Salman, Jakob, Aron and Dwoire Sigal; *Passenger and Crew Lists of Vessels Arriving at New York , NY, 1897-1957*, microfilm publication T715, (Washington: National Archives and Records Service), roll 1601, frames 222–223.

[81]1930 U.S. census, Kings County, New York, population schedule, Brooklyn borough, dwelling 78, family 78, Sam and Sylvia Siegel, Birdie and Anna Boyd; image, *Ancestry.com* (https://www.ancestry.com/interactive/6224/4638803_00974/ : accessed 24 Sep 2017).

[82]The family's data from the 1920 census is suspect: Anna is listed

as "Hannah," for example, and someone told census-takers that the whole family spoke Polish when it is almost certain they spoke Yiddish (and came from an area far from the area then recognized as Poland). Still, Sam's occupation ("fruit") is accurate, as is the name of all six children, so it's hard not to conclude it's them. 1920 U.S. census, Kings Co., NY, pop. sch., Brooklyn, dwell. 65, fam. 298, Samuel, Hannah, Jack, Bessie, Bertha, Sophia, Sylvia and Maurice Siegel.

[83] City of New York, death certificate no. 24391 (1924), Mrs. Anna Siegel; New York City Department of Records.

[84] Ginsburg to Abdill, 1 Jul 2017.

[85] 1920 U.S. census, Kings Co., NY, pop. sch., Brooklyn, dwell. 65, fam. 298, Samuel, Hannah, Jack, Bessie, Bertha, Sophia, Sylvia and Maurice Siegel.

[86] Ginsburg to Abdill, 1 Jul 2017.

[87] *Ibid.*

[88] *Ibid.*

[89] *Ibid.*

[90] 1920 U.S. census, Kings Co., NY, pop. sch., Brooklyn, dwell. 65, fam. 298, Samuel, Hannah, Jack, Bessie, Bertha, Sophia, Sylvia and Maurice Siegel.

[91] Ginsburg to Abdill, 1 Jul 2017.

[92] *Ibid.*

[93] *Ibid.*

[94] Manifest, S.S. *Birma*, 19 May 1912, line 2, Basse Sigalow; *Passenger and Crew Lists of Vessels Arriving at New York , NY, 1897-1957*, microfilm publication T715, (Washington: National Archives and Records Service), roll 1864, frames 163–164.

[95] NYC, marriage certificate no. 9315 (1928), Morris Siegel and Helen Steinman.

[96] 1920 U.S. census, Kings Co., NY, pop. sch., Brooklyn, dwell. 65, fam. 298, Samuel, Hannah, Jack, Bessie, Bertha, Sophia, Sylvia and Maurice Siegel.

[97] Ginsburg to Abdill, 1 Jul 2017.

[98] City of New York, death certificate no. 8679 (1920), Sophie Siegel; New York City Department of Records.

[99] Manifest, S.S. *Birma*, 19 May 1912, list 23, line 22, Czipe Siga-

low; *Passenger and Crew Lists of Vessels Arriving at New York ,
NY, 1897-1957*, microfilm publication T715, (Washington: National
Archives and Records Service), roll 1864, frames 253–254.

[100] Ginsburg to Abdill, 1 Jul 2017.

[101] *Ibid.*

[102] *Ibid.*

[103] *Ibid..*

[104] "Ann Ginsburg Obituary," *Legacy.com* (http://www.legacy.com/
obituaries/herald/obituary-preview.aspx?n=ann-
ginsburg&pid=176199311 : accessed 24 Sep 2017).

[105] "New York City, Marriage License Indexes, 1907-1995," database
with images, *Ancestry.com* (http://search.ancestry.com/cgi-bin/
sse.dll?indiv=1&dbid=61406&h=513069&pid=110069745618 : accessed
24 Sep 2017), entries for Berdie E Boyer and Ruben D. Prussin, marriage license 25 Mar 1938.

[106] Social Security Administration, "Social Security Death Index,"
database, *Ancestry.com* (http://search.ancestry.com/cgi-bin/sse.
dll?indiv=1&dbid=3693&h=50174381&pid=110069745620 : accessed
24 Sep 2017), entry for Ruben D. Prussin, died 20 Jul 2000, SS no.
125-30-5285.

[107] 1915 New York state census, Kings County, election district 29,
ward 30, block 4, Davis [*sic*], Annie, George, Alfred and Rubin
Prussin; image, *Ancestry.com* (https://www.ancestry.com/interactive/
2703/32848_B094164-00363/ : accessed 24 Sep 2017).

[108] "Social Security Death Index," entry for Ruben D. Prussin, SS
no. 125-30-5285.

[109] 1940 U.S. census, Kings County, New York, population schedule, Brooklyn, household 182, Rubin, Berdie, Harriet, and Joseph
Prussin, Anne Long; image, *Ancestry.com* (https://www.ancestry.
com/interactive/2442/m-t0627-02594-00146/ : accessed 24 Sep 2017);
citing NARA microfilm publication T627, roll 2594.

[110] Social Security Administration, "Social Security Death Index,"
database, *Ancestry.com* (http://search.ancestry.com/cgi-bin/sse.
dll?indiv=1&dbid=3693&h=10516114&pid=110112982696 : accessed
24 Sep 2017), entry for Sylvia Chernow, died July 1986, SS no. 056-
07-2415.

[111] "Florida Death Index, 1877–1998," database, *Ancestry.com* (http:
//search.ancestry.com/cgi-bin/sse.dll?indiv=1&dbid=7338
&h=2442518&pid=110112982696 : accessed 24 Sep 2017), entry for
Sylvia Chernow, died 22 Jul 1986.

[112] Social Security Administration, "Social Security Death Index," database, *Ancestry.com* (`http://search.ancestry.com/cgi-bin/sse.dll?indiv=1&dbid=3693&h=10516081&pid=110112983381` : accessed 24 Sep 2017), entry for Max Chernow, died June 1981, SS no. 078-20-7939.

[113] *Ibid.*

[114] Ginsburg to Abdill, 1 Jul 2017.

[115] Manifest, S.S. *Birma*, 19 May 1912, list 23, line 23, Cziwil Sigalow; *Passenger and Crew Lists of Vessels Arriving at New York , NY, 1897-1957*, microfilm publication T715, (Washington: National Archives and Records Service), roll 1864, frame 253.

[116] 1920 U.S. census, Kings Co., NY, pop. sch., Brooklyn, dwell. 65, fam. 298, Samuel, Hannah, Jack, Bessie, Bertha, Sophia, Sylvia and Maurice Siegel.

[117] 1920 U.S. census, Kings Co., NY, pop. sch., Brooklyn, dwell. 65, fam. 298, Samuel, Hannah, Jack, Bessie, Bertha, Sophia, Sylvia and Maurice Siegel.

[118] Ginsburg to Abdill, 1 Jul 2017.

[119] Polland and Soyer, 120–121.

[120] City of New York, death certificate no. 24391 (1924), Mrs. Anna Siegel.

[121] Ginsburg to Abdill, 1 Jul 2017.

[122] City of New York, death certificate no. 12359 (1944), Sam Siegel; New York City Department of Records.

Chapter 8 Steinman

[1] City of New York, death certificate no. 6632 (1927 Brooklyn), Sarah Steinman; New York City Department of Records.

[2] 1905 New York state census, Kings County, New York, election district 23, Max, Sarah, Henry, Rose, Emma, William, Amelia and Helen Steinman; image, *Ancestry.com* (`https://www.ancestry.com/interactive/7364/004296311_00503/440312` : accessed 6 Oct 2017).

[3] Manifest, S.S. *Trave*, 28 Dec 1900, stamped p. 52, index numbers 13–17, Steinfurst family; *Passenger and Crew Lists of Vessels Arriving at New York , NY, 1897-1957*, microfilm publication T715, (Washington: National Archives and Records Service), roll 166, frame 365.

⁴City of New York, death certificate no. 6632 (1927 Brooklyn), Sarah Steinman.

⁵*JewishData*, database with images (`http://jewishdata.com/secure/record_detail.php?id=170561` : accessed 6 Oct 2017), entry 170561; Marcus Steinman; Old Mt. Carmel Cemetery. Translation by Laura Munzer and Robin Meltzer: Richard Abdill, discussion thread translation of Steinman gravestones, 13 Aug 2017, "Tracing the Tribe - Jewish Genealogy on Facebook," *Facebook.com* (`https://www.facebook.com/groups/tracingthetribe/permalink/10155611973050747/` : accessed 6 Oct 2017).

⁶City of New York, death certificate no. 5193 (1912 Brooklyn), Markus Steinman; New York City Department of Records.

⁷Manifest, S.S. *Trave*, 28 Dec 1900, stamped p. 53, index numbers 13–17, Steinfirst family; *Passenger and Crew Lists of Vessels Arriving at New York , NY, 1897-1957*, microfilm publication T715, (Washington: National Archives and Records Service), roll 166, frame 364.

⁸City of New York, death certificate no. 5193 (1912 Brooklyn), Markus Steinman.

⁹*JewishData*, entry 170561; Marcus Steinman; Old Mt. Carmel Cemetery. Translation by Laura Munzer and Robin Meltzer.

¹⁰Manifest, S.S. *Trave*, 28 Dec 1900, stamped p. 52, index numbers 13–17, Steinfirst family.

¹¹1905 New York state census, Max, Sarah, Henry, Rose, Emma, William, Amelia and Helen Steinman.

¹²1910 U.S. census, Kings County, New York, population schedule, Brooklyn Borough, dwelling 66, family 266, Morris, Sarah, Henry, Rose, Emma, William, Amalie and Helen Steinman; image, *Ancestry.com* (`https://www.ancestry.com/interactive/7884/4449988_00441/` : accessed 6 Oct 2017); citing NARA microfilm publication T624, roll 969.

¹³City of New York, death certificate no. 5193 (1912 Brooklyn), Markus Steinman.

¹⁴*JewishData*, entry 170561; Marcus Steinman; Old Mt. Carmel Cemetery.

¹⁵City of New York, marriage certificate no. 71114 (1887 Manhattan), Philip Simon and Lizzie Steinfirst; New York City Department of Records.

¹⁶1930 U.S. census, Kings County, New York, population schedule, Brooklyn Borough, dwelling 44, family 132, Philip, Lizzie and Louis

Simon, Sarah, Norman and Harold Barnett; image, *Ancestry.com* (`https://www.ancestry.com/interactive/6224/4638794_00603/` : accessed 6 Oct 2017).

[17] *JewishData*, database with images (`http://jewishdata.com/secure/record_detail.php?id=170570` : accessed 6 Oct 2017), entry 170570; Lizzie Simon; Mount Carmel Cemetery.

[18] City of New York, marriage certificate no. 71114 (1887 Manhattan), Philip Simon and Lizzie Steinfirst.

[19] 1900 U.S. census, Kings County, New York, population schedule, Brooklyn Borough, family 172, Philip, Lizzie, Sarah, Louis and Norman Simon, Henry Steinman; image, *Ancestry.com* (`https://www.ancestry.com/interactive/7602/4114549_00381/` : accessed 6 Oct 2017).

[20] Mount Carmel Cemetery (Glendale, NY), online interment search (`http://www.mountcarmelcemetery.com/location.asp?id=6317975` : accessed 6 Oct 2017), entry for Lizzie Simon, died 14 Apr 1950.

[21] *JewishData*, database with images (`http://jewishdata.com/secure/record_detail.php?id=170664` : accessed 6 Oct 2017), entry 170664; Michael Steinman; Mount Carmel Cemetery.

[22] City of New York, marriage certificate no. 1630 (1892 Manhattan), Michael Stone and Rebeca [*sic*] Hoffman; New York City Department of Records.

[23] *Ibid.*, death certificate no. 6275 (1917 Brooklyn), Michael Steinman; New York City Department of Records.

[24] *Ibid.*, marriage certificate no. 1630 (1892 Manhattan), Michael Stone and Rebeca Hoffman.

[25] "United States World War I Draft Registration Cards, 1917–1918," images, Ancestry.com (`https://www.ancestry.com/interactive/6482/005262795_01853/33330199` : accessed 6 Oct 2017), card for Henry Steinman, Local Draft Board No. 34, Brooklyn, NY.

[26] Social Security Administration, "Social Security Death Index," database, *Ancestry.com* (`http://search.ancestry.com/cgi-bin/sse.dll?indiv=1&dbid=3693&h=59779311` : accessed 6 Oct 2017), entry for Henry Steinman, died Sep 1969, SS no. 099-01-7200.

[27] 1905 New York state census, Max, Sarah, Henry, Rose, Emma, William, Amelia and Helen Steinman.

[28] "New York, New York Death Index, 1862–1948," database, *Ancestry.com* (`http://search.ancestry.com/cgi-bin/sse.dll?indiv=1&dbid=9131&h=4299719` : accessed 6 Oct 2017), entry for Morris Eisenstat, certificate no. 10150 (1945 Kings).

[29] City of New York, marriage certificate no. 4755 (1912 Brooklyn), Max Eisenstat and Emma Steinman; New York City Department of Records.

[30] 1940 U.S. census, Kings County, New York, population schedule, household 277, Henry and Rose Steinman, Helen and Martin Seigel [*sic*]; image, *Ancestry.com* (https://www.ancestry.com/interactive/2442/m-t0627-02606-00250/ : accessed 1 Oct 2017); citing NARA microfilm publication T627, roll 2606.

[31] Social Security Administration, "Social Security Death Index," database, *Ancestry.com* (http://search.ancestry.com/cgi-bin/sse.dll?indiv=1&dbid=3693&h=59780131 : accessed 6 Oct 2017), entry for William Steinman, died Oct 1961, SS no. 110-07-4703.

[32] "New York City, Marriage Indexes, 1907–1995," database, *Ancestry.com* (http://search.ancestry.com/cgi-bin/sse.dll?indiv=1&dbid=61406&h=7561532 : accessed 6 Oct 2017), entries for William G Steinman and Anna Friedman, certificate no. 15641 (Manhattan 1935).

[33] Manifest, S.S. *Trave*, 28 Dec 1900, stamped p. 52, index numbers 13–17, Steinfirst family.

[34] Mark Siegel (St. Petersburg, Fla.), phone interview by Richard Abdill, 27 May 2017; transcript held privately by interviewer, Minneapolis, Minn.

[35] "New York City, Marriage Indexes, 1907–1995," database, *Ancestry.com* (http://search.ancestry.com/cgi-bin/sse.dll?indiv=1&dbid=61406&h=7661212 : accessed 6 Oct 2017), entries for Adele Steinman and Frank Katz, certificate no. 10268 (Brooklyn 1931).

[36] Moses Rischin, *The Promised City: New York's Jews, 1870–1914* (Cambridge: Harvard University Press, 1962), 20.

[37] Tobias Brinkmann, *Points of Passage: Jewish Migrants from Eastern Europe in Scandinavia, Germany, and Britain 1880–1914* (New York: Berghahn Books, 2013), 53–54.

[38] Manifest, S.S. *Scandia*, 5 Dec 1892, index number 409, Heinr. Steinfurst; *Passenger and Crew Lists of Vessels Arriving at New York , NY, 1897-1957*, microfilm publication M237, (Washington: National Archives and Records Service), roll 600, frame 485.

[39] Manifest, S.S. *Kaiser Wilhelm der Grosse*, 20 Dec 1898, list no. 15, index no. 21, Rosa Steinfirst; *Passenger and Crew Lists of Vessels Arriving at New York , NY, 1897-1957*, microfilm publication T715, (Washington: National Archives and Records Service), roll 44, frame 137.

[40] 1900 U.S. census, Kings County, New York, population schedule, Brooklyn Borough, dwelling 15, family 52, Michael, Rebecca, Lewis, Sadie and Nettie Steinman; image, *Ancestry.com* (`https://www.ancestry.com/interactive/7602/4114560_00259/` : accessed 6 Oct 2017).

[41] 1900 U.S. census, Kings County, New York, pop. sch., fam. 172, Philip, Lizzie, Sarah, Louis and Norman Simon, Henry Steinman.

[42] 1910 U.S. census, Kings County, New York, pop. sch., dwell. 66, fam. 266, Morris, Sarah, Henry, Rose, Emma, William, Amalie and Helen Steinman.

[43] City of New York, death certificate no. 5193 (1912 Brooklyn), Markus Steinman.

[44] "United States World War I Draft Registration Cards, 1917–1918," images, Ancestry.com (`https://www.ancestry.com/interactive/6482/005262795_01854/33330200` : accessed 18 Nov 2017), card for William G. Steinman, Precinct 158, Brooklyn, NY.

[45] 1920 U.S. census, Kings County, New York, population schedule, Brooklyn Borough, dwelling 117, family 318, Sarah, Henry, Rose, William, Amelia and Helen Steinman; image, *Ancestry.com* (`https://www.ancestry.com/interactive/6061/4313503-01022/` : accessed 6 Oct 2017); citing NARA microfilm publication T625, roll 1153.

[46] City of New York, death certificate no. 6632 (1927 Brooklyn), Sarah Steinman.

[47] 1900 U.S. census, Kings County, New York, pop. sch., fam. 172, Philip, Lizzie, Sarah, Louis and Norman Simon, Henry Steinman.

[48] *Ibid.*

[49] City of New York, marriage certificate no. 71114 (1887 Manhattan), Philip Simon and Lizzie Steinfirst.

[50] 1900 U.S. census, Kings County, New York, pop. sch., fam. 172, Philip, Lizzie, Sarah, Louis and Norman Simon, Henry Steinman.

[51] *Ibid.*

[52] *Ibid.*

[53] Mark Siegel, phone interview, 27 May 2017.

[54] 1920 U.S. census, Kings County, New York, population schedule, Boro of Brooklyn, dwelling 112, family 395, Herman, Sadie and Norman Barnett; image, *Ancestry.com* (`https://www.ancestry.com/interactive/6061/4313895-00759/6` : accessed 7 Oct 2017).

[55] Sarah is living with her parents in 1910, and her son Norman

was born abt 1913. 1910 U.S. census, Kings County, New York, population schedule, Brooklyn Ward 19, dwelling 11, family 59, Phillip [*sic*], Lizzie, Louis and Sadie Simon; image, *Ancestry.com* (`https://www.ancestry.com/interactive/7884/4449796_00429/` : accessed 7 Oct 2017); citing NARA microfilm publication T624, roll 968.

[56] 1940 U.S. census, Kings County, New York, population schedule, Brooklyn, household 65, Philip and Elizabeth Simon, Sadie, Norman and Harold Barnett; image, *Ancestry.com* (`https://www.ancestry.com/interactive/2442/m-t0627-02600-00407/` : accessed 7 Oct 2017); citing NARA microfilm publication T627, roll 2600.

[57] 1930 U.S. census, Kings County, New York, population schedule, Brooklyn Borough, dwelling 44, family 132, Philip, Lizzie and Louis Simon, Sarah, Norman and Harold Barnett; image, *Ancestry.com* (`https://www.ancestry.com/interactive/6224/4638794_00603/` : accessed 7 Oct 2017).

[58] *Ibid.*

[59] Mark Siegel, phone interview, 27 May 2017.

[60] "United States World War I Draft Registration Cards, 1917–1918," images, Ancestry.com (`https://www.ancestry.com/interactive/6482/005262795_01639/33329985` : accessed 7 Oct 2017), card for Louis Simon, Local Draft Board, Precinct 155, Brooklyn, NY.

[61] 1930 U.S. census, Kings County, New York, population schedule, Brooklyn Borough, dwelling 44, family 132, Philip, Lizzie and Louis Simon, Sarah, Norman and Harold Barnett; image, *Ancestry.com* (`https://www.ancestry.com/interactive/6224/4638794_00603/` : accessed 7 Oct 2017).

[62] Social Security Administration, "Social Security Applications and Claims Index, 1936–2007," database, *Ancestry.com* (`http://search.ancestry.com/cgi-bin/sse.dll?indiv=1&dbid=60901&h=8611753` : accessed 7 Oct 2017), entry for Louis Simon, SS no. 054-09-0894. (This is the record that first revealed the original name that the Steinman family used when they arrived in America—Louis's mother's name is listed here as "Lizzie Steinfurst." See the "Finding the Steinmans" appendix for more.)

[63] 1900 U.S. census, Kings County, New York, pop. sch., fam. 172, Philip, Lizzie, Sarah, Louis and Norman Simon, Henry Steinman.

[64] 1900 U.S. census, Kings County, New York, pop. sch., fam. 172, Philip, Lizzie, Sarah, Louis and Norman Simon, Henry Steinman.

[65] Italian Genealogical Group, "NYC Municipal Archives," database (`http://www.italiangen.org/records-search/deaths.php` : accessed 7 Oct 2017), search for surname "Simon" in Kings County, records

between 1887 and 1900.

[66] Mount Carmel Cemetery (Glendale, NY), online interment search, entry for Lizzie Simon.

[67] Mount Carmel Cemetery (Glendale, NY), online interment search (`http://www.mountcarmelcemetery.com/location.asp?id=6320321` : accessed 7 Oct 2017), entry for Philip Simon, died 25 Apr 1952.

[68] *JewishData*, entry 170570; Lizzie Simon; Mount Carmel Cemetery.

[69] *JewishData*, entry 170664; Michael Steinman; Mount Carmel Cemetery.

[70] 1910 U.S. census, Kings County, New York, population schedule, Brooklyn Ward 21, dwelling 23, family 73, Michael, Rebecca, Louis and Sadie Steinman, Rosie Berchock; image, *Ancestry.com* (`https://www.ancestry.com/interactive/7884/4449988_00681/` : accessed 7 Oct 2017); citing NARA microfilm publication T624, roll 969.

[71] 1900 U.S. census, Kings County, New York, pop. sch., dwell. 15, fam. 52, Michael, Rebecca, Lewis, Sadie and Nettie Steinman.

[72] *JewishData*, database with images (`http://jewishdata.com/secure/record_detail.php?id=170730` : accessed 7 Oct 2017), entry 170730; Rebecca Steinman; Old Mt. Carmel Cemetery.

[73] 1900 U.S. census, Kings County, New York, pop. sch., dwell. 15, fam. 52, Michael, Rebecca, Lewis, Sadie and Nettie Steinman.

[74] 1920 U.S. census, Kings County, New York, population schedule, Brooklyn, dwelling 142, family 305, Irving and Sylvia Jacobson, Rebecca Steinman; image, *Ancestry.com* (`https://www.ancestry.com/interactive/6061/4313503-00873/` : accessed 7 Oct 2017); citing NARA microfilm publication T625, roll 1153.

[75] 1930 U.S. census, Kings County, New York, population schedule, Brooklyn, dwelling 45, family 295, Louis H and Rebecca Steinman; image, *Ancestry.com* (`https://www.ancestry.com/interactive/6224/4638822_01118/` : accessed 7 Oct 2017).

[76] "Search," database, *CastleGarden.org* (`http://www.castlegarden.org/quick_search_detail.php?p_id=10682762` : accessed 18 Nov 2017), entry for Riwke Hoffman, arrived 23 Mar 1885.

[77] City of New York, marriage certificate no. 1630 (1892 Manhattan), Michael Stone and Rebeca Hoffman.

[78] 1900 U.S. census, Kings County, New York, pop. sch., dwell. 15, fam. 52, Michael, Rebecca, Lewis, Sadie and Nettie Steinman.

[79] "New York City, Marriage License Indexes, 1907–1995," database

with images, *Ancestry.com* (https://search.ancestry.com/cgi-bin/
sse.dll?indiv=1&dbid=61406&h=8568280 : accessed 18 Nov 2017),
entries for Louis Steinman and Miriam A Cohen, license 6844 issued
19 Mar 1919.

[80] Social Security Administration, "U.S., Social Security Applications and Claims Index, 1936–2007," database, *Ancestry.com* (https:
//search.ancestry.com/cgi-bin/sse.dll?indiv=1&dbid=60901
&h=17902229 : accessed 18 Nov 2017), entry for Barbara Jeanne
Solky, died 17 May 2007, SS no. 100-18-3358.

[81] National Archives and Records Administration, "New York, State
and Federal Naturalization Records, 1794–1940," database with images, *Ancestry.com* (https://www.ancestry.com/interactive/2280/
32126_23148330429371-00186/3435872 : accessed 18 Nov 2017), petition for citizenship, "Sylvia Jacobson nee Sylvia Steinman," born
4 Aug 1894.

[82] Social Security Administration, "Social Security Death Index,"
database, *Ancestry.com* (https://search.ancestry.com/cgi-bin/sse.
dll?indiv=1&dbid=3693&h=30286584 : accessed 18 Nov 2017), entry
for Sylvia Jacobson, died May 1974, SS no. 097-20-0418. Note: The
person in this record is recorded with the birth date 27 Sep 1894,
rather than 4 Aug, so it could be someone else.

[83] "New York, State and Federal Naturalization Records, 1794–
1940," database with images, *Ancestry.com*, petition for citizenship,
Sylvia Jacobson nee Sylvia Steinman, born 4 Aug 1894.

[84] Social Security Administration, "Social Security Death Index,"
database, *Ancestry.com* (https://search.ancestry.com/cgi-bin/sse.
dll?indiv=1&dbid=3693&h=87382992 : accessed 18 Nov 2017), entry
for Malcolm Arthur Jacobson, died 15 May 2010.

[85] 1930 U.S. census, Kings County, New York, population schedule,
dwelling 45, family 664, Irving, Sylvia, Malcolm A and Jacques F Jacobson; image, *Ancestry.com* (https://www.ancestry.com/interactive/
6224/4638822_01118/39460779 : accessed 18 Nov 2017).

[86] "Social Security Death Index," database, *Ancestry.com*, entry
for Malcolm Arthur Jacobson.

[87] "U.S. Public Records Index, 1950–1993, Volume 1," database,
Ancestry.com (https://search.ancestry.com/cgi-bin/sse.dll?indiv=
1&dbid=1788&h=385599920 : accessed 18 Nov 2017), entry for Jacques
F Jacobson, born 26 Nov 1925.

[88] Italian Genealogical Group, "New York City Births Index," database
(http://www.italiangen.org/records-search/births.php : accessed
18 Nov 2017), entry for Lina [*sic*] Steinman, certificate no. 18251

(1897).

[89] Italian Genealogical Group, "Deaths, NYC Municipal Archives," database (`http://www.italiangen.org/records-search/deaths.php` : accessed 18 Nov 2017), entry for Lena Steinman, certificate no. 11891 (1898).

[90] 1900 U.S. census, Kings County, New York, population schedule, dwell. 15, fam. 52, Michael, Rebecca, Lewis, Sadie and Nettie Steinman.

[91] City of New York, death certificate no. 6275 (1917 Brooklyn), Michael Steinman, New York City Department of Records.

[92] *JewishData*, entry 170664; Michael Steinman; Mount Carmel Cemetery.

[93] *JewishData*, entry 170730; Rebecca Steinman; Mount Carmel Cemetery.

[94] Rose, Emma and Henry Steinman, 1968; digitized by the author; privately held by Nancy Abdill, Delran, NJ, 2017.

[95] "United States World War I Draft Registration Cards, 1917–1918," card for Henry Steinman, Brooklyn, NY.

[96] "Search," *CastleGarden.org* (`http://www.castlegarden.org/searcher.php` : accessed 18 Nov 2017), entry 7024267, Himr Stenifurst.

[97] Manifest, S.S. *Scandia*, 5 Dec 1892, index no. 409, Heinr. Steinfurst, *Passenger and Crew Lists of Vessels Arriving at New York , NY, 1897-1957*, microfilm publication M237, (Washington: National Archives and Records Service), roll 600, frame 485.

[98] 1900 U.S. census, Kings County, New York, pop. sch., fam. 172, Philip, Lizzie, Sarah, Louis and Norman Simon.

[99] Joe Beine, "The Barge Office, New York City - Manhattan," *Immigrant Processing Centers for New York City* (`http://www.genealogybranches.com/ellisisland/bargeoffice.html` : accessed 18 Nov 2017).

[100] "New York, Index to Petitions for Naturalization filed in New York City, 1792–1989," database with images, *Ancestry.com* (`https://www.ancestry.com/interactive/7733/INSX_S354J_S361C-0445/538622` : accessed 18 Nov 2017), entry for Henry Steinman, b. 20 Jan 1877, card no. 5355.

[101] 1920 U.S. census, Kings County, New York, pop. sch., dwell. 117, fam. 318, Sarah, Henry, Rose, William, Amelia and Helen Steinman.

[102] 1910 U.S. census, Kings County, New York, pop. sch., dwell. 23, fam. 73, Michael, Rebecca, Louis and Sadie Steinman, Rosie Berchock.

[103] 1900 U.S. census, Kings County, New York, pop. sch., dwell. 15, fam. 52, Michael, Rebecca, Lewis, Sadie and Nettie Steinman.

[104] 1930 U.S. census, Kings County, New York, population schedule, dwelling 72, family 72, Henry, Rose, William and Adele Steinman; image, *Ancestry.com* (https://www.ancestry.com/interactive/6224/4638865_00327/90645461 : accessed 18 Nov 2017).

[105] 1940 U.S. census, Kings County, New York, pop. sch., hholds 277–278, Henry and Rose Steinman, Helen and Martin Seigal, Frank and Adele Katz.

[106] Manifest, S.S. *Trave*, 28 Dec 1900, p. 52, index nos. 13–17, Steinfirst family.

[107] Manifest, S.S. *Kaiser Wilhelm der Grosse*, 20 Dec 1898, stamped p. 95, index no. 21, Rosa Steinfurst.

[108] "New York, Index to Petitions for Naturalization filed in New York City, 1792–1989," database with images, *Ancestry.com*, entry for Henry Steinman, card no. 5355.

[109] Social Security Administration, "Social Security Death Index," database, *Ancestry.com* (https://search.ancestry.com/cgi-bin/sse.dll?indiv=1&dbid=3693&h=59779311 : accessed 18 Nov 2017), entry for Henry Steinman, died Sep 1969, SS no. 099-01-7200.

[110] 1905 New York state census, Kings County, New York, Max, Sarah, Henry, Rose, Emma, William, Amelia and Helen Steinman.

[111] Manifest, S.S. *Kaiser Wilhelm der Grosse*, 29 Aug 1900, stamped p. 124, index no. 1, Emma Steinfirst, *Passenger and Crew Lists of Vessels Arriving at New York , NY, 1897-1957*, microfilm publication T715, (Washington: National Archives and Records Service), roll 146, frame 145.

[112] 1910 U.S. census, Kings County, New York, pop. sch., dwell. 66, fam. 266, Morris, Sarah, Henry, Rose, Emma, William, Amalie and Helen Steinman.

[113] 1905 New York state census, Kings County, New York, Max, Sarah, Henry, Rose, Emma, William, Amelia and Helen Steinman.

[114] City of New York, marriage certificate no. 1995 (1927 Brooklyn), Solomon Arbeiter and Clara Reinstein.

[115] 1915 New York state census, New York City, Max and Emma Eisenstat; image, *Ancestry.com* (https://www.ancestry.com/

`interactive/2703/32848_B094077-00209/10628510` : accessed 18 Nov 2017).

[116] City of New York, marriage certificate no. 1995 (1927 Brooklyn), Solomon Arbeiter and Clara Reinstein.

[117] *Ibid.*

[118] 1915 New York state census, New York City, Max and Emma Eisenstat.

[119] Emma Eisenstadt, Rose Steinman and Mark Siegel, 1968; digitized by the author, privately held by Nancy Abdill, Delran, NJ, 2017.

[120] 1940 U.S. census, Kings County, New York, pop. sch., hhold 277, Henry and Rose Steinman, Helen and Martin Seigel.

[121] Manifest, S.S. *Kaiser Wilhelm der Grosse*, 20 Dec 1898, stamped p. 95, index no. 21, Rosa Steinfurst, *Passenger and Crew Lists of Vessels Arriving at New York , NY, 1897-1957*, microfilm publication T715, (Washington: National Archives and Records Service), roll 44, frame 642.

[122] 1920 U.S. census, Kings County, New York, pop. sch., dwell. 117, fam. 318, Sarah, Henry, Rose, William, Amelia and Helen Steinman.

[123] "United States World War I Draft Registration Cards, 1917–1918," card for William G. Steinman, Brooklyn, NY.

[124] Manifest, S.S. *Trave*, 28 Dec 1900, stamped p. 52, index numbers 13–17, Steinfirst family.

[125] 1905 New York state census, Kings County, New York, Max, Sarah, Henry, Rose, Emma, William, Amelia and Helen Steinman.

[126] 1910 U.S. census, Kings County, New York, pop. sch., dwell. 66, fam. 266, Morris, Sarah, Henry, Rose, Emma, William, Amalie and Helen Steinman.

[127] 1920 U.S. census, Kings County, New York, pop. sch., dwell. 117, fam. 318, Sarah, Henry, Rose, William, Amelia and Helen Steinman.

[128] "New York City, Marriage License Indexes, 1907–1995," database with images, *Ancestry.com* (`https://search.ancestry.com/cgi-bin/sse.dll?indiv=1&dbid=61406&h=7561532` : accessed 18 Nov 2017), entries for William G Steinman and Anna Friedman, license number 15641.

[129] 1940 U.S. census, New York, NY, population schedule, Manhattan, household 198, William, Anne and Sandra Steinman; im-

age, *Ancestry.com* (https://www.ancestry.com/interactive/2442/ m-t0627-02642-00651/ : accessed 6 Oct 2017); citing NARA microfilm publication T627, roll 2642.

[130] Mark Siegel (St. Petersburg, Fla.), phone interview by Richard Abdill, 10 Apr 2017; transcript held privately by interviewer, Minneapolis, Minn.

[131] 1940 U.S. census, New York, NY, pop. sch., hhold 198, William, Anne and Sandra Steinman.

[132] Mark Siegel, phone interview, 10 Apr 2017.

[133] Social Security Administration, "Social Security Death Index," database, *Ancestry.com* (https://search.ancestry.com/cgi-bin/sse. dll?indiv=1&dbid=3693&h=59780131 : accessed 18 Nov 2017), entry for William Steinman, died Oct 1961, SS no. 110-07-4703.

[134] Mark Siegel, phone interview, 10 Apr 2017.

[135] 1920 U.S. census, Kings County, New York, pop. sch., dwell. 117, fam. 318, Sarah, Henry, Rose, William, Amelia and Helen Steinman.

[136] 1930 U.S. census, Kings County, New York, pop. sch., dwell. 72, fam. 72, Henry, Rose, William and Adele Steinman.

[137] 1910 U.S. census, Kings County, New York, pop. sch., dwell. 66, fam. 266, Morris, Sarah, Henry, Rose, Emma, William, Amalie and Helen Steinman.

[138] 1930 U.S. census, Kings County, New York, pop. sch., dwell. 72, fam. 72, Henry, Rose, William and Adele Steinman.

[139] "New York, New York, Marriage Certificate Index 1866–1937," database, *Ancestry.com* (https://search.ancestry.com/cgi-bin/sse. dll?indiv=1&dbid=9105&h=4216431 : accessed 18 Nov 2017), entries for Frank Katz and Adele Steinman, certificate no. 7326 (Kings County).

[140] "U.S. Passport Applications, 1795-1925," record for Frank Katz, application 79129.

[141] National Archives and Records Administration, "New York, State and Federal Naturalization Records, 1794–1940," database with images, *Ancestry.com* (https://www.ancestry.com/interactive/2280/ 007792485_00791/3627076 : accessed 18 Nov 2017), declaration of intention, Frank Katz, born 14 Feb 1893.

[142] "U.S. Passport Applications, 1795-1925," database with images, *Ancestry.com* (https://www.ancestry.com/interactive/1174/USM1490_ 1327-0503/957558 : accessed 18 Nov 2017), record for Frank Katz,

b. 14 Feb 1893, application 79129.

Chapter 9 Borowski

[1] City of New York, death certificate no. 6632 (1927 Brooklyn), Sarah Steinman.

[2] "Ancestor Search Engine," *JewishData.com*, database with images (http://jewishdata.com/secure/record_detail.php?id=170595 : accessed 11 Nov 2017), entry 170595 for Sarah Steinman, died 1927.

[3] "Rajgrod Births, Marriages, Deaths," *Jewish Records Indexing – Poland* (http://jri-poland.org/jriplweb.htm : accessed 11 Nov 2017) entries for Nochym Borowski and Reuza Eufman, year 1844 akta 2.

Chapter 10 Shifting borders

[1] Agnieszka Barbara Nance, *Literary and Cultural Images of a Nation Without a State: The Case of Nineteenth-century Poland* (Bern, Switzerland: Peter Lang, 2008), 8.

[2] Joseph Ehrenfried, *Colloquial Phrases and Dialogues in German and English* (Philadelphia: Joseph A. Speel, 1834), 91.

[3] Lida Clara Schem, *The Hyphen*, volume 1 (New York: E.P. Dutton, 1920), 467.

[4] Gustav Liek, *Die Stadt Schippenbeil* (Konigsberg: Commissions-Verlag von Braun Weber, 1874).

[5] Information via "Medzhibozh," *History of Jewish Communities in Ukraine* (http://jewua.org/medzhibozh/ : accessed 8 Oct 2017). Photograph from Wikimedia Commons, "Medzhybizh,Bach's Synagogue.jpg" (https://commons.wikimedia.org/wiki/File:Medzhybizh, Bach%27s_Synagogue.jpg : accessed 8 Oct 2017), uploaded by user Irenmatye.

Chapter 11 Wyszogród memories

[1] Jack Kugelmass and Jonathan Boyarin, eds., *From a Ruined Garden: The Memorial Books of Polish Jewry*, second expanded edition (Indiana University Press, 1998), 1.

[2] Kugelmass and Boyarin, 2.

³Lawrence A. Hoffman, "9/11: Remembering How We Remembered," *Life and a Little Liturgy* (`https://blog.lawrenceahoffman.com/2011/09/11/911-remembering-how-we-remembered/` : accessed 19 Nov 2017).

⁴Marc Kaminsky, "All That Our Eyes Have Witnessed: Memories of a Living History Workshop in the South Bronx," *Twenty-Five Years of the Life Review: Theoretical and Practical Considerations*, ebook (`https://books.google.com/books?id=83psBAAAQBAJ` : accessed 19 Nov 2017), 105.

⁵Email communication between the author and Lance Ackerfeld, JewishGenYizkor Book Project supervisor, 16–17 Sep 2017.

⁶Joyce Field, "Zachor: Yizkor Books as Collective Memory of a Lost World," *Yizkor Book Insights* (`https://www.jewishgen.org/yizkor/ybinsights.html` : accessed 19 Nov 2017).

⁷Ida Selavan Schwarcz, "Yizker Bikher as Preservers of Family and Community History," *Yizkor Book Insights*.

⁸`http://yizkor.nypl.org/index.php?id=1401`

⁹Ackerfeld to Abdill.

¹⁰Simon bar Kokhba was the leader of the last of the wars between Judea and the Roman Empire. His connection in this case to "Shulamit" is unclear. Bar Kokhba was the subject of a play by Yiddish playwright Avrom Goldfadn, who also write an operetta called *Shulamis*; this is the only ready answer, though not a satisfying one.

Chapter 12   HaShoah

¹Yad Vashem, "The Holocaust: Definition and Preliminary Discussion," *The Holocaust Resource Center* (`http://www.yadvashem.org/yv/en/holocaust/resource_center/the_holocaust.asp` : accessed 18 Nov 2017).

²Wyszogrod PSA Books of Residence, entry for Haim Aron Bilgoraj, house 124.

³"Central Database of Shoah Victims' Names," database with images, *Yad Vashem* (`http://yvng.yadvashem.org/nameDetails.html?language=en&itemId=3937635` : accessed 18 Nov 2017), entry 3937635, Surah Bilgraj [*sic*]. An administrator at Yad Vashem said they had no record indicating the identities of the people in the photo. Email communication between the author and Ariela Koppelman, Yad Vashem Hall of Names, 1 Aug 2017.

[4] "Medzhibozh," *The Untold Stories: The Murder Sites of the Jews in the Occupied Territories of the Former USSR* (http://yadvashem.org/untoldstories/database/index.asp?cid=497 : accessed 7 Oct 2017).

[5] "Central Database of Shoah Victims' Names," database with images, *Yad Vashem* (http://yvng.yadvashem.org/ : accessed 18 Nov 2017), entry 893238, Avadya Veinshtein.

[6] *Ibid.*, entry 1119555, Reizl Veinshtein.

[7] *Ibid.*, entry 7223768, Evede Vaynshteyn.

[8] *Ibid.*, entry 5646068, Gregory Veinshtein.

[9] Yahad-In Unum, "Execution Sites of Jewish Victims" (http://yahadmap.org/ : accessed 18 Nov 2017), entries for Medzhybizh.

[10] "Medzhibozh, Ukraine, Postwar, A mass grave," digital scan of photograph, *Yad Vashem*, item ID 39131. Photo courtesy of Dr. Gindos.

[11] "Central Database of Shoah Victims' Names," database with images, *Yad Vashem* (http://yvng.yadvashem.org/ : accessed 18 Nov 2017), entry 3956392, Brucha Bilgraj.

[12] American-Israeli Cooperative Enterprise, "Wyszogrod," *Jewish Virtual Library* (http://www.jewishvirtuallibrary.org/wyszogrod : accessed 18 Nov 2017.

[13] "Central Database of Shoah Victims' Names," database with images, *Yad Vashem* (http://yvng.yadvashem.org/ : accessed 18 Nov 2017), entry 7371701, Alek Arbajter.

[14] *Ibid.*, entry 7371870, Hirsz Iccak Arbajter.

[15] *Ibid.*, entry 7372048, Hagar Arbajter.

[16] *Ibid.*, entry 7700830, Joseph Arbajter.

[17] *Ibid.*, entry 10685269, Yitzchak Arbeiter.

[18] *Ibid.*, entry 10685270, Hungara Arbeiter.

[19] *Ibid.*, entry 10685268, Elek Arbeiter.

[20] David Filipov, "Izzy and Anna Arbeiter found—and saved—each other," *Boston Globe*, online edition, 3 Jun 2012 (https://www.bostonglobe.com/metro/2012/06/02/izzy-and-anna-arbeiter-found-and-saved-each-other/KTQR8DY91nuKaNkuqcCnMP/story.html : accessed 14 Oct 2017).

[21] "Central Database of Shoah Victims' Names," database with images, *Yad Vashem* (http://yvng.yadvashem.org/ : accessed 18

Nov 2017), entry 1274890, Ihezkel Arbeiter.

[22] *Ibid.*, entry 1852979, Lea Arbeiter.

[23] *Ibid.*, entry 4116092, Mordekhai Arbeiter.

[24] *Ibid.*, entry 7244272, Aaron Arbeiter.

[25] *Ibid.*, entry 5076549, Ziskind Arbeiter.

[26] *Ibid.*, entry 9823046, Khana Arbeiter.

[27] *Ibid.*, entry 5076550, Khaim Arbeiter.

[28] *Ibid.*, entry 402883, Khava Florman.

[29] *Ibid.*, entry 1707415, Moshe Florman.

[30] *Ibid.*, entry 1242417, Itka Florman.

[31] *Ibid.*, entry 1242421, Israel Florman.

[32] *Ibid.*, entry 5410374, Jacob Bilgora.

[33] Wyszogrod PSA Births, Marriages, Deaths 1886-1906, entries for Brucha Poznanski and Aron Bilgoraj, document 2.

[34] *Ibid.*, entry 3956392, Brucha Bilgraj.

[35] Wyszogrod PSA Books of Residence, entry for Haja Rykla Bilgoraj, house 124.

[36] *Ibid.*, entry 3935469, Chaia Bilgraj.

[37] Wyszogrod PSA Books of Residence, entry for Izrael Bilgoraj, house 124.

[38] *Ibid.*, entry 3931440, Israel Bilgraj

[39] No birth record has been found for Surah, but she is described in testimony from her cousin as being about five years younger than her sister Haja, who we know was born in 1905. (It should be noted that the cousin seems to have guessed their ages incorrectly, likely because she did not know their exact dates of birth: She estimated that Haja was 43 when she died, which, to be true, would have meant she died three years after the end of the war.)

[40] *Ibid.*, entry 3937635, Surah Bilgraj

[41] Ada Holtzman, translator, "List of the Deceased before the Holocaust, as Submitted by the Relatives," *Book to the Martyrs of Wyszogrod*, partially transcribed by JewishGen (https://www.jewishgen.org/yizkor/Wyszogrod/Wyszogrod.html : accessed 18 Nov 2017).

[42] "Israel Arbeiter's Biography," *America.gov*, U.S. State Department (http://photos.state.gov/libraries/poland/788/pdfs/izzybio.

pdf : accessed 18 Nov 2017).

[43] "Studio portrait of religious grandparents and their young grandson.," digital scan of photograph, *United States Holocaust Memorial Museum*, photograph no. 66109 (https://collections.ushmm.org/search/catalog/pa1159045 : accessed 18 Nov 2017). Photo courtesy of Israel Arbeiter.

[44] Israel Arbeiter (Newton, Mass.), phone interview by Richard Abdill, 9 Aug 2017; transcript held privately by interviewer, Minneapolis, Minn.

[45] Wyszogrod PSA Books of Residence, entry for Josek Arbajter, house 218.

[46] "Plock, Poland, An SS soldier supervising the deportation of Jews," digital scan of photograph, *Yad Vashem*, item ID 8732. Photo via Alexander Bernfas.

[47] "Plock, Poland, Jews, wearing armbands, inside open train cars at the time of their deportation," digital scan of photograph, *Yad Vashem*, item ID 98492. Photo by Shlomo Margalit, via Ephraim Zorof.

[48] "MEDVIN: Bohuslavskyi Raion, Kyiv Oblast," *International Jewish Cemetery Project* (https://www.iajgsjewishcemeteryproject.org/ukraine/medvin.html : accessed 14 Oct 2017).

[49] "Central Database of Shoah Victims' Names," database with images, *Yad Vashem* (http://yvng.yadvashem.org/ : accessed 18 Nov 2017), entry 1644556, Sizel (Sigalov) Shubinskaya.

[50] *Ibid.*, entry 11131562, Matvey Sigalov.

[51] *Ibid.*, entry 3906785, Iosiph Sigalov.

[52] *Ibid.*, entry 9826665, Iosiph Sigalov.

[53] *Ibid.*, entry 3566676, Freida Sigalov.

[54] *Ibid.*, entry 1674246, Braina (Geller) Sigalova.

[55] *Ibid.*, entry 9826663, Ben Sigalov.

[56] "Ilya Levitas," *Jewish Confederation of Ukraine* (http://www.jewukr.org/biograf/levitas_e.html : accessed 17 Oct 2017).

[57] "Central Database of Shoah Victims' Names," database with images, *Yad Vashem* (http://yvng.yadvashem.org/ : accessed 18 Nov 2017), entry 9826662, Aryl Sigalov.

[58] *Ibid.*, entry 9826664, Duved Sigalov.

[59] *Ibid.*, entry 9826666, Zus Sigalov.

[60] *Ibid.*, entry 9826667, Kutz Sigalov.

[61] *Ibid.*, entry 9826668, Leyba Sigalov.

[62] *Ibid.*, entry 9826669, Nusik Sigalov.

[63] *Ibid.*, entry 9826670, Moshko Sigalov.

[64] *Ibid.*, entry 9826671, Osvey Sigalov.

[65] *Ibid.*, entry 9826672, Srul Sigalov.

[66] *Ibid.*, entry 9826674, Yakov Sigalov.

[67] *Ibid.*, entry 9826673, First name unknown Sigalov.

[68] *Ibid.*, entry 9826675, Pyrlya Sigalova.

[69] *Ibid.*, entry 9826676, Sophia Sigalova.

[70] *Ibid.*, entry 9826677, Khava Sigalova.

[71] "Historia," *Urzad Gminy Raczki* (http://www.raczki.pl/art, 83,historia.html : accessed 7 Oct 2017).

Chapter 13   Genetic testing

[1] Baruch Dziedzic photo, from his gravestone at Waldheim Cemetery, Forest Park, Illinois; image privately held by Mitch Gordon, St. Paul, Minn., 2017.

[2] Richard Abdill, Scott Gordon and Mitch Gordon, St. Paul, Minn., 27 Sep 2017. Digital photo, held by the author, Minneapolis, Minn., 2017.

Chapter A   Translated documents

[1] Wyszogrod vital records, entry for marriage of Zelman Arbayter and Ryfka Chrzanowska, year 1843, akta 2, FHL microfilm 730,157, image 334. Original in Polish.

[2] Wyszogrod vital records, entry for birth of Chana Ita Biłgoray, year 1846, akta 60; FHL microfilm 730,208, image 102. Original in Polish.

[3] Wyszogrod vital records, entry for death of Szymon Biłgoraj, year 1846, akta 187; FHL microfilm 730,208, image 166. Original in Polish.

[4] Wyszogrod vital records, entry for death of Berek Arbejter, year 1855, akta 31; FHL microfilm 730,209, image 277. Original in Polish.

[5]The original translation by Dr. Rzymska put this year as 1864; a follow-up confirmed this was an error, and the correct year is 1855.

[6]Wyszogrod vital records, entry for marriage of Dawid Arbajter and Chana Ita Biłgoraj, year 1864, akta 13; FHL microfilm 730,210, image 387. Original in Polish.

[7]Wyszogrod vital records, entry for birth of Abram Arbajter, year 1878, akta 3; FHL microfilm 1,201,500, image 854. Original in Russian.

[8]Wyszogrod vital records, entry for birth of Nauma Arbajter, year 1881, akta 3; FHL microfilm 1,733,681, image 7. Original in Russian.

[9]Wyszogrod vital records, entry for birth of Jakob Arbajter, year 1883, akta 93; FHL microfilm 1,733,681, image 360. Original in Russian.

Chapter B   Arrivals

[1]Abraham Cahan, *The Rise of David Levinsky*; original published 1917, online transcription via Project Gutenberg, 2001 (`http://www.gutenberg.org/cache/epub/2803/pg2803-images.html` : accessed 19 Nov 2017).

[2]Manifest, S.S. *Scandia*, 5 Dec 1892, index number 409, Heinr. Steinfurst.

[3]Manifest, S.S. *Kaiser Wilhelm der Grosse*, 20 Dec 1898, stamped p. 95, index no. 21, Rosa Steinfurst.

[4]Manifest, S.S. *Kaiser Wilhelm der Grosse*, 29 Aug 1900, stamped p. 124, index no. 1, Emma Steinfirst.

[5]Manifest, S.S. *Trave*, 28 Dec 1900, stamped p. 52, index numbers 13–17, Steinfurst family.

[6]Manifest, S.S. *Corinthian*, 11 Mar 1904, index no. 14, Hersch Reinstein.

[7]Manifest, S.S. *Astoria*, 3 Jul 1905, index nos. 19–22, Edel, Perl, David and Chane Reinstein.

[8]Manifest, S.S. *Celtic*, 27 May 1907, stamped p. 94, index number 17, Abraham Arbeiter.

[9]Manifest, S.S. *Livonia*, 23 Jun 1907, list 22, index no. 20, Schmiel Reinstein.

[10]Manifest, S.S. *St. Paul*, 17 Nov 1907, stamped p. 19, index numbers 5–8, Sarah, Rebecca, Salomon and Benny Arbeiter.

¹¹Manifest, S.S. *Kaiserin Auguste Victoria*, 28 Nov 1910, list 18, Salman, Jakob, Aron and Dwoire Sigal.

¹²Manifest, S.S. *Birma*, 19 May 1912, list 23, lines 18–23, Sigalow family.

¹³Manifest, S.S. *Gothland*, 29 Jul 1913, written p. 27, index no. 21, Chaim Renistein.

Chapter C Burials

¹"Mount Zion Cemetery" (`http://www.mountzioncemetery.com/` : accessed 19 Nov 2017).

²Photographs from Kevin LaCherra, Mount Zion Cemetery, 25 Jun 2017.

³Mount Zion Cemetery office staff, phone conversation with the author, July 2017.

⁴Mount Hebron Cemetery, "Contact" (`http://www.mounthebroncemetery.com/` : accessed 19 Nov 2017).

⁵Mount Hebron Cemetery (Flushing, NY), online interment search (`http://www.mounthebroncemetery.com/interment/?id=37652` : accessed 19 Nov 2017), entry for Morris Seigel.

⁶*Ibid.* (`http://www.mounthebroncemetery.com/interment/?id=74504` : accessed 19 Nov 2017), entry for Sam Siegel.

⁷*Ibid.* (`http://www.mounthebroncemetery.com/interment/?id=144698` : accessed 19 Nov 2017), entry for Abraham Arbeiter.

⁸*Ibid.* (`http://www.mounthebroncemetery.com/interment/?id=124602` : accessed 19 Nov 2017), entry for Blanche Arbeiter.

⁹*Ibid.* (`http://www.mounthebroncemetery.com/interment/?id=31651` : accessed 19 Nov 2017), entry for Sylvia Arbeiter.

¹⁰*Ibid.* (`http://www.mounthebroncemetery.com/interment/?id=71889` : accessed 19 Nov 2017), entry for Louis Buchalter.

¹¹"Mount Carmel Cemetery" (`http://www.mountcarmelcemetery.com/` : accessed 19 Nov 2017).

¹²Mount Carmel Cemetery (Glendale, NY), online interment search (`http://www.mountcarmelcemetery.com/location.asp?id=6287319` : accessed 19 Nov 2017), entry for Markus Steinman.

¹³*Ibid.* (`http://www.mountcarmelcemetery.com/location.asp?id=6287420` : accessed 19 Nov 2017), entry for Sarah Steinman.

[14] *Ibid.* (`http://www.mountcarmelcemetery.com/location.asp?id=6324998` : accessed 19 Nov 2017), entry for Michel [*sic*] Steinman.

[15] *Ibid.* (`http://www.mountcarmelcemetery.com/location.asp?id=6301476` : accessed 19 Nov 2017), entry for Rebecca Steinman.

[16] *Ibid.* (`http://www.mountcarmelcemetery.com/location.asp?id=6317975` : accessed 19 Nov 2017), entry for Lizzie Simon.

[17] *Ibid.* (`http://www.mountcarmelcemetery.com/location.asp?id=6320321` : accessed 19 Nov 2017), entry for Philip Simon.

[18] Montefiore Springfield Long Island Cemetery Society, "Contact Us" (`http://montefiorecemetery.org/contact/` : accessed 19 Nov 2017).

[19] Montefiore Cemetery (Springfield, NY), online interment search (`http://montefiorecemetery.org/interment/?id=5451093` : accessed 19 Nov 2017), entry for Esther Reinstein, died 17 Apr 1950.

[20] Montefiore Cemetery (Springfield, NY), online interment search (`http://montefiorecemetery.org/interment/?id=5482014` : accessed 19 Nov 2017), entry for Hyman Dreizen, died 20 Oct 1964.

[21] "Beth David Cemetery," *FindAGrave* (`https://www.findagrave.com/cgi-bin/fg.cgi?page=cr&CRid=63964` : accessed 19 Nov 2017).

[22] City of New York, death certificate no. 2236 (1938 Brooklyn), Nathan Reinstein.

[23] "Cemetery Information," database, *JewishGen Online Worldwide Burial Registry* (`http://data.jewishgen.org/wconnect/wc.dll?jg~jgsys~admin~&system=jowbr&Action=SHOWUSER&ID=USA-01159` : accessed 19 Nov 2017), entry for Medgibosh Progressive Solidarity, Beth David Cemetery, Elmont, NY.

[24] Ginsburg to Abdill, 1 Jul 2017.

[25] "JewishGen Online Worldwide Burial Registry," database, *JewishGen* (`http://www.jewishgen.org/databases/jowbr.php?rec=J_NY_0014982` : accessed 19 Nov 2017), entry for Sam Reinstein, died 1975.

[26] "Washington Cemetery (Brooklyn)," *Facebook Pages* (`https://www.facebook.com/pages/Washington-Cemetery-Brooklyn/146654905366993` : accessed 19 Nov 2017).

[27] Marisa Tarantino, phone interview, 15 Sep 2017.

[28] *Ibid.*

[29] *Find A Grave*, memorial 161272866; Pearl Reinstein Gitlin.

[30] *Find A Grave*, memorial 161273035; Harry Joseph Gitlin; Washington Cemetery.

[31] "Mount Ararat Cemetery" (http://www.mountararatcemetery.com : accessed 11 Oct 2017).

[32] Mount Ararat Cemetery (Lindenhurst, NY), online interment search, entry for Goldie Task.

[33] *Ibid.* (http://www.mountararatcemetery.com/location.asp?id=1132224 : accessed 19 Nov 2017), entry for Joseph Task, died 3 Jul 1970.

[34] *Ibid.* (http://www.mountararatcemetery.com/location.asp?id=1140522 : accessed 19 Nov 2017), entry for Rose Newman, died 25 Jul 1949.

[35] "Wellwood Cemetery," *Star of David Memorial Chapels* (http://www.jewish-funeral-home.com/wellwood-cemetery/ : accessed 19 Nov 2017).

[36] City of New York, death certificate no. 156-95-051851 (1995), Martin Siegel.

[37] All interments at this location confirmed by Mark Siegel.

[38] "Cemetery and Chevra Kadisha," *Congregation Agudas Israel* (http://www.congregationagudasisrael.org/Cemetery.html : accessed 19 Nov 2017).

[39] "Online Worldwide Burial Registry," entry for Sarah (Arbeiter) Finkel and Samuel Finkel, Congregation Agudas Israel Cemetery, New Windsor, NY.

[40] *Ibid.*

[41] "Beth Israel Cemetery/Woodbridge Memorial Gardens," *BurialPlanning.com* (http://www.burialplanning.com/cemeteries/beth-israel-cemetery/ : accessed 19 Nov 2017).

[42] Forest Lawn Cemetery office staff, phone conversation with the author, September 2017.

[43] *Ibid.*

[44] "Memorial Gardens," *Temple Beth El of Hollywood* (http://www.templebethelhollywood.org/memorial-garden/ : accessed 19 Nov 2017).

[45] *Find A Grave*, memorial 147972312; Betty Jarwood; Temple Beth El Memorial Gardens; gravestone added by T. Jason Brown.

[46] "Sylvan Abbey Funeral Home and Sylvan Abbey Cemetery," *Dignity Memorial* (http://www.dignitymemorial.com/sylvan-abbey-funeral-home/en-us/index.page : accessed 19 Nov 2017).

[47] *Find A Grave*, database with images (https://www.findagrave.

com/memorial/89470042 : accessed 19 Nov 2017), memorial 89470042; Anna B Gladstone; Sylvan Abbey Memorial Park; gravestone added by Audrey.

[48] *Ibid.*, memorial 89469992; Arthur Gladstone; Sylvan Abbey Memorial Park; gravestone added by Audrey.

[49] "Contact Us," *Temple Emanuel* (https://www.teroanoke.org/ : accessed 19 Nov 2017).

[50] Commonwealth of Virginia, death certificate no. 71-028225, David Reinstein.

[51] "Our Cemeteries: East Ham Cemetery," *US Burial* (https://www.theus.org.uk/article/east-ham-cemetery : accessed 11 Oct 2017).

[52] "Find a Grave," *US Burial*; entry for Davis Arbiter; East Ham Cemetery.

[53] *Ibid.*

[54] *Ibid.*, entry for Isaac Arbeiter [*sic*]; East Ham Cemetery.

[55] Wyszogrod PSA Births, Marriages, Deaths 1886-1906, entry for death of Ryfka Arbajter, document 24.

[56] Wyszogrod PSA Books of Residence, entry for Szmul Haim Bilgoraj, house 124.

[57] *Ibid.*, entry for Sura Estera (Wejs) Bilgoraj, house 124.

[58] Translated death record of Szymon Biłgoraj; see "Translations" appendix.

[59] Wyszogrod Births, Marriages, Deaths; entry for Rasza Bilgoraj death, 1864, akta 13.

[60] Translated death record of Berek Arbajter; see "Translations" appendix.

[61] "European Jewish Cemeteries Initiative," database, *Lo Tishkach Foundation* (http://www.lo-tishkach.org/database : accessed 18 Nov 2017), entry for "Biezun Jewish Cemetery," Zuromin County, Poland.

[62] Biezun PSA Births, Marriages, Deaths, entry for Jakob Szoel Chrzanowski, died 1857, akta 7.

[63] *Ibid.*, entry for Ester Chrzanowska, died 1843, akta 186.

[64] *Ibid.*, entry for Chaim Chrzanowski, died 1837, akta 109.

[65] Photo by the author.

Chapter D Finding the Steinmans

[1] 1905 New York state census, Kings County, New York, election district 23, Max, Sarah, Henry, Rose, Emma, William, Amelia and Helen Steinman.

[2] 1900 U.S. census, Kings County, New York, pop. sch., Brooklyn, fam. 172, Philip, Lizzie, Sarah, Louis and Norman Simon, Henry Steinman.

[3] *Ibid.*

[4] 1930 U.S. census, Kings County, New York, pop. sch., Brooklyn, dwell. 44, fam. 132, Philip, Lizzie and Louis Simon, Sarah, Norman and Harold Barnett.

[5] Social Security Administration, "Social Security Applications and Claims Index, 1936–2007," database, *Ancestry.com*, entry for Louis Simon, SS no. 054-09-0894.

[6] Manifest, S.S. *Trave*, 28 Dec 1900, p. 52, index nos. 13–17, Steinfirst family.

[7] Manifest, S.S. *Kaiser Wilhelm der Grosse*, 20 Dec 1898, stamped p. 95, index no. 21, Rosa Steinfurst.

[8] Manifest, S.S. *Kaiser Wilhelm der Grosse*, 29 Aug 1900, stamped p. 124, index no. 1, Emma Steinfirst.

[9] "Search," database, *CastleGarden.org* (`http://www.castlegarden. org/quick_search_detail.php?p_id=7024267` : accessed 18 Nov 2017), entry for Heinrich Steinfuerst, arrived 5 Dec 1892.

[10] Manifest, S.S. *Scandia*, 5 Dec 1892, index no. 409, Heinr. Steinfurst.

[11] Mount Carmel Cemetery (Glendale, NY), online interment search (`http://www.mountcarmelcemetery..com/location.asp?id=6287319` : accessed 18 Nov 2017), entry for Markus Steinman, location 1-E-17-5-11.

[12] *Ibid.* (`http://www.mountcarmelcemetery.com/location.asp?id=6324998` : accessed 18 Nov 2017), entry for Michel [*sic*] Steinman, location 1-E-17-9-13.

[13] *Ibid.* (`http://www.mountcarmelcemetery.com/location.asp?id=6301476` : accessed 18 Nov 2017), entry for Rebecca Steinman, died 1 Sep 1937.

[14] *JewishData*, entry 170561; Marcus Steinman; Old Mt. Carmel Cemetery. Translation by Laura Munzer and Robin Meltzer.

[15] *JewishData*, entry 170664; Michael Steinman; Mount Carmel Cemetery.

Chapter E   Siegel to Sigalow

[1] 1920 U.S. census, Kings County, New York, pop. sch., dwell. 65, fam. 298, Samuel, Hannah, Jack, Bessie, Bertha, Sophia, Sylvia and Maurice Siegel.

[2] Ginsburg to Abdill, 1 Jul 2017.

[3] 1930 U.S. census, Kings County, New York, pop. sch., dwell. 78, fam. 78, Sam and Sylvia Siegel, Birdie and Anna Boyd.

[4] "Ancestor Search Engine," *JewishData.com*, database with images (http://jewishdata.com/secure/record_detail.php?id=384691 : accessed 18 Nov 2017), entry 384691 for Anna Siegel, died 1924.

[5] Ginsburg to Abdill, 1 Jul 2017.

[6] *Ibid.*

[7] City of New York, death certificate no. 2292 (1932), Morris Seigel.

[8] *Ibid.*, death certificate no. 8679 (1920), Sophie Siegel.

[9] Ginsburg to Abdill, 1 Jul 2017.

[10] "Florida Death Index, 1877–1998," database, *Ancestry.com*, entry for Sylvia Chernow, died 22 Jul 1986.

[11] 1920 U.S. census, Kings County, New York, pop. sch., dwell. 65, fam. 298, Samuel, Hannah, Jack, Bessie, Bertha, Sophia, Sylvia and Maurice Siegel.

[12] 1930 U.S. census, Kings County, New York, pop. sch., dwell. 78, fam. 78, Sam and Sylvia Siegel, Birdie and Anna Boyd.

[13] City of New York, death certificate no. 2292 (1932), Morris Seigel.

[14] *Ibid.*

[15] Mount Hebron Cemetery (Queens, New York, NY), online interment search, entry for Morris Seigel.

[16] Jewish Genealogical Society, "AJHS [American Jewish Historical Society] Incorporation Data," (https://www.jgsny.org/index.php/new-exclusive-benefits/back-dorots-2/127-spring-2014 : accessed 18 Nov 2017).

[17] "Medvin, Ukraine," *JewishGen Communities Database* (https://www.jewishgen.org/Communities/community.php?usbgn=-1046393 : accessed 18 Nov 2017).

[18] Ginsburg to Abdill, 1 Jul 2017.

[19] Warren Blatt, "Hebrew to English Adaptations," digital presentation slides, *JewishGen* (https://www.jewishgen.org/infofiles/GivenNames/slide66.html : accessed 18 Nov 2017), slide 66.

[20] Manifest, S.S. *Birma*, 19 May 1912, list 23, Sigalow family.

[21] Edward Smedley, Hugh James Rose, Henry John Rose, eds., *Encyclopædia Metropolitana; Or, Universal Dictionary of Knowledge*, volume XVI (London, 1845), 48.

[22] "Past Auction: June 2008," Cherrystone Philatelic Auctioneers (https://www.cherrystoneauctions.com/_auction/results.asp?auction=200806&searchtext=&country=RUSSIA++Flight+Covers : accessed 18 Nov 2017), lot 5120, "RUSSIA Flight Covers."

[23] 1920 U.S. census, Kings County, New York, pop. sch., dwell. 65, fam. 298, Samuel, Hannah, Jack, Bessie, Bertha, Sophia, Sylvia and Maurice Siegel.

[24] City of New York, death certificate no. 8679 (1920), Sophie Siegel.

[25] Marisa Tarantino (Brooklyn, NY), general manager, Washington Cemetery; phone interview by Richard Abdill, 15 Sep 2017; transcript held privately by interviewer, Minneapolis, Minn.

[26] *Ibid.*

[27] Marisa Tarantino, phone interview, 15 Sep 2017.

[28] "Ancestor Search Engine," *JewishData.com*, database with images, entry 384691 for Anna Siegel, died 1924.

[29] City of New York, death certificate no. 24391 (1924), Mrs. Anna Siegel.

[30] "Passenger Search," database with images, *Statue of Liberty–Ellis Island Foundation* (https://www.libertyellisfoundation.org/passenger-result).

[31] Manifest, S.S. *Kaiserin Auguste Victoria*, 28 Nov 1910, list 18, Salman, Jakob, Aron and Dwoire Sigal.

[32] Record of Detained Aliens, S.S. *Livonia*, 23 Jun 1907, Schmiel Reinstein.

[33] Record of detained aliens, S.S. *Westernland*, 26 Mar 1906, stamped p. 51, index no. 43, Ruchel Reinstein, *Passenger and Crew Lists of*

Vessels Arriving at New York , NY, 1897-1957, microfilm publication T715, (Washington: National Archives and Records Service), roll 681, frame 320.

[34] "Ancestor Search Engine," *JewishData.com*, database with images (http://jewishdata.com/secure/record_detail.php?id=384697 : accessed 18 Nov 2017), entry 384697 for Sophie Siegel, died 1920.

Chapter F Rasza's father

[1] Translated death record of Szymon Biłgoraj, see "Translations" appendix.

[2] Wyszogrod PSA Books of Residence, entry for Zelmen Ber Bilgoraj (and the couple's other children), house 126.

[3] *Ibid.*, entry for Sura Estera (Wejs) Bilgoraj, house 124.

[4] Translated birth record of Hana Itta Biłgoraj, see "Translations" appendix.

[5] Translated marriage record of Dawid Arbajter and Hana Itta Biłgoraj, see "Translations" appendix.

[6] Wyszogrod PSA Books of Residence, entry for Icek Bilgoraj, house 124.

[7] Translated death record of Szymon Biłgoraj, see "Translations" appendix.

[8] Wyszogrod PSA Books of Residence, entry for Szymon Boruch Bilgoraj, house 123.

[9] Translated death record of Abram Arbajter, see "Translations" appendix.

[10] Wyszogrod PSA Births, Marriages, Deaths 1886-1906, entry for birth of Ryfka Arbajter, document 43.

[11] Wyszogrod PSA Books of Residence, entry for Rasza Arbajter, house 166.

[12] General Register Office of England, birth registration no. 402 (1903 Mile End, London), Solomon Arbeiter.

[13] *Ibid.*, birth registration no. 175 (1900 Mile End New Town, London), Rebecca Arbiter.

[14] 1911 England census, Davis and Annie Arbieter.

Bibliography

Books and documents

Alexander, Scott, *The Red Hot Jazz Archive*. `http://www.redhotjazz.com` : 2017.

"Baltic American Line Steamship Brochures and Historical Archives," *Gjenvick-Gjonvik Archives*. `http://www.gjenvick.com/SteamshipLines/BalticAmericaLine/` : 2017.

Barr, Jason and Teddy Ort, "Population Density across the City: The Case of 1900 Manhattan," Department of Economics, Rutgers University. `http://andromeda.rutgers.edu/~jmbarr/skyscrapers/tenementsdraftv1_18aug2013.pdf` : 2017.

Bartlett Scholl of Architecture (London), *Survey of London: Histories of Whitechapel*, interactive map and collection, `https://surveyoflondon.org/map/feature/443/detail/`

Behar, Doron M., et. al, "Multiple Origins of Ashkenazi Levites: Y Chromosome Evidence for Both Near Eastern and European Ancestries," *American Journal of Human Genetics*. `https://www.ncbi.nlm.nih.gov/pmc/articles/PMC1180600/` : 2017.

Beine, Joe, "The Barge Office, New York City - Manhattan," *Immigrant Processing Centers for New York City*. `http:`

//www.genealogybranches.com/ellisisland/
bargeoffice.html : 2017.

Bennett, Arnold, "Your United States," *Hearst's International*, vol. 23. New York: World Review Company, 1913.

Berrol, Selma, *East Side/East End: Eastern European Jews in London and New York, 1870–1920*. Westport, Conn.: Praeger, 1994.

Birmingham, Stephen, *The Rest of Us: The Rise of America's Eastern European Jews*, first Syracuse University Press edition. Syracuse University Press, 1999.

Blatt, Warren, "Polish-Jewish Genealogy: Questions and Answers," *JewishGen.com*. https://www.jewishgen.org/InfoFiles/Poland/Questions.htm : 2017.

Block, Susana Leistner "Polish Patronymics and Surname Suffixes," *KehilaLinks*. https://kehilalinks.jewishgen.org/Suchostaw/polish_patronymics_and_surname_suffixes.htm : 2017.

Braunstein, Susan L. and Jenna Weissman Joselit, eds., *Getting Comfortable in New York: The American Jewish Home, 1880–1950*. New York: The Jewish Museum, 1991.

Burns, Charles, *Galician Traces*. http://galiciantraces.com : 2017.

Charles E. Goad Ltd., "Insurance Plan of London Vol. XI," *British Library Online Gallery*, online images of maps, http://gallery.bl.uk/

Cohen, Jocelyn and Daniel Soyer, eds., *My Future Is In America: Autobiographies of Eastern European Jewish Immigrants*. New York: NYU Press, 2006.

Crockett, Davy, *An Account of Col. Crockett's Tour to the North and Down East.* Baltimore: Carey, Hart, and Co., 1835.

Cudahy, Brian J., *Over and Back: The History of Ferryboats in New York Harbor.* New York: Fordham University Press, 1990.

Davis, Marni, *Jews and Booze: Becoming American in the Age of Prohibition.* New York: New York University Press, 2012.

Dawidowicz, David, "The Vishogrod Synagogue," anthologized in Vishogrod yizkor book. `http://www.jewishgen.org/yizkor/Wyszogrod/wyse003.html`

Ehrenfried, Joseph, *Colloquial Phrases and Dialogues in German and English.* Philadelphia: Joseph A. Speel, 1834.

Encyclopedia Titanica, online encyclopedia. `https://www.encyclopedia-titanica.org` : 2017.

Fidelholtz, James L., "Stress in Polish – With Some Comparisons to English Stress," *Papers and Studies in Contrastive Linguistics,* edition 9 (1979); version available online, `http://ifa.amu.edu.pl/psicl/files/9/04_Fidelholtz.pdf` : 2017.

Figes, Orlando, *A People's Tragedy.* New York: Penguin Books, 1998.

Frank, Rusty E., *TAP! The Greatest Tap Dance Stars and Their Stories, 1900–1955.* Cambridge: Da Capo Press, 1995.

Freeze, ChaeRan Y., *Jewish Marriage and Divorce in Imperial Russia.* London: Brandeis University Press, 2001.

Fried, Albert, *The Rise and Fall of the Jewish Gangster in America.* New York: Columbia University Press, 1980.

George, Henry, *Social Problems.* New York: Henry George

& Co., 1886.

Gilbert, Martin, *The Routledge Atlas of the Holocaust*, third edition. London: Routledge, 2002.

Glazier, Ira A., *Migration from the Russian Empire: June 1889–July 1890*. Baltimore: Genealogical Publishing Co., 1998.

Greenspoon, Leonard J., ed., *Fashioning Jews: Clothing, Culture, and Commerce*. West Lafayette, Ind: Purdue University Press, 2013.

Grose, Howard B., *Aliens or Americans?*. New York: Presbyterian Home Missions, 1906.

Gurock, Jeffrey S., *When Harlem Was Jewish, 1870–1930*. New York: Columbia University Press, 1979.

History of Jewish Communities in Ukraine. `http://jewua.org/medzhibozh/` : 2017.

Hoffman, Lawrence A., "9/11: Remembering How We Remembered," *Life and a Little Liturgy*. `https://blog.lawrenceahoffman.com/2011/09/11/911-remembering-how-we-remembered/` : 2017.

Holtzman, Ada, translator, "List of the Deceased before the Holocaust, as Submitted by the Relatives," *Book to the Martyrs of Wyszogrod*. Partially transcribed by JewishGen, `https://www.jewishgen.org/yizkor/Wyszogrod/Wyszogrod.html` : 2017.

Howe, Irving, *World of Our Fathers: The Journey of the East European Jews to America and the Life They Found and Made*. New York: NYU Press, reprinted 2005.

Hundert, Gershon David, *Jews in Poland-Lithuania in the Eighteenth Century: A Genealogy of Modernity*. Berkeley: University of California Press, 2004.

Jenkins, Terence, *The Most Dangerous Woman in Europe (And Other Londoners)*. Leicester, UK: Matador

Publishing, 2016.

Joseph, Samuel, "Jewish Immigration to the United States from 1881 to 1910," *Studies in History, Economics and Public Law*, volume 59. New York: Columbia University, 1914.

Kaminsky, Marc, "All That Our Eyes Have Witnessed: Memories of a Living History Workshop in the South Bronx," *Twenty-Five Years of the Life Review: Theoretical and Practical Considerations*. E-book, `https://books.google.com/books?id=83psBAAAQBAJ` : 2017.

Kavieff, Paul R., *The Life and Times of Lepke Buchalter: America's Most Ruthless Labor Racketeer*. Fort Lee, NJ: Barricade Books, 2006.

Kizilov, Mikhail, *The Sons of Scripture: The Karaites in Poland and Lithuania in the Twentieth Century*. Warsaw: De Gruyter Open, 2005.

Klier, John, *Russians, Jews, and the Pogroms of 1881–1882*. New York: Cambridge University Press, 2011.

Kugelmass, Jack and Jonathan Boyarin, eds., *From a Ruined Garden: The Memorial Books of Polish Jewry*, second expanded edition. Indiana University Press, 1998.

Kulczyk, Sylwia, "Mini Guidebook: The north-western Mazovia." Warsaw: Mazowieckie Voivodeship, 2009. Web copy of print pamphlet, `https://www.mazovia.pl/gfx/mazovia/userfiles/m.guzowska/linki_nie_usuwac/mazowsze_polnocno-zachodnie_en_2.pdf`

Lawson, Ellen NicKenzie, *Smugglers, Bootleggers, And Scofflaws: Prohibition And New York City*. Albany: Excelsior Editions, 2013. Online addenda, "Geographical List of Manhattan Prohibition Sites." `http://smugglersbootleggersandscofflaws.com/geography-significant-sites-prohibition-new-york-city/` : 2017.

Lee, Paul, *Titanic Pages*. `http://www.paullee.com/`

titanic/ : 2017.

Library of Congress, "A People At Risk," article, *Immigration: Polish/Russian.* `https://www.loc.gov/teachers/classroommaterials/presentationsandactivities/presentations/immigration/polish5.html`

Liek, Gustav, *Die Stadt Schippenbeil.* von Braun & Weber, 1874.

London Borough of Tower Hamlets, "Stepney Green Conservation Area," *Conservation Area Character Appraisals and Management Guidelines*, digital image of report, `http://democracy.towerhamlets.gov.uk/mgConvert2PDF.aspx?ID=7773`

London School of Economics & Political Science, "Charles Booth's London," online images of maps, `https://booth.lse.ac.uk/map/18/-0.0703/51.5174/100/0?marker=534132.0,181694.0`

Manbeck, John B., consulting ed., *The Neighborhood of Brooklyn.* New Haven: Yale University Press, 1998.

MacDougall, Philip, *London and the Georgian Navy.* Stroud, United Kingdom: The History Press, 2013.

Michaels, Marc, *The East London Synagogue: Outpost Of Another World*, fourth edition. London: Kulmus Publishing, 2013.

Millgram, Abraham, "Pre-Modern Synagogue Architecture and Interior Design," *My Jewish Learning.* `http://www.myjewishlearning.com/article/synagogue-architecture-and-interior-design/`

Miln, Louise Jordan, *Wooings and Weddings in Many Climes.* Chicago: Herbert S. Stone & Company, 1900.

Morris, George Pope, *Poems*, Project Gutenberg edition. `http://www.gutenberg.org/ebooks/2558` : 2017.

"Multiculture," *Muzeum of Vistula in Wyszogrod.* `http://`

muzeumwyszogrod.pl/en/ekspozycje/wielokulturowosc/
: 2017.

Nance, Agnieszka B., *Literary and Cultural Images of a Nation Without a State: The Case of Nineteenth-Century Poland*. Bern, Switzerland: Peter Lang, 2008.

Nicholls, Geoff, *The Drum Book: A History of the Rock Drum Kit*. London: Backbeat Books, 2008.

Passenger and Crew Lists of Vessels Arriving at New York, NY, 1897–1957. Micropublication T715, 8,537 rolls. Washington, D.C.: National Archives and Records Service.

Pelo, June, *Genealogy Research*. Self-published online, http://sydaby.eget.net/swe/genealogy.html

"'From Pickle Day Exhibits: What is a Pickle?" *New York Food Museum*. http://www.nyfoodmuseum.org/ _pkwhat.htm : 2017.

Polland, Annie and Daniel Soyer, *Emerging Metropolis: New York Jews in the Age of Immigration, 1840–1920*. New York: New York University Press, 2015.

Polish Genealogical Society of America, *How to Begin Your Family Research*. https://pgsa.org/how-to/ : 2017.

"Reading Hebrew Tombstones," *JewishGen InfoFiles*. http://www.jewishgen.org/InfoFiles/tombstones.html : 2017.

Riis, Jacob A., *How The Other Half Lives: Studies Among the Tenements of New York*. New York: Charles Scribner's Sons, 1897.

The Royal Castle In Warsaw - Museum, "For Independence. Year 1914," https://www.zamek-krolewski.pl/en/ your-visit/temporary-exhibitions/for-independence.-year-1914-institute-of-national-remembrances-exhibition : 2017.

Schauss, Hayyim, "History of Bar Mitzvah," *My Jewish*

Learning. `http://www.myjewishlearning.com/article/history-of-bar-mitzvah/`

Schem, Lida Clara, *The Hyphen*, volume 1. New York: E.P. Dutton, 1920.

Seward, Josiah Lafayette, *A History of the town of Sullivan, New Hampshire*, vol. 1. Keene, NH: published by the author, 1921.

Sherwin, Byron L., *Sparks Amidst the Ashes: The Spiritual Legacy of Polish Jewry.* New York: Oxford University Press, 1997.

Shyovitz, David, "History & Development of Yiddish," *Jewish Virtual Library.* `http://www.jewishvirtuallibrary.org/history-and-development-of-yiddish` : 2017.

Singer, Isidore et. al, eds., *The Jewish Encyclopedia*, volume 10. New York: Funk and Wagnalls Company, 1907.

Sifakis, Carl, *The Mafia Encyclopedia*, third edition. New York: Facts On File, 1999.

Smith, Marian L., *Manifest Markings.* `https://www.jewishgen.org/InfoFiles/Manifests/`

Smedley, Edward, Hugh James Rose, Henry John Rose, eds., *Encyclopædia Metropolitana; Or, Universal Dictionary of Knowledge*, volume XVI. London, 1845.

Sokolov, Nahum, "Vishogrod, Town of 'Schools,'" anthologized in Vishogrod yizkor book. `http://www.jewishgen.org/yizkor/Wyszogrod/wyse003.html`

Soyer, Daniel, *Jewish Immigrant Associations and American Identity in New York, 1880–1939.* Detroit: Wayne State University Press, 1997.

Spitalfields Life, blog, `http://spitalfieldslife.com` : 2017.

Stone, Peter, *The History of the Port of London: A Vast Emporium of All Nations.* South Yorkshire, England:

Pen & Sword, 2017.

Swartz, Sarah Silberstein, "Return to Poland: In Search of My Parents' Memories," *From Memory to Transformation: Jewish Women's Voices*. Toronto: Second Story Press, 1998.

Tucker, Mark, *Ellington: The Early Years*. Champaign, Ill.: University of Illinois Press, 1995.

Turkus, Burton B. and Sid Feder, *Murder, Inc.* New York: Tenacity Media Books, 1951.

United States Holocaust Memorial Museum, *Holocaust Encyclopedia*, `https://www.ushmm.org/learn/holocaust-encyclopedia` : 2017.

U.S. Citizenship and Immigration Services, "Immigrant Name Changes," *Genealogy Notebook*. `https://www.uscis.gov/history-and-genealogy/genealogy/genealogy-notebook/immigrant-name-changes` : 2017.

Weintraug, Joel, "The Ellis Island Name Change Myth," *JewishGen InfoFiles*. `http://www.jewishgen.org/InfoFiles/ellismythnames.html` : 2017.

Wilson, Keith, ed., *Decisions for War 1914*. London: Routledge, 2016.

Yad Vashem, *The Holocaust Resource Center*. `http://www.yadvashem.org/yv/en/holocaust/resource_center/the_holocaust.asp` : 2017.

Yad Vashem, *The Untold Stories: The Murder Sites of the Jews in the Occupied Territories of the Former USSR*. `http://yadvashem.org/untoldstories/index.html` : 2017.

YIVO Encyclopedia of Jews in Eastern Europe. `http://www.yivoencyclopedia.org` : 2017.

Yizkor Book Insights, online essay collection. `https://www.jewishgen.org/yizkor/ybinsights.html` : 2017.

Collections

"19th Century Russian Maps," database with images, *WWII Aerial Photos and Maps*, `http://www.wwii-photos-maps.com/19thcenturyrussianmaps/`

"Bomb Sight: Mapping the WW2 bomb census," database and interactive map, `http://bombsight.org`

Castle Garden database, `http://www.castlegarden.org`

"Cmentarze," database with images, *kirkuty.xip.pl*, `http://www.kirkuty.xip.pl/fotogalerie.htm`

"England Wales, Civil Registration Birth Index, 1837–1915," database with images, *Ancestry.com*, `https://search.ancestry.com/search/db.aspx?dbid=8912` : 2017).

"England Wales, National Probate Calendar," database with images, *Ancestry.com*, `https://search.ancestry.com/search/db.aspx?dbid=1904` : 2017).

"European Jewish Cemeteries Initiative," database, *Lo Tishkach Foundation*, `http://lo-tishkach.org`

Federal Bureau of Investigation, *FBI Records: The Vault*, database with images, `https://vault.fbi.gov/`

Find A Grave. Database with images. `http://www.findagrave.com`

"Find a Grave," database with images, *US [United Synagogue] Burial*, `https://www.theus.org.uk/category/find-grave`

"Florida Death Index, 1877–1998," database with images, *Ancestry.com*, `https://search.ancestry.com/search/db.aspx?dbid=7338`

Florida Department of Health, "Florida Divorce Index, 1927–2001," database with images, *Ancestry.com*, `https://search.ancestry.com/search/db.aspx?dbid=8837`

Florida Department of Health, vital records collections.

FreeBMD, vital records index, `https://www.freebmd.org.uk`

General Register Office of England, vital records collections. Her Majesty's Passport Office, London, England.

International Jewish Cemetery Project, database with images, `https://www.iajgsjewishcemeteryproject.org`

Italian Genealogical Group, "Bronx, Kings, Manhattan, Richmond, and Queens County Brides," database, `http://www.italiangen.org/records-search/brides.php`

Italian Genealogical Group, "Deaths, NYC Municipal Archives," database, `http://www.italiangen.org/records-search/deaths.php`

Italian Genealogical Group, "New York City Births Index," database, `http://www.italiangen.org/records-search/births.php`

"Jewish Communities & Records," database, *JewishGen*, `https://www.jewishgen.org/jcr-uk/`

JewishData, database with images, `http://jewishdata.com`

Jewish Genealogical Society, "AJHS [American Jewish Historical Society] Incorporation Data," database, `https://www.jgsny.org/index.php/new-exclusive-benefits/back-dorots-2/127-spring-2014`

"JewishGen Online Worldwide Burial Registry," database, *JewishGen*, `https://www.jewishgen.org/databases/cemetery/`

"Jewish Records Indexing - Poland," database with images. `http://jri-poland.org/jriplweb.htm`

"Kiev Gubernia Duma Voters Lists Database," database, *JewishGen*, `https://www.jewishgen.org/databases/Ukraine/KievDuma.htm`

Montefiore Cemetery, interment search, database. `http:`

//montefiorecemetery.org

Mount Ararat Cemetery, interment search, database. `http://www.mountararatcemetery.com`

Mount Hebron Cemetery, interment search, database. `http://www.mounthebroncemetery.com`

New Jersey State Department of Health, vital records collections.

New York City Department of Records, vital records collections.

"New York City, Marriage License Indexes, 1907–1995," database, *Ancestry.com* (`https://search.ancestry.com/search/db.aspx?dbid=61406`

"New York, Index to Petitions for Naturalization filed in New York City, 1792–1989," database with images, *Ancestry.com*, `https://search.ancestry.com/search/db.aspx?dbid=7733`

"New York, New York, Birth Index 1878–1909," database, *Ancestry.com*, `https://search.ancestry.com/search/db.aspx?dbid=9089`

"New York, New York, Death Index 1862–1948," database, *Ancestry.com*, `https://search.ancestry.com/search/db.aspx?dbid=9131`

"New York, New York, Marriage Certificate Index 1866–1937," database, *Ancestry.com*, `https://search.ancestry.com/search/db.aspx?dbid=9105`

"New York, State and Federal Naturalization Records, 1794–1940," database, *Ancestry.com*, `https://search.ancestry.com/search/db.aspx?dbid=2280`

"Ohio, Birth Index, 1908–1964," database, *Ancestry.com*, `https://search.ancestry.com/search/db.aspx?dbid=3146`

"Ohio, Deaths, 1908–1932, 1938–2007," database, *Ances-*

try.com, `https://search.ancestry.com/search/db.aspx?dbid=5763`

"Passenger Search," database with images, *Statue of Liberty–Ellis Island Foundation*, `https://www.libertyellisfoundation.org/passenger-result`

"The Photo Archive," database with images, *Yad Vashem*, `http://collections1.yadvashem.org/search.asp?lang=ENG&rsvr=7`

Registrar of Vital Statistics of Wrightstown Borough, vital records collections. Burlington County, NJ.

"Selected U.S. Naturalization Records, Original Documents, 1790–1974," database with images, *Ancestry.com*, `https://www.ancestry.com/interactive/1554/32126_22319183132018-00378/3311426`

Social Security Administration, "Social Security Applications and Claims Index, 1936–2007" database, *Ancestry.com*, `https://search.ancestry.com/search/db.aspx?dbid=60901`

Social Security Administration, "Social Security Death Index," database, *Ancestry.com*, `https://search.ancestry.com/search/db.aspx?dbid=3693`

"StreetEasy," database with maps, `https://streeteasy.com`

"Sweden, Emigrants Registered in Church Books, 1783–1991," database, *Ancestry.com*, `https://search.ancestry.com/search/db.aspx?dbid=61085`

"UK, Outward Passenger Lists, 1890–1960," database with images, *Ancestry.com*, `https://search.ancestry.com/search/db.aspx?dbid=2997`

"United States World War II Draft Registration Cards, 1942," database with images, *Ancestry.com*, `https://search.ancestry.com/search/db.aspx?dbid=1002`

"U.S. City Directories, 1822–1995," database, *Ancestry.com*, `https://search.ancestry.com/search/db.aspx?dbid=2469`

"U.S., Department of Veterans Affairs BIRLS Death File, 1850–2010," database, *Ancestry.com*, `https://search.ancestry.com/search/db.aspx?dbid=2441`

"U.S. Passport Applications, 1795-1925," database with images, *Ancestry.com*, `https://search.ancestry.com/search/db.aspx?dbid=1174`

"U.S. Public Records Index, 1950–1993, Volume 1," database, *Ancestry.com*, `https://search.ancestry.com/search/db.aspx?dbid=1788`

"U.S., World War I Draft Registration Cards, 1917–1918," database, *Ancestry.com*, `https://search.ancestry.com/search/db.aspx?dbid=6482`

"U.S., World War II Draft Registration Cards, 1942," database, *Ancestry.com*, `https://search.ancestry.com/search/db.aspx?dbid=1002`

Virginia Department of Health, vital records collections.

"Virginia, Divorce Records, 1918–1991," database, *Ancestry.com*, `https://search.ancestry.com/search/db.aspx?dbid=9280`

"Wills and Probate 1858–1996," vital records collections. Her Majesty's Courts & Tribunals Service, London, England.

"WWII Draft Registration Cards," database with images, *Fold3*, `https://www.fold3.com`

"Wyszogród," database with images, *Fotopolska*, `http://wyszogrod.fotopolska.eu/`

Yad Vashem, "The Central Database of Shoah Victims' Names," database with images, `http://yvng.yadvashem.org/index.html?language=en`

Yahad-In Unum, "Execution Sites of Jewish Victims," database with maps, `http://yahadmap.org/`

Census records

All via Ancestry.com; *databases with images, accessed 2016–2017, as cited in the text.*

England. Mile End Old Town civil parish. 1901.

England. Whitechapel civil parish. 1901.

England. City of London civil parish. 1911.

New York. Kings County. 1905.

New York. Kings County. 1915.

New York. New York City. 1925.

New York. Sullivan County. 1925.

United States. Kings County, New York. 1900.

United States. Kings County, New York. 1910.

United States. Manhattan, New York. 1910.

United States. Manhattan, New York. 1920.

United States. Bronx County, New York. 1930.

United States. Kings County, New York. 1930.

United States. Queens County, New York. 1930.

United States. Bronx County, New York. 1940.

United States. Kings County, New York. 1940.

United States. Manhattan, New York. 1940.

United States. Nassau County, New York. 1940.

United States. Queens County, New York. 1940.

News publications

Arutz Sheva, Israel, `http://www.israelnationalnews.com`

Asbury Park Press, Asbury Park, NJ, clippings via News-papers.com.

BBC News, London, England, `https://www.bbc.com`

Boston Globe, Boston, Mass., `https://www.bostonglobe.com`

Daily Mail, Hagerstown, Md., clippings via Newspapers.com.

Deep Baltic, `https://deepbaltic.com/`

Fremont News-Messenger, Fremont, Ohio, clippings via Rutherford B. Hayes Presidential Library.

The Independent, London, England, `http://www.independent.co.uk`

Lima News, Lima, Ohio, clipping via Ancestry.com.

New Statesman, London, England, `http://www.citymetric.com`

New York Sun, New York, NY, clippings via Newspapers.com.

New York Times, New York, NY, `https://www.nytimes.com`

Politico, Arlington, Va., `https://www.politico.com`

The Press and Sun-Bulletin, Binghamton, NY, clippings via Newspapers.com.

Rochester Democrat and Chronicle, Rochester, NY, clippings via Newspapers.com.

Tablet, New York, NY, `http://www.tabletmag.com`

Times of Israel, Jerusalem, Israel, `https://www.timesofisrael.com`

Washington Post, Washington, DC, `https://www.washingtonpost.`

com

Interviews

All interviews conducted 2017 via phone by the author. Transcripts privately held by Richard Abdill, Minneapolis, Minn.

Abdill, Nancy: 28 Jun, 26 Aug, 21 Oct.

Arbeiter, Jay: 10 Jun.

Siegel, Mark: 10 Apr, 27 May, 17 Jun, 25 Jul, 19 Nov.

Tarantino, Marisa, general manager, Washington Cemetery, 15 Sep.

Index

317

"The riches of a soul are stored up in its memory...
When we want to understand ourselves,
to find out what is most precious in our lives,
we search our memory."

—Abraham Joshua Heschel,
   Man Is Not Alone

www.ingramcontent.com/pod-product-compliance
Lightning Source LLC
Chambersburg PA
CBHW022329280326
41934CB00006B/580